Healed and Released

Equipping the Believer for Ministry

By

Dorothy Parker

Copyright © 2013 by Dorothy Parker

Healed and Released
Equipping the Believer for Ministry
by Dorothy Parker

Printed in the United States of America

ISBN 9781625096081

All rights reserved solely by the author. The author guarantees all contents are original and do not infringe upon the legal rights of any other person or work. No part of this book may be reproduced in any form without the permission of the author. The views expressed in this book are not necessarily those of the publisher.

Unless otherwise indicated, Bible quotations are taken from The King James Version; The Amplified (AMP), The Message (MSG), The Young's Literal Translation (YLT), and The Weymouth New Testament (WYN). Copyright © 2011 by Rick Meyers.

All are from e-Sword, www.esword.net.

The content of Healed and Released is based on the teachings and publications of Rev. Cheryl Schang. Quotes and indirect quotes are with her permission.

www.xulonpress.com

Table of Contents

Table of Contents	v
Acknowledgements	ix
Introduction	xi
LESSON 1 – His Presence	**13**
Introduction	13
Created for His Presence	14
Halal Praise	18
Why God Wants this Kind of Praise	19
Benefits of *Halal* Praise	19
Salvation Opportunity	24
Activation Time	25
Assignment	25
Salvation Scriptures	27
LESSON 2 – Healing and the Holy Spirit	**30**
Introduction	30
The Holy Spirit in the Old Testament	31
The Holy Spirit in the New Testament	33
Jesus and the Holy Spirit	34
Disciples and the Holy Spirit	36
The Early Church and the Holy Spirit	39
The Holy Spirit and the Church Today	45
Summary	47
Activation Time	49
Assignment	49
Baptism of the Holy Spirit	51
LESSON 3 – The Gift	**53**
Introduction	53
I Corinthians 12	55
Historical Setting	56
The Church at Corinth	56
Context of 1 Corinthians 12	57
Analysis of Chapter 12	59

  The Holy Spirit is the Gift **62**
  Summary **67**
  Activation Time **69**
  Assignment **70**
LESSON 4 – Healing in the Atonement **73**
  Introduction **73**
  Old Testament Types and Shadows **74**
    Passover: Exodus 12 .... **75**
    2 Chronicles 28 – 30 .... **76**
    Rebellion in the Camp: Numbers 16 .... **77**
    The Brazen Serpent: Numbers 21 .... **79**
    Isaiah 53:4-5 .... **80**
  Jesus: The fulfillment of O.T. Types **83**
  Sozo **88**
  Activation Time **90**
  Assignment. **92**
  Communion Scriptures **94**
  Seven Redemptive Names of God **95**
LESSON 5 – Unbelief vs. Faith **96**
  Introduction **96**
  Ignorance **97**
  Unbelief **98**
  Faith **100**
    What Is Faith **101**
    Where Is Faith **103**
    How Do We Get Faith **104**
  Summary. **108**
  Activation Time **109**
  Assignment **109**
LESSON 6 – Faith That Receives **111**
  Faith Acts **111**
    Eye of Faith **112**
  Faith Speaks **114**
  The Prayer of Faith **118**
    Thanksgiving **121**
    No Faith **123**
  Activation Time **125**
  Assignment **126**
LESSON 7 – Hinderances to Faith **128**
  Introduction **128**
  Traditions of Men **129**
    God Is the Author of Sickness and Disease **130**
    Sickness Brings Glory to God **134**
    The Age of Miracles Has Passed Away **134**
    Praying If It Be Thy Will **136**

Table Of Contents

      Sickness Is God's Way of Teaching Us...136
      If You Only Have Enough Faith 138
         Paul's Thorn 140
   Rejection 144
   Spiritual Interference 145
   Activation Time. 147
   Assignment 148

LESSON 8 – Spiritual Interference...150
   Introduction 150
   You're In the Army Now 153
      Military Briefing 154
      Demonic and Sickness/Disease Connection 155
   Activation Time 162
   Assignment 164
   Psalms 139 & Romans 8:35, 38, 39..166

LESSON 9 – Heal the Sick..167
   Introduction 167
   Diversity in Methods...168
   Ministering Healing and Deliverance 169
      The Process 171
         Identify the Enemy..171
         Repent, Renounce, and Break Your Agreement.........................176
         Cast the Enemy Out 178
         Command the Body 180
         Thanksgiving..180
         Staying Free 183
   Activation Time 184
   Assignment 184
   How to Keep Your Healing/Deliverance 188
   Common Issues and Spirits...190

LESSON 10 – Dealing with Issues..191
   Introduction 191
   Unforgiveness 194
   Depression...195
   Abuse/Violence 195
   Fear 196
   Sexual Sins..196
      Soul Ties..197
   Generational Curses 200
   False Religion/Idolatry 201
   Breaking Covenant..201
   Summary 202
   Activation Time 204
   Assignment 204
   Common Illnesses and Demonic Roots 206

LESSON 11 – Healing for the Unbeliever 208
    Kingdom of God Has Come to You 208
    The Messianic Miracles 210
        Healing of a Jewish Leper 211
        Healing of a Man Blind from Birth 213
        Casting Out of a Dumb Spirit 216
        A Fourth-Day Man, Raised from the Dead 217
    Our Mission 219
    Summary 224
    Love Chapter 225
    Activation Time 226
    Assignment 226

LESSON 12 – Be Released 228
    Personal Release 228
    Released for Ministry 230
    Activation and Assignment 232

ACKNOWLEDGMENTS

This manual, "Healed and Released," is the result of the grace of God and His faithfulness. At a time when I was struggling to complete the last two or three chapters and was even questioning if I was really suppose to write the book at all, God in His faithfulness used several of His prophetic servants to bring words of encouragement that assured me "Healed and Released" was part of His plan for my life. I'm grateful for those who were obedient and allowed Holy Spirit to use them to speak those words of encouragement into my life at a time when I desperately needed to hear them. Those words supplied the encouragement I needed to press on and complete the task.

I want to also express my heart felt gratitude to Rev. Cheryl Schang, a special friend and mentor to me. A large portion of the material in "Healed and Released" has its foundation from the teaching I received while sitting under her ministry. Much of the content is information that I gleaned from notes and tapes of her teachings. I especially appreciate Cheryl's diligence in digging into the truth of God's Word. I will be eternally thankful for her faith in me. Cheryl's ability to not only teach but her unselfish willingness to release those she taught into ministry can only be described as a God-given gift that is rare.

Kitty Williams is another person who played on important part in the completion of "Healed and Released." Kitty is a long time personal friend who has always been there to encourage and support me. Her faith in me and her financial support has helped to make the publication of "Healed and Release" possible. Her support and friendship is very precious to me. Thank you, Kitty.

Special thanks to Gary Stripling who did the final editing for me. Thank You, Gary, for your time, expertise, and support. In addition, there are others, too many to name, who spent their time reading "Healed and Released" and helping me with formatting and early editing. Your acts of kindness and love will not be forgotten.

Last but certainly not least I want to thank Charles Parker, my loving husband, best friend, and most enthusiastic cheerleader. Charles has always encouraged me to stretch myself beyond what I thought I could do. He believes in me when I question my own abilities. It was his encouragement that started me on the path of writing "Healed and Released" and it was his faith in me that motivated me to press on to the finish when it would have been much easier to quit. Thank you, Charles, for not giving up on me. We did it!

My prayer is that "Healed and Released" will be instrumental in bringing healing to those who are in need of healing and that it will be an encouragement and resource tool for " Equipping the Believer" for the work of the ministry (Ephesians 4:11-12).

INTRODUCTION

*W*elcome to an exciting journey through the Word of God which focuses on healing for the believer and for the unbeliever. My purpose for writing "Healed and Released" is, first and foremost, to lay a Biblical foundation for the believer to receive physical healing and walk in divine heath in the same way they received their spiritual healing, eternal life. Jesus made atonement for both at the Cross of Calvary (Isaiah 53:4-5; I Peter 2:24).

The second purpose for "Healed and Released" is to equip and release the *believer* to do the works of Jesus (John 14:12) in their sphere of influence: in their home, on the job, in the market place, etc.

In order for group study to achieve the full potential from this manual, lessons need to be held weekly and be two and a half to three hours in length. Each lesson is divided into three sections: Biblical teachings, activations, and weekly assignments.

The first half of the lesson time is spent in Bible study and instruction. It is during this time that the student will learn foundational Biblical truths upon which their faith can be established.

The second half of the lesson time is given to activation. The student will receive instructions in activities and drills designed to activate and develop the learned material in their personal life. Each student will have the opportunity to put into practice the truths he/she learned during the time of instruction.

At the end of each lesson is a weekly assignment section. Each student will be encouraged to put into practice during that week the truths and activities learned in the lesson and record the results of their experience.

This lesson format is designed to create a safe place for the student to (1) grow in the knowledge of the Word of God, (2) develop their ability to allow the manifestations of the Holy Spirit to flow through them, and (3) experience God using them to minister to others.

My prayer is that upon completion of this study the student will be fully convinced that it is God's will for everybody, everywhere, all the time, to be healed and that He wants to use them, the believer, to release the power and manifestations of the Holy Spirit into their world.

The world is waiting for the Body of Christ to begin to walk in the demonstration of the power of the Holy Spirit which will usher in the "end time" harvest. It is my hope that this journey through "Healed and Released" will help prepare the Body of Christ for that harvest time.

LESSON 1 - His Presence

Memory Verse

Thou wilt shew me the path of life: in thy presence is fullness of joy; at thy right hand there are pleasures for evermore. (Psalms 16:11 KJV)

Introduction

When ministering healing, deliverance, and in the supernatural realm, there are many Biblical truths to be studied and understood: faith, knowledge of what the Bible says on the subject, the anointing, authority of the believer, power of the tongue, etc. We will study many of these topics in the lessons contained in this manual.

The first Biblical truth I want us to look at is: Ministry is to flow out of an intimate relationship with the Father.

So Jesus answered them by saying, I assure you, most solemnly I tell you, the Son is able to do nothing of Himself (of His own accord); but He is able to do only what He sees the Father doing, for whatever the Father does is what the Son does in the same way [in His turn]. (John 5:19 AMP)

Jesus did only what He saw the Father doing and He did it the same way He saw the Father doing it. He did nothing of Himself. Everything Jesus did flowed out of the relationship He had with the Father.

Believest thou not that I am in the Father, and the Father in me? The words that I speak unto you I speak not of myself: but the Father that dwelleth in me, he doeth the works. (John 14:10 KJV)

Jesus tells us that the words He spoke and the works He did were not of Himself rather they were of the Father and the Holy Spirit, who dwelled in Him doing the works.

Verily, verily, I say unto you, He that believeth on me, the works that I do shall he do also; and greater works than these shall he do; because I go unto my Father. (John 14:12 KJV)

If we, as believers, are going to heal all manner of sickness and disease, cast out devils, raise the dead, work miracles, control the elements, multiply food, walk on water, turn water into wine, and accomplish anything we undertake to do in the natural and spiritual realm as Jesus did, it is vital that we pursue an intimate relationship with the Fath

Created for His Presence

Ministry, in the supernatural, flows out of His presence.

Surely the righteous shall give thanks unto thy name: the upright shall dwell in thy presence. (Psalms 140:13 KJV)

Mankind was created to dwell in His presence. Therefore, it is important that we learn how to develop a lifestyle of walking in His presence.

Before the fall Adam and Eve walked and talked face to face with God. They were filled with the very breath, life, and presence of God. All their thought life flowed out of His presence. His thoughts were their thoughts. They had access to the tree of life and to the complete mind of God. His desires were their desires. All their provision came from His presence. Everything they needed flowed out of His presence from within them. They were clothed with His glory.

And they were both naked, the man and his wife, and were not ashamed. (Genesis 2:25 KJV)

Unfortunately, Adam and Eve chose to disobey God and they ate of the tree of the knowledge of good and evil.

And when the woman saw that the tree was good for food, and that it was pleasant to the eyes, and a tree to be desired to make one wise, she took of the fruit thereof, and did eat, and gave also unto her husband with her; and he did eat. (Genesis 3:6 KJV)

For the first time, mankind received instruction, knowledge, and wisdom from a source other than God. They began to look and depend on the creation rather than the Creator. They committed spiritual idolatry and mankind died spiritually. To be spiritually dead is to be separated from the presence of God. The glory that once clothed Adam and Eve left them.

And the eyes of them both were opened, and they knew that they were naked; and they sewed fig leaves together, and made themselves aprons. (Genesis 3:7 KJV)

And they heard the voice of the LORD God walking in the garden in the cool of the day: and Adam and his wife hid themselves from the presence of the LORD God amongst the trees of the garden. (Genesis 3:8 KJV)

The presence of the Lord that once gave life, health, protection, peace, joy, and security to Adam and Eve brought fear.

And he said, I heard thy voice in the garden, and I was afraid, because I was naked; and I hid myself. (Genesis 3:10 KJV)

Instead of the Life of God ruling mankind, sin and death entered the world and death was passed on to all mankind. Mankind instantly died spiritually. To be spiritually dead is to be separated from God the Father.

Therefore, as sin came into the world through one man, and death as the result of sin, so death spread to all men, [no one being able to stop it or to escape its power] because all men sinned. (Romans 5:12 AMP)

For the wages which sin pays is death, but the [bountiful] free gift of God is eternal life through (in union with) Jesus Christ our Lord. (Romans 6:23 AMP)

The good news is: God the Father loves mankind so much that He provided a way for us to be restored back into fellowship with Him.

But God shows and clearly proves His [own] love for us by the fact that while we were still sinners, Christ (the Messiah, the Anointed One) died for us. (Romans 5:8 AMP)

God sent Jesus, the sinless Son of God, to pay the price for the sin of all mankind on the Cross of Calvary so we could again have fellowship with Him and the life of God could again rule and reign in our lives.

For he hath made him to be sin for us, who knew no sin; that we might be made the righteousness of God in him. (2 Corinthians 5:21 KJV)

Well then, as one man's trespass [one man's false step and falling away led] to condemnation for all men, so one Man's act of righteousness [leads] to acquittal and right standing with God and life for all men. (Romans 5:18 AMP)

We have been restored to right standing with God through the Blood of Jesus Christ. God restored to man the two things he lost in the garden. As Christians, Father God has made it possible for us to dwell (live) in His presence (healing for our spirit and soul) here on the earth, and He has made it possible for us to walk in divine health in our body.

I have been crucified with Christ [in Him I have shared His crucifixion]; it is no longer I who live, but Christ (the Messiah) lives in me; and the life I now live in

> *the body I live by faith in (by adherence to and reliance on and complete trust in) the Son of God, Who loved me and gave Himself up for me. (Galatians 2:20 AMP)*
>
> *Therefore if any person is [ingrafted] in Christ (the Messiah) he is a new creation (a new creature altogether); the old [previous moral and spiritual condition] has passed away. Behold, the fresh and new has come! (2 Corinthians 5:17 AMP)*
>
> *Do you not know that your body is the temple (the very sanctuary) of the Holy Spirit Who lives within you, Whom you have received [as a Gift] from God? You are not your own. (1 Corinthians 6:19 AMP)*

Father God has made a way for us to dwell in His presence. We have the Holy Spirit on the inside of us to lead, guide and empower us. However, it does not happen automatically just because we are Christians. We must pursue Him.

> *Seeing then that we have a great high priest that is passed into the heavens, Jesus the Son of God, let us hold fast our profession. (Hebrews 4:14 KJV)*
>
> *For we have not a high priest which cannot be touched with the feeling of our infirmities; but was in all points tempted like as we are, yet without sin. (Hebrews 4:15 KJV)*
>
> *Let us therefore come boldly unto the throne of grace, that we may obtain mercy, and find grace to help in time of need. (Hebrews 4:16 KJV)*

The word boldly in verse 16 does not mean that we can just go to God any way we please. It means that because of what Jesus did for us on the Cross we can now approach the throne of grace without fear or intimidation and with full assurance that He will be merciful to us in a time of need. We approach Him not on our own merit but through the precious Blood of Jesus and His finished work of the Cross. However, we must follow His instructions on how to approach the throne.

I remember a friend telling how one day she was angry and she went to God with an attitude about the situation. She said she heard the Holy Spirit say, "Stop! Young lady, do not you ever approach Me with that attitude again." We have access to His presence but we must come according to His instructions.

God has always given His people clear instructions as to how He is to be approached and how we are to worship Him.

> *Let us come before his presence with thanksgiving, and make a joyful noise unto him with psalms. (Psalms 95:2 KJV)*
>
> *Serve the LORD with gladness: come before his presence with singing. (Psalms 100:2 KJV)*

God is omnipresent but we must, as an act of our will, choose to enter into and walk in His presence. Scripture teaches us that the way we enter into His presence is through praise.

Lesson 1 - His Presence

As you read through the Old Testament you will find different Hebrew words translated as the word "praise" in English. Each of those words described a different type of praise and are designed to be used in different situations.

- *Barak*: to kneel as an act of adoration; to bless God
- *Zamar*: to celebrate in song and music; to touch the strings or parts of a musical instrument
- *Yadah*: to worship with waving hands as if to throw a stone or arrow
- *Todah*: worship with extended hands; specifically a choir of worshippers
- *Shabach*: praise in a loud tone
- *Hillul*: a celebration of thanksgiving for harvest; comes from the root word *halal*
- *Tehillah*: *halal* to music; a hymn of praise
- *Halal:* to shine, to make a show, to boast, to be clamorously foolish, to rave, to celebrate, to stultify (Webster's Dictionary: Stultify = to cause to appear to be stupid, foolish, or absurdly illogical).

These definitions of praise make it very clear that praise of any kind is not just something we say. Rather, praise is something we do. Further study reveals that the type of praise being expressed was dependent on the situation.

For example: when expressing thanksgiving for what God has done, the word *yadah* is used and is often translated "give thanks or thanksgiving." When a choir of worshippers is expressing thanksgiving, the word *todah* is used and is often translated "thanksgiving."

> *Enter into his gates with thanksgiving* **(todah)**, *and into his courts with praise* **(tehillah or halal with music)**: *be thankful* **(yadah)** *unto him, and bless* **(barak)** *his name. (Psalms 100:4 KJV)*

Most Christians would agree that this verse of Scripture is giving instructions on how to enter into the presence of God. However, very few Christians have a full understanding of those instructions, and those who may have an understanding rarely actually follow the instructions.

This verse tells us that *todah* (choir of worshipers with extended hands) praise gets us in the gate and *halaling* (wild crazy praise) with music gets us into His courts. As you approach His throne, *yadah* (waving hands like you are throwing a stone or arrow), and once you are in His presence, bow low, *barak*.

Sadly, many of God's people are worshipping Him at the gate because they do not have an understanding of *halal* or *tehillah* praise. They never get past the gates.

Most of the Church in general expresses *zamar* praise, celebrating Him in song and musical instruments. It is also familiar with *barak* praise, kneeling as an act of adoration to God. In some Churches that are considered to go a little overboard in their praise, you will see *yadah* praise, worship with the waving of the hands (as if to throw a stone) and even *todah* praise, a choir of worshippers praising with extended hands, expressed among the congregation. If the Church is considered to be a little radical, you may even see and hear *shabach* praise, praising in a loud tone. However, few Churches experience this *halal* praise or the *hillul* and *tehillah* praise, which comes from the Hebrew root word *halal*.

They leave off one of the wheels of their vehicle - *halal* - thereby doing all their praise at the gate and never reaching the throne room and His presence.

Halal Praise

God has ordained praise as the vehicle to take us into His presence. Our destination is His presence. Our vehicle is praise. If our vehicle, our car, is missing a wheel, we probably will not reach our destination.

If *halal* praise is one of the wheels of our vehicle into His presence, we need a Biblical understanding of:

- What it is;
- What to do;
- Why God wants us to *halal* praise;
- What the benefits are.

Halal praise is a quick and direct access to the manifest presence of God and it is a powerful weapon that God has given to us to defeat the enemy in our lives.

Definition of *Halal*

Halal praise is a wild kind of praise. I heard someone who understands the Hebrew language much better than me say that if you take the words describing *halal* from the Strong's Dictionary and put them into a sentence, it would sound something like this: "Give to the Lord a bright shining celebration with ranting and raving and boasting and bragging and clamorous foolishness, appearing to be somebody who is drunk or temporarily gone insane while praising God."

Truly we cannot *halal* with our mouth closed, or sitting down, or standing still. When we *halal*, we will look like we are drunk or have lost our minds. (Example: The Day of Pentecost)

A study of the word *halal* reveals that *halal* praise is a command, not a suggestion. The book of Psalms alone is filled with commands to *halal* the Lord.

> *Ye that fear the lord, praise* **(halal)** *him. . . (Psalms 22:23 KJV)*

> *Let the heaven and earth praise* **(halal)** *him, the seas, and everything that moves therein. (Psalms 69:34 KJV)*

> *Let the poor and needy praise* **(halal)** *thy name. (Psalms 74:21 KJV)*

> *Praise* **(halal)** *ye the Lord. Praise* **(halal)**, *o ye servants of the Lord, praise* **(halal)** *the name of the Lord. (Psalms 113:1 KJV)*

> *O praise* **(halal)** *the Lord, all ye nations. . . (Psalms 117:1 KJV)*

> *Praise* **(halal)** *ye the Lord, praise* **(halal)** *ye the name of the Lord; praise him, O ye servants of the Lord. (Psalms 135:1 KJV)*

> *Praise* **(halal)** *ye the Lord, o my soul. (Psalms 146:1 KJV)*

The entire chapter of Psalms 148 is (*halal*) praise, as well as Psalms 150.

If we want to dwell in His presence we must first learn to move into His court with *tehillah* or *halal* praise.

Why God Wants This Kind of Praise

In Isaiah 14 the prophet begins by describing the defeat of the king of Babylon. Then in verses 12-15 he describes the fall of Lucifer.

Satan's name before he was kicked out of heaven was Lucifer. Lucifer is the Hebrew word *hallel* which comes from the root word *halal*, meaning wild and crazy praise. Lucifer's very name was wild praise. He led *halal* or wild praise in heaven. He not only led wild praise, he was wild praise.

Lucifer lost his position in heaven and his name was changed to Satan. His position has been given to us. As Christians we are now responsible for filling the earth with *halal* praise and releasing God's manifest presence into the earth.

Benefits of *Halal* Praise

Halal praise can quickly take you into the Throne Room and into His presence, but there is another benefit of *halaling*.

All praise blesses God but it seems that different kinds of praise accomplish different things in the spirit realm.

In modern Biblical studies we know that the first mention of a name or word is significant and everything about that situation where it is used is significant. If you have a word and you are trying to determine the correct or best interpretation of it, go back to the place in the Bible where it is first used and look at the context. That's the general rule for interpretation.

The first use of *halal* was used in connection with the overthrow of Israel's enemies. Is it not just like God to ordain *halal* praise or wild praise (Lucifer's name) to be the instrument we are to use to destroy the works of our enemy (Satan himself)? God really does have a sense of humor!

King David

> *And he appointed certain of the Levites to minister before the ark of the LORD, and to record, and to thank* **(yadah)** *and praise* **(halal)** *the LORD God of Israel: (1 Chronicles 16:4 KJV)*

This is the first mention of *halal* in the Bible. David had just defeated the Philistines and had brought the ark of God back to the City of David, Jerusalem. After offering burnt sacrifices and peace offerings before the Lord, the first thing David did was to appoint Levites to minister before the ark of the Lord and to thank (*yadah*) and praise (*halal*) the Lord God of Israel.

It was the same kind of praise that caused Michal to despise King David in her heart when she saw him dancing and playing as they brought the ark of God into the city. David had stripped himself of his kingly robes and was dancing before the ark. He was dancing so wildly that his wife thought he was making a public spectacle of himself to the point that he was a total embarrassment to her. That is *halal* praise.

Give thanks unto the LORD, call upon his name, make known his deeds among the people. (1 Chronicles 16:8 KJV)

David gives us clear instructions as to how to halal. We are to call upon His name and make known His deeds among the people. Then in verses 9-35 he begins to halal: declaring the works of God among the people (Psalms 104 and 105).

Halal praise is declaring who God is in our situation. It is extolling Him. It is ranting and raving, not like a lunatic, but ranting and raving about God. You make known His deeds among the people.

Throughout the Scriptures God is consistent in His use of *halal* praise in situations dealing with the defeat of an enemy.

Jehoshaphat: 2 Chronicles 20

In 2 Chronicles 20 three kings came against Jehoshaphat and Judah.

And Jehoshaphat feared, and set himself to seek the LORD, and proclaimed a fast throughout all Judah. (2 Chronicles 20:3 KJV)

And Judah gathered themselves together, to ask help of the LORD: even out of all the cities of Judah they came to seek the LORD. (2 Chronicles 20:4 KJV)

Verse 3 tells us Jehoshaphat feared and decided to seek the Lord. He called a fast throughout Judah and all Judah gathered together to ask help of the Lord. In verse 6 we see that Jehoshaphat's idea of asking the Lord for help was halaling.

And said, O LORD God of our fathers, art not thou God in heaven? and rulest not thou over all the kingdoms of the heathen? And in thine hand is there not power and might, so that none is able to withstand thee? (2 Chronicles 20:6 KJV)

In verses 6-12 he continues to declare who God is in their situation. He proclaimed the deeds and the works of the Lord among the people, lifting God up and making Him bigger than their problem.

Then upon Jahaziel the son of Zechariah, the son of Benaiah, the son of Jeiel, the son of Mattaniah, a Levite of the sons of Asaph, came the Spirit of the LORD in the midst of the congregation; (2 Chronicles 20:14 KJV)

And he said, Hearken ye, all Judah, and ye inhabitants of Jerusalem, and thou king Jehoshaphat, Thus saith the LORD unto you, Be not afraid nor dismayed by reason of this great multitude; for the battle is not yours, but God's. (2 Chronicles 20:15 KJV)

While they were *halaling* the Spirit of God manifested in the midst of the congregation through a Levite named Jahaziel and he began to prophesy. First he gave a word of *encouragement* saying,

Lesson 1 - His Presence

"Be not afraid, nor dismayed by reason of this great multitude; for the battle is not yours, but God's." (verse 15). Then in verse 16 he spoke a Word of Knowledge:

> *Tomorrow go ye down against them: behold, they come up by the cliff of Ziz; and ye shall find them at the end of the brook, before the wilderness of Jeruel. (2 Chronicles 20:16 KJV)*

God revealed to them the location of their enemy. Then God, speaking through Jahaziel, gave these instructions (verse 17):

> *Ye shall not need to fight in this battle: set yourselves, stand ye still, and see the salvation of the LORD with you, O Judah and Jerusalem: fear not, nor be dismayed; tomorrow go out against them: for the LORD will be with you. (2 Chronicles 20:17 KJV)*

All Judah fell before the Lord, worshipping Him (verse 18). The Levites stood up and praised (*halaled*) the Lord God of Israel with a loud voice (verse 19).

The next morning Jehoshaphat instructed the army to believe in the Lord and to believe His prophets so they would prosper:

> *And when he had consulted with the people, he appointed singers unto the LORD, and that should praise **(halal)** the beauty of holiness, as they went out before the army, and to say, Praise **(yadah)** the LORD; for his mercy endureth forever. (2 Chronicles 20:21 KJV)*

> *And when they began to sing and to praise **(tehillah),** the LORD set ambushments against the children of Ammon, Moab, and mount Seir, which were come against Judah; and they were smitten. (2 Chronicles 20:22 KJV)*

The word sing in verse 22 is a Hebrew word meaning to shout or to sing out for joy. The word praise is *tehillah*, meaning to *halal* to music.

When they began to sing out for joy and to *halal* to music the Lord set ambushments and destroyed all the enemy of Judah. Something was triggered by their praise and the enemy destroyed themselves.

When Jehoshaphat and his army arrived at the place where their enemy was, they were all dead; there was an abundance of riches and jewels found with their dead bodies and verse 25 tells us it took them three days to gather and carry away the spoils. Pretty awesome, don't you think? It took over a million men (2 Chronicles 17:14-19) three days to carry away the spoils and they did not even have to raise a sword!

When we *halal* something happens in the spirit realm and the reward is unbelievable. In Psalms 149 David devotes the entire chapter to *halal* praise and the overthrow of our enemies.

Psalms 149

> *Praise **(halal)** ye the LORD. Sing unto the LORD a new song, and his praise **(tehillah)** in the congregation of saints. (Psalms 149:1 KJV)*
>
> *Let Israel rejoice in him that made him: let the children of Zion be joyful in their King. (Psalms 149:2 KJV)*
>
> *Let them praise **(halal)** his name in the dance: let them sing praises **(zamar)** unto him with the timbrel and harp. (Psalms 149:3 KJV)*
>
> *For the LORD taketh pleasure in his people: he will beautify the meek with salvation. (Psalms 149:4 KJV)*
>
> *Let the saints be joyful in glory: let them sing aloud upon their beds. (Psalms 149:5 KJV)*
>
> *Let the high praises of God be in their mouth, and a two-edged sword in their hand;(Psalms 149:6 KJV)*
>
> *To execute vengeance upon the heathen, and punishments upon the people; (Psalms 149:7 KJV)*
>
> *To bind their kings with chains, and their nobles with fetters of iron; (Psalms 149:8 KJV)*
>
> *To execute upon them the judgment written: this honor have all his saints. Praise **(halal)** ye the LORD. (Psalms 149:9 KJV)*

In verse 8 David tells us that "*We bind kings with chains and their nobles with fetters of iron*" when we *halal*.

We know we cannot bind earthly kings with praise. David is talking about spiritual kings or rulers and we can bind them with our *halal* praise. The entire chapter is talking about defeating the enemy through *halal* praise.

Psalms 149 is the only Scripture that tells us we can bind things in the spirit realm and the only way is through *halal* praise. *Halal* praise is one of the key weapons of our spiritual warfare.

Matthew 18:18 is a Scripture that almost every one quotes thinking they can to do spiritual warfare with it.

> *Truly I say unto you, whatsoever you shall bind on earth shall be bound in heaven; and whatsoever ye shall loose on earth shall be loosed in heaven. (Matthew 18:18 KJV)*

Lesson 1 - His Presence

This verse taken in the proper original context is a lecture on Church government. Do not permit what God has forbidden. Do not forbid what God has permitted. Do not put vain obligations on the people. The Amplified Bible gives us better interpretation:

> *Truly I tell you, whatever you forbid and declare to be improper and unlawful on earth must be what is already forbidden in heaven, and whatever you permit and delare proper and lawful on earth must be what is already permitted in heaven. (Matthew 18:18 AMP)*

I used to do what we call normal spiritual warfare, binding this spirit and that spirit. Even if you can get some results why would you want to battle and struggle with the enemy all the time when Jesus has already defeated him? How about acting foolish for a short period of time and then just collecting the spoil?

Can we bind things in the spirit realm? Yes! But not by saying "I bind you." Psalms 149 is the only Scripture that gives instructions on how we are to do that. We do it through *halal* praise. The kind of praise that is appropriate for overcoming the enemy is wild praise.

- ➢ Lost your job and have no paycheck – what are you going to do? *HALAL!*
- ➢ You need a breakthrough and you do not want it to take a long time. *HALAL!*
- ➢ Got a bad doctor's report? Declare who He is in that situation. *HALAL!*

> *Neither murmur ye, as some of them also murmured, and were destroyed of the destroyer. (1 Corinthians 10:10 KJV)*

Murmuring and complaining causes you to be destroyed. Thanking and *halaling* gets you the victory. Anytime the enemy attacks you, do not murmur and complain. Declare who God is in your situation. Make God bigger than your problem. (This is where it is beneficial to be rooted and grounded in the Word of God.)

When we are ministering healing and deliverance to others, we are taking back territory from Satan, the enemy of their souls. *Halaling* before we minister ensures the victory. *Halaling* after maintains the victory.

Halaling brings the presence of God into our situation. His presence destroys the work of our enemy.

> *When mine enemies are turned back, they shall fall and perish at thy presence. (Psalms 9:3 KJV)*

If our desire is to do as Jesus did — heal them all — it is absolutely vital for us to develop a lifestyle of *halal* praise so we can walk and minister from His manifest presence. We must daily spend time in His presence as preparation for ministering healing and deliverance to the sick people we encounter every day.

Salvation Opportunity

Our acceptance of Jesus' finished work on the Cross of Calvary gives us access to the presence of Father God.

Before we go any further, I want to ask, "If Jesus were to return or you were to die tonight, would you go to heaven?" If your answer is not YES and you want to be absolutely sure of your eternal destination, please stand to your feet. I want to pray for you.

Jesus answered, Verily, verily, I say unto thee, Except a man be born of water and of the Spirit, he cannot enter into the kingdom of God. (John 3:5 KJV)

Prayer: Father God, I confess that I am a sinner. I repent for my sins. This day I turn away from them. I ask You, Lord, to forgive me and to cleanse me from all unrighteousness. I confess that I believe Jesus Christ died for me, rose from the dead, is alive, and seated at the right hand of God the Father. Come into my heart, Lord Jesus and be my Lord and my Savior. I give my life to You and I will serve You all the days of my life. Thank You, Lord Jesus, for forgiving me, giving me a new life, and giving me eternal life with You. In the name of my Lord, Jesus Christ, I pray. Amen.

Activation Time

Salvation Opportunity:

- Read the salvation Scriptures and pray the prayer provided at the end of this lesson.
- If manual is being used in a group, ask if there is anyone who would like to be born again. Read the Scriptures and lead them in the salvation prayer.
- Signs and wonders point to Jesus and who He is. Once a person receives a miracle or healing from Jesus they are often open to receive Him as their Lord and Savior. The believer should be equipped and ready to lead them to the Lord. A list of Scriptures and an example of a prayer is provided at the end of this lesson for you to use as a guideline for leading someone to Jesus.

Attributes of God:

The purpose of the following activation is to have the person experience how *halaling* brings them into the presence of God and increase the awareness, of the believer, of what God's voice sounds like on the inside of them.

- Make a list of at least 5 attributes of God, words describing who God is in your life, using the handout provided at the end of this lesson. (Example: Savior, healer, counselor, etc.) If using manual to teach a group, make a copy of the handout for each student.
- Spend time practicing entering into His presence, *halaling* using your list. Declare who God is in your life for 1 minute. Be silent and listen. Record the thoughts that come to you. Repeat the process 5 times.

Assignment

- Meditate on and memorize the memory verse.
- Add 5 more attributes of God to your list.
- Begin your daily prayer time by *halaling* for at least 2 minutes using your list of attributes of God.
- Pray and ask God to give you somebody to lead to the Lord.

Assignment Result and Comments

Salvation Scriptures

All have sinned:

Since all have sinned and are falling short of the honor and glory which God bestows and receives. (Romans 3:23 AMP)

The wages of sin:

For the wages which sin pays is death, but the [bountiful] free gift of God is eternal life through (in union with) Jesus Christ our Lord. (Romans 6:23 AMP)

Jesus died for our sins:

But God shows and clearly proves His [own] love for us by the fact that while we were still sinners, Christ (the Messiah, the Anointed One) died for us. (Romans 5:8 AMP)

God's provision for eternal life:

For God so greatly loved and dearly prized the world that He [even] gave up His only begotten (unique) Son, so that whoever believes in (trusts in, clings to, relies on) Him shall not perish (come to destruction, be lost) but have eternal (everlasting) life. (John 3:16 AMP)

Accept the work of the Cross:

Because if you acknowledge and confess with your lips that Jesus is Lord and in your heart believe (adhere to, trust in, and rely on the truth) that God raised Him from the dead, you will be saved. (Romans 10:9 AMP)

For with the heart a person believes (adheres to, trusts in, and relies on Christ) and so is justified (declared righteous, acceptable to God), and with the mouth he confesses (declares openly and speaks out freely his faith) and confirms [his] salvation. (Romans 10:10 AMP)

Salvation Prayer of Repentance

Lead them in a prayer of repentance and acceptance of the work of the Cross.

> **Prayer:** Father God, I confess that I am a sinner. I repent for my sins. This day I turn away from them. I ask You, Lord, to forgive me and to cleanse me from all unrighteousness. I confess that I believe Jesus Christ died for me, rose from the dead, is alive, and seated at the right hand of God the Father. Come into my heart, Lord Jesus and be my Lord and my Savior. I give my life to You and I will serve You all the days of my life. Thank You, Lord Jesus, for forgiving me, giving me a new life, and giving me eternal life with You. In the name of my Lord, Jesus Christ, I pray. Amen.

Lesson 1 - His Presence

My List of Attributes of God

LESSON 2 - Healing and the Holy Spirit

Memory Verse

How God anointed Jesus of Nazareth with the Holy Ghost and with power: who went about doing good and healing all that were oppressed of the devil; for God was with him. (Acts 10:38 KJV)

Introduction

*I*n Lesson 1 we discussed at length the fact that Jesus' intimate relationship with the Father was a vital part of His ministry. He only did what He saw the Father do and He did it the way the Father said to do it.

> *"In most solemn truth I tell you," replied Jesus, "that the Son can do nothing of Himself—He can only do what He sees the Father doing; for whatever He does, that the Son does in like manner." (John 5:19 WNT)*

Jesus is our example. Therefore, it is important for us to develop and practice a lifestyle of spending time in His presence if we want the supernatural power of God to operate in our lives. All supernatural ministry must flow out of an intimate relationship with the Father.

We have learned that *halal* praise is a key to entering into the very Throne Room of God and that it is our major weapon in defeating our enemy, the devil. Therefore, it is important for the believer to develop and practice a lifestyle of spending time in His presence through *halal* praise on a daily basis.

Further study of the ministry of Jesus reveals another key to operating in the supernatural. It is found in our memory verse. (Read Memory Verse)

Jesus was anointed by God with the Holy Ghost. His power or ability to do the signs and wonders, miracles, healings, and deliverances came from His intimate relationship with the Holy Spirit. All the works of Jesus were done as the Son of Man empowered by the Holy Ghost.

Jesus never healed one person nor did He do one miracle before He was baptized in the Holy Spirit. Jesus not only had an intimate relationship with the Father, He had an intimate relationship with the Holy Spirit.

Lesson 2 - Healing And The Holy Spirit

A relationship with the Holy Spirit is the springboard into ministry in the supernatural. Therefore, it is vital for the believer to get to know the Holy Spirit and to develop an intimate relationship with Him.

The Holy Spirit in the Old Testament

From the beginning we see the Holy Spirit at work.

In the beginning God created the heaven and the earth. (Genesis 1:1 KJV)

And the earth was without form, and void; and darkness was upon the face of the deep. And the Spirit of God moved upon the face of the waters. (Genesis 1:2 KJV)

And God said, Let there be light: and there was light. (Genesis 1:3 KJV)

Creation itself gives us a picture of God, the Word of God, and the Spirit of God working together to bring about the plans and purposes of God.

And God said, Let us make man in our image, after our likeness: and let them have dominion over the fish of the sea, and over the fowl of the air, and over the cattle, and over all the earth, and over every creeping thing that creepeth upon the earth. (Genesis 1:26 KJV)

Mankind, Adam, was created after the image of God the Father, God the Son, and God the Holy Spirit.

And the LORD God formed man of the dust of the ground, and breathed into his nostrils the breath of life; and man became a living soul. (Genesis 2:7 KJV)

God formed man from the dust of the earth, but the impartation of the Breath of God, the Breath of Life, or Holy Spirit of God, made man a living soul. From the beginning it was God's intention for His Holy Spirit to reside or dwell in mankind.
Before the fall, Adam thought like God; he had the mind of Christ in its fullness. He received all his instructions from Holy Spirit who was within him. In Him, God, Adam truly moved, lived, and had his being (Acts 17:28).
After the fall, the Holy Spirit was still in the earth, but He could no longer dwell in mankind because of sin.
However, throughout the Old Testament was see the Holy Spirit manifesting Himself upon chosen individuals, usually kings, priests, or prophets, for the purpose of giving direction to God's people, bringing healing and deliverance to His people, establishing the plans and purposes of God, and declaring future events in the earth.

Zechariah — Priest

And the Spirit of God came upon Zechariah the son of Jehoiada the priest, which stood above the people, and said unto them, Thus saith God, Why transgress ye the commandments of the LORD, that ye cannot prosper? Because ye have forsaken the LORD, he hath also forsaken you. (2 Chronicles 24:20 KJV)

David — King

Then Samuel took the horn of oil, and anointed him in the midst of his brethren: and the Spirit of the LORD came upon David from that day forward. So Samuel rose up, and went to Ramah. (1 Samuel 16:13 KJV)

Ezekiel — Prophet

And the Spirit of the LORD fell upon me, and said unto me, Speak; Thus saith the LORD; Thus have ye said, O house of Israel: for I know the things that come into your mind, every one of them. (Ezekiel 11:5 KJV)

Samson

And the woman bore a son, and called his name Samson: and the child grew, and the LORD blessed him. (Judges 13:24 KJV)

And the Spirit of the LORD began to move him at times in the camp of Dan between Zorah and Eshtaol. (Judges 13:25 KJV)

Samson was born to a woman who was the wife of *Monaoh* from the tribe of Dan. She was barren until an angel of the Lord appeared to her (Judges 13:3). The Spirit of God came on Samson to fulfill the plans and purposes of God until he disobeyed God and fell into sin.

These are just a few examples of the Spirit of God coming on certain individuals in order that the plans and purposes of God might be done on the earth.

And it shall come to pass afterward, that I will pour out my spirit upon all flesh; and your sons and your daughters shall prophesy, your old men shall dream dreams, your young men shall see visions. (Joel 2:28 KJV)

And also upon the servants and upon the handmaids in those days will I pour out my spirit. (Joel 2:29 KJV)

The prophet Joel prophesied of a time that would come when God would pour out His Spirit on all flesh, mankind.

The Holy Spirit in the New Testament

Before Jesus' death, burial and resurrection, we see the Holy Spirit manifesting in much the same way He did in the Old Testament.

John the Baptist: Luke 1:15

For he shall be great in the sight of the Lord, and shall drink neither wine nor strong drink; and he shall be filled with the Holy Ghost, even from his mother's womb. (Luke 1:15 KJV)

John the Baptist was filled with the Holy Spirit from his mother's womb. His father, Zacharias, was a Jewish priest from the tribe of Levi.

Jesus' Conception: Luke 1:34-35

Then said Mary unto the angel, "How shall this be, seeing I know not a man?" (Luke 1:34 KJV)

And the angel answered and said unto her, "The Holy Ghost shall come upon thee, and the power of the Highest shall overshadow thee: therefore also that holy thing which shall be born of thee shall be called the Son of God." (Luke 1:35 KJV)

Jesus was conceived by the Holy Spirit. He was born of the Spirit. The Holy Spirit came upon Mary to bring about the plan of God in the earth.

Elizabeth: Luke 1:41-45

In Luke 1:41 Elizabeth, the mother of John the Baptist, was filled with the Holy Ghost when she heard Mary's voice and then she gave Mary a confirming prophetic word. (verse 45)

And it came to pass, that, when Elisabeth heard the salutation of Mary, the babe leaped in her womb; and Elisabeth was filled with the Holy Ghost. (Luke 1:41 KJV)

And she spake out with a loud voice, and said, "Blessed art thou among women, and blessed is the fruit of thy womb." (Luke 1:42 KJV)

And whence is this to me, that the mother of my Lord should come to me? (Luke 1:43 KJV)

For, lo, as soon as the voice of thy salutation sounded in mine ears, the babe leaped in my womb for joy. (Luke 1:44 KJV)

And blessed is she that believed: for there shall be a performance of those things which were told her from the Lord. (Luke 1:45 KJV)

Zacharias: Luke 1:67

Zacharias, who was a Jewish priest (Luke 1:5), was filled with the Spirit after the birth of John the Baptist and he prophesied.

And his father Zacharias was filled with the Holy Ghost, and prophesied. (Luke 1:67 KJV)

Simeon: Luke 2:25-26

And, behold, there was a man in Jerusalem, whose name was Simeon; and the same man was just and devout, waiting for the consolation of Israel: and the Holy Ghost was upon him. (Luke 2:25 KJV)

And it was revealed unto him by the Holy Ghost, that he should not see death, before he had seen the Lord's Christ. (Luke 2:26 KJV)

The Holy Spirit came upon Simeon and revealed to him that he would not die until he saw the Lord's Christ.

As you can see by these examples, the Holy Spirit manifested in and through specific individuals at various times in order to declare and accomplish the Father's plans and purposes for mankind.

Jesus and the Holy Spirit

Matthew 1:18

Now the birth of Jesus Christ was on this wise: When as his mother Mary was espoused to Joseph, before they came together, she was found with child of the Holy Ghost. (Matthew 1:18 KJV)

Then Joseph her husband, being a just man, and not willing to make her a public example, was minded to put her away privily. (Matthew 1:19 KJV)

But while he thought on these things, behold, the angel of the Lord appeared unto him in a dream, saying, Joseph, thou son of David, fear not to take unto thee Mary thy wife; for that which is conceived in her is of the Holy Ghost. (Matthew 1:20 KJV)

Jesus was conceived and born of the Holy Spirit. He was the only Son of God. He was also Son of Man because He was born in the flesh. Jesus was one hundred percent man and one hundred percent God.

In the beginning was the Word, and the Word was with God, and the Word was God. (John 1:1 KJV)

> *And the Word was made flesh, and dwelt among us, (and we beheld his glory, the glory as of the only begotten of the Father,) full of grace and truth. (John 1:14 KJV)*

Jesus was born of the Spirit. He was the Son of God. He stripped himself of all His divine ability and chose to limit himself as a man. Jesus, the Son of Man, was baptized with the Holy Spirit before He began His ministry.

> *Now when all the people were baptized, it came to pass, that Jesus also being baptized, and praying, the heaven was opened, (Luke 3:21 KJV)*

> *And the Holy Ghost descended in a bodily shape like a dove upon him, and a voice came from heaven, which said, Thou art my beloved Son; in thee I am well pleased. (Luke 3:22 KJV)*

When the Holy Spirit came upon Jesus, He stayed.

> *And John bare record, saying, I saw the Spirit descending from heaven like a dove, and it abode upon him. (John 1:32 KJV)*

After Jesus' baptism the Holy Spirit led Him into the wilderness to be tempted by the devil.

> *And Jesus being full of the Holy Ghost returned from Jordan, and was led by the Spirit into the wilderness. (Luke 4:1 KJV)*

When the devil was finished tempting Jesus, he departed from Him for a season and Jesus returned to Galilee in the power of the Holy Spirit.

> *And Jesus returned in the power of the Spirit into Galilee: and there went out a fame of him through all the region round about. (Luke 4:14 KJV)*

Three days after His return to Galilee Jesus and Mary attended a wedding in Cana. We all know the story. The family ran out of wine and Jesus miraculously turned the water into wine (John 2). In the Book of John Chapter 2, verse 11 John tells us this was the beginning of the miracles that Jesus performed.

> *This beginning of miracles did Jesus in Cana of Galilee, and manifested forth his glory; and his disciples believed on him. (John 2:11 KJV)*

Jesus never did a miracle until He was baptized in the Holy Ghost. He operated as the Son of Man filled with the Holy Ghost. His entire ministry on the earth was a demonstration of the Son of Man operating under the influence of the Holy Spirit.

> *How God anointed Jesus of Nazareth with the Holy Ghost and with power: who went about doing good, and healing all that were oppressed of the devil; for God was with him. (Acts 10:38 KJV)*

Jesus was born of the Holy Spirit and yet He was baptized in the Holy Spirit before He began His ministry. He is our example. Jesus came to earth to demonstrate how mankind is to live in partnership with Holy Spirit. When we are born again we are born of the Spirit. However, we still need the baptism of the Holy Spirit that we might walk in the supernatural power of God.

Disciples and the Holy Spirit

And when he had called unto him his twelve disciples, he gave them power against unclean spirits, to cast them out, and to heal all manner of sickness and all manner of disease. (Matthew 10:1 KJV)

Behold, I give unto you power to tread on serpents and scorpions, and over all the power of the enemy: and nothing shall by any means hurt you. (Luke 10:19 KJV)

Jesus gave His twelve disciples and seventy other of His followers power over the enemy before He sent them out. The word *power* in Matthew and the first *power* in Luke is the Greek word *exousia*. It means authority. Jesus gave them authority over all the power of the enemy. The word power in the phrase "*power of the enemy*" in Luke 10:19 is the Greek word *dunamis*. It is where we get our English word dynamite. It means ability. Jesus gave them authority over all the ability of the enemy. They ministered under the anointing and delegated authority of Jesus.

He that believeth on me, as the Scripture hath said, out of his belly shall flow rivers of living water. (John 7:38 KJV)

(But this spake he of the Spirit, which they that believe on him should receive: for the Holy Ghost was not yet given; because that Jesus was not yet glorified.) (John 7:39 KJV)

In these two verses Jesus, speaking to his disciples, foretells the coming of the Holy Spirit to live and dwell in the believer. In John Chapter 13 Jesus foretells His upcoming betrayal and death.
Then in Chapter 14 Jesus tells them He is returning to the Father and the Father will send them the Comforter, the Holy Spirit, who they know for He dwells with them, but He will be in them.

Verily, verily, I say unto you, He that believeth on me, the works that I do shall he do also; and greater works than these shall he do; because I go unto my Father. (John 14:12 KJV)

And I will pray the Father, and he shall give you another Comforter, that he may abide with you forever; (John 14: 16 KJV)

Even the Spirit of truth; whom the world cannot receive, because it seeth him not, neither knoweth him: but ye know him; for he dwelleth with you, and shall be in you. (John 14: 17 KJV)

Lesson 2 - Healing And The Holy Spirit

The Holy Spirit could not dwell in the disciples because they were not as yet born of the Spirit. The Holy Spirit was only with them in the same way He was with the kings, priests, and prophets of the Old Testament.

> *Then said Jesus to them again, Peace be unto you: as my Father hath sent me, even so send I you. (John 20:21 KJV)*

> *And when he had said this, he breathed on them, and saith unto them, Receive ye the Holy Ghost. (John 20:22 KJV)*

The evening after Jesus' resurrection He appeared to the disciples, breathed on them, and commanded them to receive the Holy Spirit. I believe this is when they were born again. They knew Jesus died for their sins, and that God had raised Him from the dead. Jesus was alive.

> *That if thou shalt confess with thy mouth the Lord Jesus, and shalt believe in thine heart that God hath raised him from the dead, thou shalt be saved. (Romans 10:9 KJV)*

According to Romans 10:9 the disciples were saved. They were born of the Spirit. Yet Jesus instructed them not to do anything until they received the Holy Spirit.

Acts 1:2-5

> *Until the day in which he was taken up, after that he through the Holy Ghost had given commandments unto the apostles whom he had chosen. (Acts 1:2 KJV)*

> *To whom also he shewed himself alive after his passion by many infallible proofs, being seen of them forty days, and speaking of the things pertaining to the kingdom of God. (Acts 1:3 KJV)*

> *And, being assembled together with them, commanded them that they should not depart from Jerusalem, but wait for the promise of the Father, which, saith he, ye have heard of me. (Acts 1:4 KJV)*

> *For John truly baptized with water; but ye shall be baptized with the Holy Ghost not many days hence. (Acts 1:5 KJV)*

For forty days Jesus showed himself alive and spent time with the disciples speaking of things pertaining to the Kingdom of God (verse 3).

One of the last things Jesus said to His disciples before His ascension was, "Do not depart from Jerusalem until you receive the promise of the Holy Spirit (verse 4)." Notice it was a command; not a suggestion.

It was during this time that He gave them what the Church of our day calls the Great Commission.

Matthew 28:18-20

> *And Jesus came and spake unto them, saying, All power **(authority)** is given unto me in heaven and in earth. (Matthew 28:18 KJV)*
>
> *Go ye therefore, and teach all nations, baptizing them in the name of the Father, and of the Son, and of the Holy Ghost, (Matthew 28:19 KJV)*
>
> *Teaching them to observe all things whatsoever I have commanded you: and, lo, I am with you always, even unto the end of the world. Amen. (Matthew 28:20 KJV)*

Jesus told His disciples that all authority (power) had been given to Him in heaven and in earth. He then instructed them to go in His delegated authority and teach all nations, baptizing them in the name of the Father, and of the Son, and of the Holy Ghost. The disciples were to teach new converts to observe and to guard from loss all the things that Jesus had commanded them, the disciples, to do. Not just until the Church got started, but to the end of the world.

Why did they need to wait in Jerusalem for the Holy Ghost? Although the disciples were born of the Spirit, born-again children of God, they needed the baptism of the Holy Spirit so they could walk in the power of the Holy Ghost and be witnesses in their community and in the nations.

> *But ye shall receive power, after that the Holy Ghost is come upon you: and ye shall be witnesses unto me both in Jerusalem, and in all Judea, and in Samaria, and unto the uttermost part of the earth. (Acts 1:8 KJV)*

One hundred twenty disciples, men and women, gathered in Jerusalem to pray and wait for the promise of the Holy Spirit, as Jesus had commanded (Acts 1:12-15).

Acts 2:2-4

> *And suddenly there came a sound from heaven as of a rushing mighty wind, and it filled all the house where they were sitting. (Acts 2:2 KJV)*
>
> *And there appeared unto them cloven tongues like as of fire, and it sat upon each of them. (Acts 2:3 KJV)*
>
> *And they were all filled with the Holy Ghost, and began to speak with other tongues, as the Spirit gave them utterance. (Acts 2:4 KJV)*

On the day of Pentecost, the one-hundred and twenty were all in one accord in one place. They were all filled with the Holy Ghost and spoke with other tongues. The Holy Ghost was poured out and rested on them just as He did on Jesus at His baptism. They became the temple, the dwelling place, of the Holy Ghost.

The Early Church and the Holy Spirit

Peter

Acts 2:14-41

After receiving the Baptism of the Holy Spirit we see Peter, who had denied Jesus three times, stand up and preach the Gospel with boldness which resulted in 3,000 souls being added to the Church (verse 41).

> *Then they that gladly received his word were baptized: and the same day there were added unto them about three thousand souls. (Acts 2:41 KJV)*

Cripple at Gate Beautiful

In Acts 3:1-8 we see Peter and John on their way to the temple to worship and a man who was lame from his mother's womb was begging for alms at the gate called Beautiful.

Acts 3:6-8

> *Then Peter said, Silver and gold have I none; but such as I have give I thee: In the name of Jesus Christ of Nazareth rise up and walk. (Acts 3:6 KJV)*

> *And he took him by the right hand, and lifted him up: and immediately his feet and ankle bones received strength. (Acts 3:7 KJV)*

> *And he leaping up stood, and walked, and entered with them into the temple, walking, and leaping, and praising God. (Acts 3:8 KJV)*

Peter's Shadow

Multitudes brought their sick and laid them in the streets in hopes that Peter's shadow would overshadow them as he walked by. They came from cities around Jerusalem bringing sick people and those vexed with unclean spirits and they were all healed.

Acts 5:14-16

> *And believers were the more added to the Lord, multitudes both of men and women. (Acts 5:14 KJV)*

> *Insomuch that they brought forth the sick into the streets, and laid them on beds and couches, that at the least the shadow of Peter passing by might overshadow some of them. (Acts 5:15 KJV)*

> *There came also a multitude out of the cities round about unto Jerusalem, bringing sick folks, and them which were vexed with unclean spirits: and they were healed every one. (Acts 5:16 KJV)*

Dorcas Resurrected

Peter even raised the dead. In Joppa there was a disciple named Tabitha, or *Dorcas* in Greek, who did many good works and gave alms. She made coats and garments for those who had need of them. She became sick and died. The disciples in Joppa sent for Peter.

> *But Peter put them all forth, and kneeled down, and prayed; and turning him to the body said, Tabitha, arise. And she opened her eyes: and when she saw Peter, she sat up. (Acts 9:40 KJV)*

> *And he gave her his hand, and lifted her up, and when he had called the saints and widows, presented her alive. (Acts 9:41 KJV)*

Peter Takes the Gospel to the Gentiles

In Chapter 10 we have the account of Peter and Cornelius. Cornelius was a Gentile, a centurion or a captain of a hundred men. He was a godly man who feared God and always prayed to God. Cornelius had a vision and an angel of Lord instructed him to go to Joppa to get Peter.

At the same time in Joppa Peter was on a housetop praying. He became hungry and would have eaten but he fell into a trance and saw a vision of a great sheet being let down to the earth. In this sheet were all kind of four-footed animals, wild beasts, creeping things, and fowls of the air (Acts 10:9-12).

Acts 10:13-15

> *And there came a voice to him, Rise, Peter; kill, and eat. (Acts 10:13 KJV)*

> *But Peter said, Not so, Lord; for I have never eaten anything that is common or unclean. (Acts 10:14 KJV)*

> *And the voice spoke unto him again the second time, what God hath cleansed, that call not thou common. (Acts 10:15 KJV)*

The vision came to Peter three times. As he thought on this vision and what it meant, the three men Cornelius sent were asking for Peter. After hearing that the angel of the Lord had instructed Cornelius to send for Peter to come, Peter went with the men and preached Christ to Cornelius and his household.

Acts 10:44-47

> *While Peter yet spoke these words, the Holy Ghost fell on all them which heard the word. (Acts 10:44 KJV)*

> *And they of the circumcision which believed were astonished, as many as came with Peter, because that on the Gentiles also was poured out the gift of the Holy Ghost. (Acts 10:45 KJV)*

> *For they heard them speak with tongues, and magnify God. Then answered Peter, (Acts 10:46 KJV)*

> *Can any man forbid water, that these should not be baptized, which have received the Holy Ghost as well as we? (Acts 10:47 KJV)*

This is the same Peter who had denied Christ three times rather than let others know he even knew Jesus. After being baptized in the Holy Spirit we see him doing the same signs and wonders that Jesus did when He was on earth.

Peter was not the only one who did signs and wonders after this encounter with the Holy Spirit on the day of Pentecost. Signs and wonders were done by the hands of all the apostles.

> *And by the hands of the apostles were many signs and wonders wrought among the people; (and they were all with one accord in Solomon's porch. (Acts 5:12 KJV)*

Stephen

As the number of disciples grew, the Grecians began to murmur against the Hebrews because their widows were not having their needs met in the daily ministration. The twelve called the multitude together and instructed them to choose seven men of honest report and full of the Holy Ghost and appoint them over this business of serving tables (Acts 6 & 7).

> *And the saying pleased the whole multitude: and they chose Stephen, a man full of faith and of the Holy Ghost, and Philip, and Prochorus, and Nicanor, and Timon, and Parmenas, and Nicolas a proselyte of Antioch. (Acts 6:5 KJV)*

Stephen was one of the seven that was chosen for the job of serving. Stephen, who was not one of the apostles, being full of the Holy Ghost, did great signs and wonders among the people as he was ministering to the widows.

Acts 6:6-8

> *Whom they set before the apostles: and when they had prayed, they laid their hands on them. (Acts 6:6 KJV)*

And the word of God increased; and the number of the disciples multiplied in Jerusalem greatly; and a great company of the priests were obedient to the faith. (Acts 6:7 KJV)

And Stephen, full of faith and power, did great wonders and miracles among the people. (Acts 6:8 KJV)

Stephen caused such a stir among those in the synagogue that in Chapter 7, he is stoned to death. He was an ordinary born-of-the-Spirit believer who was filled with the Holy Spirit.

Philip

Because of the persecution against the Church in Jerusalem, the disciples were scattered throughout the regions of Judea and Samaria, except the apostles. Philip went to Samaria and preached Christ to them. (Acts 8:5-19)

Acts 8:6-8

And the people with one accord gave heed unto those things which Philip spake, hearing and seeing the miracles which he did. (Acts 8:6 KJV)

For unclean spirits, crying with loud voice, came out of many that were possessed with them: and many taken with palsies, and that were lame, were healed. (Acts 8:7 KJV)

And there was great joy in that city. (Acts 8:8 KJV)

When the apostles, who were still in Jerusalem, heard that Samaria had received the Word of God, they sent Peter and John down to pray for them that they might receive the Holy Ghost.

Acts 8:15-17

Who, when they were come down, prayed for them, that they might receive the Holy Ghost: (Acts 8:15 KJV)

(For as yet he was fallen upon none of them: only they were baptized in the name of the Lord Jesus.) (Acts 8:16 KJV)

Then laid they their hands on them, and they received the Holy Ghost. (Acts 8:17 KJV)

Verse 16 tells us they were baptized in the name of the Lord Jesus (Baptism of Repentance). The Samaritans were saved, born again, and yet they needed to receive the Holy Spirit.

Philip Goes to the Desert, Gaza

Later in this same chapter the Lord spoke to Philip and instructed him to go to Gaza, which is a desert. So Philip left the revival in Samaria to go to the desert, where he saw a eunuch from Ethiopia sitting in his chariot reading Isaiah the prophet. Philip joined him and from the Scripture in Isaiah preached Christ to him. The eunuch got saved and Philip baptized him. Then Philip was translated to *Azotus*.

> *And when they were come up out of the water, the Spirit of the Lord caught away Philip, that the eunuch saw him no more: and he went on his way rejoicing. (Acts 8:39 KJV)*

> *But Philip was found at Azotus: and passing through he preached in all the cities, till he came to Caesarea. (Acts 8:40 KJV)*

Paul

Saul, later known as Paul, was a Pharisee who was persecuting the Church in Jerusalem. He was a witness to Stephen's stoning (Acts 7:58-59). Saul was on his way to Damascus looking for any disciples of the Lord Jesus Christ that he might bring them bound to Jerusalem for punishment.

Road to Damascus: Acts 9:1-9

As he approached Damascus a light from heaven appeared. Saul fell to the earth and Jesus spoke to him. Jesus instructed Saul to go into the city and he would be told what to do. When Saul arose he was blind and had to be led into the city. For three days Saul fasted and was without sight.

> *And Ananias went his way, and entered into the house; and putting his hands on him said, Brother Saul, the Lord, even Jesus, that appeared unto thee in the way as thou camest, hath sent me, that thou mightest receive thy sight, and be filled with the Holy Ghost. (Acts 9:17 KJV)*

Saul was saved on the road to Damascus when he called Jesus Lord and obeyed what He told him to do. The Lord sent a disciple named Ananias, who lived in Damascus, to pray for Saul's healing and that he might receive the Holy Spirit. From chapter 13 of Acts on Saul is called Paul.

Iconium: Acts 14:1-3 (Paul and Barnabas)

> *And it came to pass in Iconium, that they went both together into the synagogue of the Jews, and so spake, that a great multitude both of the Jews and also of the Greeks believed. (Acts 14:1 KJV)*

> *But the unbelieving Jews stirred up the Gentiles, and made their minds evil affected against the brethren. (Acts 14:2 KJV)*

> *Long time therefore abode they speaking boldly in the Lord, which gave testimony unto the word of his grace, and granted signs and wonders to be done by their hands. (Acts 14:3 KJV)*

Many signs and wonders were done by the hands of Paul and Barnabas in Iconium. They caused such a stir in the city that both Gentiles and Jews made plans to stone them. Paul and Barnabas, being aware of their plans, fled to Lystra where they preached Christ to the people.

Lystra: Acts 14:8-10 (A creative miracle by Paul)

> *And there sat a certain man at Lystra, impotent in his feet, being a cripple from his mother's womb, who never had walked: (Acts 14:8 KJV)*

> *The same heard Paul speak: who stedfastly beholding him, and perceiving that he had faith to be healed, (Acts 14:9 KJV)*

> *Said with a loud voice, stand upright on thy feet. And he leaped and walked. (Acts 14:10 KJV)*

Thyatira: Acts 16:16-18

In the city of Thyatira Paul and Silas visited a women's prayer group and a woman named Lydia got saved and invited them to stay with her.

> *And it came to pass, as we went to prayer, a certain damsel possessed with a spirit of divination met us, which brought her masters much gain by soothsaying: (Acts 16:16 KJV)*

> *The same followed Paul and us, and cried, saying, These men are the servants of the most high God, which shew unto us the way of salvation. (Acts 16:17 KJV)*

> *And this did she many days. But Paul, being grieved, turned and said to the spirit, I command thee in the name of Jesus Christ to come out of her. And he came out the same hour. (Acts 16:18 KJV)*

When the masters of the girl saw their hope of gain was lost they had Paul and Silas thrown into a Philippian jail (Acts 16:25-30).

Ephesus: Acts 19:1-7

Twenty years after Pentecost the Holy Ghost was still vital to the believer. Paul began his third missionary journey and in Ephesus he meets twelve disciples.

He said unto them, Have ye received the Holy Ghost since ye believed? And they said unto him, We have not so much as heard whether there be any Holy Ghost. (Acts 19:2 KJV)

And he said unto them, Unto what then were ye baptized? And they said, Unto John's baptism. (Acts 19:3 KJV)

Then said Paul, John verily baptized with the baptism of repentance, saying unto the people, that they should believe on him which should come after him, that is, on Christ Jesus. (Acts 19:4 KJV)

When they heard this, they were baptized in the name of the Lord Jesus. (Acts 19:5 KJV)

And when Paul had laid his hands upon them, the Holy Ghost came on them; and they spake with tongues, and prophesied. (Acts 19:6 KJV)

Paul, once the persecutor of the Church of Jesus Christ, is now preaching Jesus as the Messiah and he is doing the same signs and wonders among the people that Jesus did by the power of the Holy Spirit.

Special Miracles

And God wrought special miracles by the hands of Paul: (Acts 19:11 KJV)

So that from his body were brought unto the sick handkerchiefs or aprons, and the diseases departed from them, and the evil spirits went out of them. (Acts 19:12 KJV)

For our gospel came not unto you in word only, but also in power, and in the Holy Ghost, and in much assurance; as ye know what manner of men we were among you for your sake. (1 Thessalonians 1:5 KJV)

Miracles, signs and wonders, were normal happenings in the First Century Church. The Apostles and disciples of Jesus were born-of-the-Spirit believers being directed and influenced by the Holy Spirit. They were examples for the Church today. If we are to walk in the same demonstration of power that the First Century Church operated in we must know the Holy Spirit and how He operates in the believer.

The Holy Spirit and the Church Today

As believers it would be advantageous for us to remember that Jesus received His authority, direction, and power from the Holy Spirit. He instructed the disciples to do the same, and they were to teach all converts to do what He (Jesus) had commanded them (the disciples) to do. We are to walk in the same power of the Holy Spirit that Jesus, the disciples, and the early Church walked in.

> *Then Peter said unto them, Repent, and be baptized every one of you in the name of Jesus Christ for the remission of sins, and ye shall receive the gift of the Holy Ghost. (Acts 2:38)*

> *For the promise is unto you, and to your children, and to all that are afar off even as many as the LORD our God shall call. (Acts 2:39)*

The promise of the Holy Spirit is for the Body of Christ today. Once we receive Jesus as our Lord and Savior, the Holy Spirit is available to those who ask.

> *If ye then, being evil, know how to give good gifts unto your children: how much more shall your heavenly Father give the Holy Spirit to them that ask him? (Luke 11:13 KJV)*

Just as eternal life is a gift that is available to us but must be received, the Holy Spirit is a gift that is available to us, as believers, but we must ask for Him.

> *And I will pray the Father, and he shall give you another Comforter, that he may abide with you forever; (John 14:16 KJV)*

> *Even the Spirit of truth; whom the world cannot receive, because it seeth him not, neither knoweth him: but ye know him; for he dwelleth with you, and shall be in you. (John 14:17 KJV)*

Today the Holy Spirit does not just dwell with us, He is in us. We are the temple of the Holy Ghost.

> *What? Know ye not that your body is the temple of the Holy Ghost which is in you, which ye have of God, and ye are not your own? (1 Corinthians 6:19 KJV)*

Holy Spirit is our sanctifier. He is the One who is purifying us and making us holy.

> *That I should be the minister of Jesus Christ to the Gentiles, ministering the gospel of God, that the offering up of the Gentiles might be acceptable, being sanctified by the Holy Ghost. (Romans 15:16 KJV)*

Holy Spirit is our teacher.

> *But the Comforter, which is the Holy Ghost, whom the Father will send in my name, he shall teach you all things, and bring all things to your remembrance, whatsoever I have said unto you. (John 14:26 KJV)*

Which things also we speak, not in the words which man's wisdom teacheth, but which the Holy Ghost teacheth; comparing spiritual things with spiritual. (1 Corinthians 2:13 KJV)

It is the Holy Spirit who builds us up in our faith.

But ye, beloved, building up yourselves on your most holy faith, praying in the Holy Ghost, (Jude 1:20 KJV)

It is the Holy Spirit who gives us the power, the ability to be witnesses in our city, state, nation, and other nations.

But you shall receive power (ability, efficiency, and might) when the Holy Spirit has come upon you, and you shall be My witnesses in Jerusalem and all Judea and Samaria and to the ends (the very bounds) of the earth. (Acts 1:8 AMP)

Mark 16:15-18

And he said unto them, Go ye into all the world, and preach the gospel to every creature. (Mark 16:15 KJV)

He that believeth and is baptized shall be saved; but he that believeth not shall be damned. (Mark 16:16 KJV)

And these signs shall follow them that believe; In my name shall they cast out devils; they shall speak with new tongues; (Mark 16:17 KJV)

They shall take up serpents; and if they drink any deadly thing, it shall not hurt them; they shall lay hands on the sick, and they shall recover. (Mark 16:18 KJV)

Summary

Jesus promised that when He returned to Heaven, Father God would send the Holy Spirit in His name to remind us of the things Jesus did and teach us all things. Jesus called the Holy Spirit the "Spirit of Truth" which comes from the Father God to testify of Jesus and show us things to come (John 14:6; 15:26; 16:13-14).

The promise of the Holy Spirit is for all who believe in the name of the Lord Jesus Christ. This was the promise Jesus spoke of in the Book of Acts when He told the disciples to not leave Jerusalem after He ascended to Heaven, but to wait for the Baptism of the Holy Spirit (Acts 1:4-5; 2:38-39).

The Holy Spirit fills the believer with power to be a witness. Believers receive their prayer language which is the Holy Spirit praying through them (Acts 2:4). In addition, praying in their prayer language edifies them (Jude 1:20).

Developing a lifestyle of spending time in His presence and spending time praying in the Holy Spirit are keys to successfully doing the works of Jesus and fulfilling the Great Commission.

The Holy Spirit is God's agent on earth today performing signs and wonders, miracles, healings, deliverance, etc. But He only does so in partnership or cooperation with the faith of believers.

Activation Time

Receiving the Baptism of the Holy Spirit

If you have not received the Baptism of the Holy Spirit, with the evidence of praying in tongues,

- *Halal* for 2 minutes, using your list of attributes of God.
- Read the Scriptures that have been provided for you at the end of this lesson.
- Pray the Prayer to Receive the Holy Spirit, also provided at the end of this lesson. God will give you the utterance, the words, but you must, by faith, speak those words. If you are using the manual for a group teaching, ask any who would like to receive the Holy Spirit to stand, read the Scriptures to them, lead them in the Prayer to Receive the Holy Spirit, then lay hands on them and release the Holy Spirit. Begin to pray in tongues and encourage them to do the same as the Spirit gives them the utterance.
- Pray in the Spirit out loud and with passion for one minute. Be quiet and listen. Record anything you hear. Repeat – but pray for 2 minutes before listening and recording. Repeat, increasing your praying time 1 minute each time until you reach praying for 5 consecutive minutes.

Assignment

- Meditate on and memorize memory verse.
- Add 5 more attributes to your attributes of God list.
- Begin your daily prayer time by *halaling* for at least 2 minutes using your list of attributes of God.
- Pray in the Spirit a minimum of 5 minutes a day.
- Ask the Lord for a divine appointment with somebody you can lead to Jesus and pray for them to be filled with the Holy Spirit

Assignment Results and Comments

Baptism of the Holy Spirit

The Promise, the Holy Spirit, Dwelling in You

And I will pray the Father, and he shall give you another Comforter, that he may abide with you forever; (John 14: 16 KJV)

Even the Spirit of truth; whom the world cannot receive, because it seeth him not, neither knoweth him: but ye know him; for he dwelleth with you, and shall be in you. (John 14: 17 KJV)

Disciples Told to Wait for Holy Spirit

And, being assembled together with them, commanded them that they should not depart from Jerusalem, but wait for the promise of the Father, which, saith he, ye have heard of me. (Acts 1:4 KJV)

For John truly baptized with water; but ye shall be baptized with the Holy Ghost not many days hence. (Acts 1:5 KJV)

Day of Pentecost

And suddenly there came a sound from heaven as of a rushing mighty wind, and it filled all the house where they were sitting. (Acts 2:2 KJV)

And there appeared unto them cloven tongues like as of fire, and it sat upon each of them. (Acts 2:3 KJV)

And they were all filled with the Holy Ghost, and began to speak with other tongues, as the Spirit gave them utterance. (Acts 2:4 KJV)

The Promise Is for Us Today

Then Peter said unto them, Repent, and be baptized every one of you in the name of Jesus Christ for the remission of sins, and ye shall receive the gift of the Holy Ghost. (Acts 2:38 KJV)

For the promise is unto you, and to your children, and to all that are afar off, even as many as the Lord our God shall call. (Acts 2:39 KJV)

We Must Ask for the Baptism of the Holy Spirit

If ye then, being evil, know how to give good gifts unto your children: how much more shall your heavenly Father give the Holy Spirit to them that ask him? (Luke 11:13 KJV)

Prayer to Receive the Holy Spirit

> Father God, as your child, I come to You, in faith, to receive the gift of the Holy Spirit. I ask You, in the Name of Jesus Christ, to baptize me with the Holy Spirit. Fill me with the power to be a witness for You. I receive the fullness and power of the Holy Spirit with the evidence of speaking in tongues. I yield my voice to You and declare I will pray in the Holy Spirit as the Spirit gives me utterance. Thank You for filling me with Your Holy Spirit. I confess, in the name of Jesus, that I am baptized with the Holy Spirit, just as You promised. Amen!

Explain that God will give them the utterance, the words, but they must, by faith, speak those words. Lay hands on them and release the Holy Spirit. Begin to pray in tongues and encourage them to do the same as the Spirit gives them the utterance.

Declaration: I declare by faith that Holy Spirit is working in my life. I know His voice; I discern His leading; and I boldly do what He tells me to do. Because I am obedient to His voice, the life of Jesus Christ is manifest in me. Just as Holy Spirit worked miracles through the apostles in the book of Acts, He works miracles through me today – healing the sick, casting out devils, and bringing salvation to the lost through Jesus Christ. I declare this by faith in the name of Jesus.

LESSON 3 - The Gift

Memory Verse

Then Peter said unto them, Repent, and be baptized every one of you in the name of Jesus Christ for the remission of sins, and ye shall receive the gift of the Holy Ghost. (Acts 2:38 KJV)

Introduction

*I*n Lesson 2 we discussed the fact that Jesus did nothing of Himself. He did not perform miracles because He was the Son of God. Jesus willingly stripped himself of His divinity and came to earth as the Son of Man. He did everything as the Son of Man under the influence and direction of the Holy Spirit.

How God anointed Jesus of Nazareth with the Holy Ghost and with power: who went about doing good, and healing all that were oppressed of the devil; for God was with him. (Acts 10:38 KJV)

Jesus is our example of how all mankind is to live under the control and influence of the Holy Spirit.

Then said Jesus unto them, When ye have lifted up the Son of man, then shall ye know that I am he, and that I do nothing of myself; but as my Father hath taught me, I speak these things. (John 8:28 KJV)

Believest thou not that I am in the Father, and the Father in me? The words that I speak unto you I speak not of myself: but the Father that dwelleth in me, he doeth the works. (John 14:10 KJV)

Jesus knew how to cooperate with the Holy Spirit of God. That's how He knew to spit and make mud, or say, *"Arise, take up your bed and walk,"* or *"Your sins are forgiven."*

And, being assembled together with them, commanded them that they should not depart from Jerusalem, but wait for the promise of the Father, which, saith he, ye have heard of me. (Acts 1:4 KJV)

For John truly baptized with water; but ye shall be baptized with the Holy Ghost not many days hence. (Acts 1:5 KJV)

Jesus commanded the disciples not to depart from Jerusalem until they received the Baptism of the Holy Spirit. Notice it was a command— not a suggestion.

Acts 2:1-4

And when the day of Pentecost was fully come, they were all with one accord in one place. (Acts 2:1 KJV)

And suddenly there came a sound from heaven as of a rushing mighty wind, and it filled all the house where they were sitting. (Acts 2:2 KJV)

And there appeared unto them cloven tongues like as of fire, and it sat upon each of them. (Acts 2:3 KJV)

And they were all filled with the Holy Ghost, and began to speak with other tongues, as the Spirit gave them utterance. (Acts 2:4 KJV)

After the Day of Pentecost Scripture records that the Apostles and even ordinary believers demonstrated the same signs, wonders, miracles, healings, etc., that were operating in the ministry of Jesus. The same Holy Spirit that manifested in the life of Jesus also manifested Himself in and through the lives of the believers of the First Century Church.

Go ye therefore, and teach all nations, baptizing them in the name of the Father, and of the Son, and of the Holy Ghost: (Matthew 28:19 KJV)

Teaching them to observe all things whatsoever I have commanded you: and, lo, I am with you always, even unto the end of the world. Amen. (Matthew 28:20 KJV)

The disciples were to teach new converts to observe, to guard from injury or loss, all the things Jesus commanded them to do.

Therefore being by the right hand of God exalted, and having received of the Father the promise of the Holy Ghost, he hath shed forth this, which ye now see and hear. (Acts 2:33 KJV)

For the promise is unto you, and to your children, and to all that are afar off, even as many as the LORD our God shall call. (Acts 2:39 KJV)

In verse 33 Peter identifies the "promise" as the Holy Spirit. Verse 39 tells us the promise of the gift of the Holy Spirit is still available to us today. We are still in the Church Age. The Holy Spirit wants to manifest Himself in the Church of today in the same manner in which He did in the First Century Church.

1 Corinthians 12

Any time the subject of the gifts of the Holy Spirit, miracles, signs and wonders, healings, etc. are discussed the first Scripture that comes to mind is usually 1 Corinthians 12.

Any student of the Bible who has studied anything concerning the ministry of the Holy Spirit is familiar with 1 Corinthians 12. They have heard many teachings using this chapter as the foundational text.

If we are to be used by God to minister in the supernatural as it relates to healing and deliverance, proper Biblical understanding of this chapter is vital.

> *These were more noble than those in Thessalonica, in that they received the word with all readiness of mind, and searched the Scriptures daily, whether those things were so. (Acts 17:11 KJV)*

Paul, speaking of the Jews in Berea, said they were nobler than the Jews in Thessalonica because they not only received the word that was taught, but they searched the Scriptures to see if those things Paul taught were so or not. With that in mind, let's take a fresh look at this very familiar chapter.

A foundational principle for proper Biblical exegesis of the Scripture is: Scripture can never mean to us what it could not have meant to the original audience. In order to properly understand what a Scripture meant to the original audience, the student must ask three questions:

(1) Who is speaking?
(2) To whom is the author speaking?
(3) What is going on at the time it was written?

All of these things are important if we want to understand the message in the same way those who heard it for the first time would have understood it.

Scripture tells us that Paul is the author (1 Corinthians 1:1). Paul was a Roman citizen, a scholar, and a skilled lawyer. He was also a student of the Law of Moses. As a member of the Sanhedrin before his conversion, it was Paul's job to prosecute Christians; those whom the Sanhedrin believed were in doctrinal error. After his conversion Paul became an Apostle of Jesus Christ and not only the author of First Corinthians, but the author of a major part of the New Testament.

Scripture also clearly states that Paul was writing to the First Century Church of Corinth (1 Corinthians 1:2). Therefore, as students, we should approach our study of Chapter 12 from the standpoint of the context of the events in the First Century.

Historical Setting

Ancient Corinth, the original Corinth, was the richest port and the largest city in ancient Greece. It was a powerful commercial center located near two seaports only four miles apart. The western harbor was a trading port to Italy and Sicily and the eastern harbor was the port for the eastern Mediterranean countries. The city was known for its idolatry and sexual perversion.

This wealthy Greek city-state was completely destroyed by Rome in 146 BC. The city lay dormant for a hundred years or more and was established again in 44 BC by Julius Caesar as a Roman colony. This former Greek city was re-populated mostly with Italian, Greek, Syrian, Egyptian, and Judean slaves who had been freed from Rome.

Corinth's strategic location caused the city to quickly regain popularity. In just a few years it, again, became a crossroad for trade and known as a financial institution. The enormously profitable commerce of this crossroads of the nations was a great attraction and brought thousands of eager new settlers from all over the known world of that time. People from many different religious beliefs, economic status, and ethical backgrounds lived in this first century city. Corinth's population rapidly became very diverse.

When Paul arrived in Corinth it was a little more than a hundred years old but was five times larger than Athens and the capitol of the province. The atmosphere in Corinth did not intimidate him since it shared many characteristics with his hometown, Tarsus and his home Church city, Syrian Antioch.

As would be expected, the profitable commerce of the city not only attracted more wealth it attracted a lot of vice as well. The first century city of Corinth, not unlike ancient Corinth, was also well known for its sexual vices, especially fornication. In fact, one of the Greek verbs for fornicate was the word *korinthiazomai,* a word derived from the city's name.

All kinds of sexual immorality were common in Corinth during the first century. Sexually transmitted diseases were rampant in the city. Even its art and pottery depicts people giving sacrifice to the idols of the city, asking them to remove the plague of venereal diseases from their midst.

The heart of the city was filled with temples and shrines to the emperor and various members of his family, which were built alongside temples of older Greek gods such as *Asklepios*, the god of healing and *Aphrodite*, the goddess of love. A thousand sacred prostitutes were associated with the temple of *Aphrodite*. One worshipped the goddess of love by having sexual relations with these prostitutes.

Historically it is safe to say that the city of Corinth was very diverse ethnically and financially. One can also conclude that it was intellectually astute, financially prosperous and morally corrupt.

The Church at Corinth

The Church at Corinth mirrored what was going on in the city. It is clear from the content of Paul's first letter to the Corinthians that there was quite a mixture of people in the Church of Corinth. The names that are recorded throughout Paul's letter indicate there were Jews, Latinos, and Greeks in the congregation. It is also evident by some of those mentioned (Stephanas, Titus, and Justus) that there were wealthy people in the Church. Chapter 7, verses 20-24, indicates that slaves or freed slaves were also a part of the Church. The Church at Corinth seemed to be just as diverse as the city, both ethnically and financially.

Lesson 3 - The Gift

There were also other influences of the city in the Church at Corinth such as idolatry, a leaning toward sexual vices, and an independent spirit. This is evident to even a casual reader of this letter to the Corinthians.

Paul had received reports from various sources that the diversity of the people and influence of the city was causing division and disorder in the Church. It is to this diverse, conflicted congregation that Paul addresses this letter. The language and style he uses, according to theologians, are especially rhetorical and combative. Some of the problems he attacks are:

(1) A serious lack of unity in the Church.
(2) Differential treatment among the Uncorrected sexual sin in the Church.
(3) Uncorrected sexual sin in the Church.
(4) Misconceptions about marriage.
(5) Use of freedom from the law as an excuse to sin.
(6) An over-emphasis on speaking in tongues as an indication of spirituality and not enough value given to other manifestations of the Holy Spirit.
(7) Disorder in worship.
(8) False teaching concerning the resurrection.

One can conclude that the Church of Corinth had become a congregation of believers who had allowed the corruption and immorality of the city and the cultural practices of its converts to bring division and disorder into the Church.

Context of 1 Corinthians 12

From the very beginning of his letter, Paul is dealing with the problem of division in the Church at Corinth. After a short introduction and greeting, Paul introduces and sets the theme for the entire letter: the necessity for unity in the Church.

> *But I urge and entreat you, brethren, by the name of our Lord Jesus Christ, that all of you be in perfect harmony and full agreement in what you say, and that there be no dissensions or factions or divisions among you, but that you be perfectly united in your common understanding and in your opinions and judgments. (1 Corinthians 1:10 AMP)*

We find this theme throughout the entire book of First Corinthians. In Chapters 1 through 4 Paul addresses the divisions in the Church. In Chapters 5 and 6 he addresses the disorders in the Church. Then in Chapters 7-15, at the request of the Church at Corinth, Paul responds to eleven difficulties in the Church. Only one of these issues is considered to be theological in nature. Chapter 15 is a discussion on the doctrine of the resurrection. The other ten issues are behavioral issues which some scholars believe were, in part, a result of the influence of a First Century religious practice known as *Gnosticism*.

Gnosticism

The word *Gnosticism* comes from the Greek word *Gnosis* which means knowledge. *Gnosticism* is a religion based on getting to God through knowledge. *Gnostics* believe:

- ➢ The only way to get to God was through knowledge. Their number one goal was to allow their spirits to ascend to God and they believed this could only happen through knowledge. According to the *Gnostics*, there were different levels of enlightenment and at each level they received secret keys that would move them on to the next level. The idea was to reach the next level first and ultimately get to God first. Naturally, this mindset created an air of competition, which was consistent with what was going on in Corinth at the time.
- ➢ Angel worship. Since tongues or *Glossolalia* was considered to be the language of the angels, the *Gnostic* walked around speaking in tongues. Their purpose was to be or appear to be super spiritual. This over-emphasis of speaking in tongues all the time was one of the issues Paul addresses in this letter.
- ➢ The physical body as a whole is of no importance to the believer. They believed that individual men were at one time parts of one heavenly being. This unified being was overpowered by lower powers that were hostile toward God. These lower powers tore the individuals apart and captured them in individual material bodies and robbed them of their memories of their heavenly origins. For this reason the *Gnostics* disdained the flesh which they believed was holding them captive and preventing them from returning to the unity they once knew in the spirit. Since flesh was a prison they did not agree with the idea of a resurrection, either of man or of Christ. The last thing a Gnostic would want is the resurrection of the body from the dead, which would again imprison their spirit in flesh. Paul deals with this issue in Chapter 15.

Gnosticism pre-dates Christianity. However, it had the ability to adapt to its current environment. Therefore, *Gnostics* easily incorporated the idea of a Christ, although none existed in the religion until Christianity. The problem was they denied that Christ came in the flesh. To them the flesh was bad, a prison, and could not hold the spirit of Christ. This logic led them to the belief that Jesus could not have died in the flesh since He did not really come in the flesh.

> *Hereby know ye the Spirit of God: Every spirit that confesseth that Jesus Christ is come in the flesh is of God: (1 John 4:2 KJV)*

> *And every spirit that confesseth not that Jesus Christ is come in the flesh is not of God: and this is that spirit of antichrist, whereof ye have heard that it should come; and even now already is it in the world. (1 John 4:3 KJV)*

> *For many deceivers are entered into the world, who confess not that Jesus Christ is come in the flesh. This is a deceiver and an antichrist. (2 John 1:7 KJV)*

Gnostics were made to curse Jesus before being accepted in their fellowship. This curse did not apply to the heavenly Christ but only to the man Jesus.

Lesson 3 - The Gift

Although Paul does not use the word *Gnosticism* in his writing, as you read through First Corinthians one quickly discovers that the behavioral issues or spiritual matters he discusses in Chapters 7-15, in response to the letter he received from the Church at Corinth, are consistent with the practice of *Gnosticism*.

One of the proofs scholars use to support their view that Paul was addressing *Gnosticism* is 1 Corinthians 7.

Now concerning the things whereof ye wrote unto me: It is good for a man not to touch a woman. (1 Corinthians 7:1 KJV)

Nevertheless, to avoid fornication, let every man have his own wife, and let every woman have her own husband. (1 Corinthians 7:2 KJV)

The word *woman* in verse 1 is the Greek word for wife. The same Greek word is translated wife in verse 2. One of the questions the Church at Corinth had asked Paul was, "Is it okay for a man to have sex with his wife?" Where did that kind of question come from? Remember, *Gnostics* believed that any desire of the flesh was profane and ungodly. Sex is a pleasure of the body (flesh). Therefore, the *Gnostic* would carry their spirituality to the extreme and would refrain from having sex even with his own wife.

Paul's response was, "Of course It is okay for a man to have sex with his wife. Your body is not your own. It is your duty." (verses 3-5)

In the following chapters, Paul's tone continues to be corrective, not instructional or informational. Several times he refers to the Church as the Body of Christ (10:7; 11:29; 12:12-26). Using this imagery, Paul makes essentially two points:

➢ The necessity of unity in the Church; and
➢ The key to unity was their common experience of the Spirit (12:13).

As we come to Chapter 12, Paul's focus of correction appears to be with the Corinthians' understanding of what it means to be spiritual.

Analysis of Chapter 12

Now concerning spiritual "gifts," brethren, I would not have you ignorant. (1 Corinthians 12:1 KJV)

Look at the word gifts in verse 1. Is it in italics in your Bible? It should be. Any time you see a word in *italics* in your Bible, it is an indication of that particular word not being in the original text. The word gift *is* not in the original Greek text. It was added to the text by the translator, in an attempt to give clarity of interpretation.

The word spiritual in this verse is the Greek word *pneumatikos* and it does not mean spiritual gifts. It means spiritual or non-carnal matters. A better translation of verse 1 is found in Young's Literal Translation.

And concerning the spiritual things, brethren, I do not wish you to be ignorant; (1 Corinthians 12:1 YLT)

Paul begins Chapter 12 by saying that he did not want the Church at Corinth to be ignorant concerning spiritual matters.

Ye know that ye were Gentiles, carried away unto these dumb idols, even as ye were led. (1 Corinthians 12:2 KJV)

Wherefore I give you to understand, that no man speaking by the Spirit of God calleth Jesus accursed: and that no man can say that Jesus is the Lord, but by the Holy Ghost. (1 Corinthians 12:3 KJV)

Paul is drawing a contrast in verses 2 and 3. He says as Gentiles we served dumb idols who could not speak. But we now serve a God who does speak. He is contrasting speaking in tongues by the Spirit (God speaking through the believer) versus serving dumb idols who do not speak. Paul wants the believer to know about speaking by the Spirit of God and how to discern Him.

I Corinthians 12:4-6

Now there are diversities of gifts, but the same Spirit. (1 Corinthians 12:4 KJV)

And there are differences of administrations, but the same Lord. (1 Corinthians 12:5 KJV)

And there are diversities of operations, but it is the same God which worketh all in all. (1 Corinthians 12:6 KJV)

In verses 4 through 6 Paul paints a picture of the triune Godhead. Notice the word *diversities* and the word *same.* Paul is emphasizing, through his choice and arrangement of words, that even though there are differences of administrations and operations in the Godhead, they are still one.

Paul continues to stress unity and to set them up for his argument concerning the extreme use of speaking in tongues. In verses 7 through 10 Paul points out that just as there is diversity in the Godhead there is diversity in the Holy Spirit and the way He manifests in the believer, yet by the same Spirit.

I Corinthians 12:7-11

But the manifestation of the Spirit is given to every man to profit withal. (1 Corinthians 12:7 KJV)

For to one is given by the Spirit the word of wisdom; to another the word of knowledge by the same Spirit; (1 Corinthians 12:8 KJV)

Lesson 3 - The Gift

> *To another faith by the same Spirit; to another the gifts of healing by the same Spirit; (1 Corinthians 12:9 KJV)*
>
> *To another the working of miracles; to another prophecy; to another discerning of spirits; to another divers kinds of tongues; to another the interpretation of tongues: (1 Corinthians 12:10 KJV)*
>
> *But all these worketh that one and the selfsame Spirit, dividing to every man severally as he will. (1 Corinthians 12:11 KJV)*

Paul usually tends to be very systematic in his writing. However, the structure in verses 8-10 is not typical of Paul's writing. According to Greek scholars, the language in these verses is noticeably unstructured or non-systematic. The list in these verses is neither carefully organized nor exhaustive. It is as if Paul goes into a very passionate kind of speech and gives this list of different ways the Holy Spirit manifests Himself in the life of the believer.

The list is merely representative of the diversity of the Spirit is manifestations. Paul is most likely offering a considerable list so they would stop focusing on just one manifestation: speaking in tongues. Did you notice that Paul put speaking in tongues at the end of the list? He seems to be saying to the *Gnostic*. "Why are you focused on this one thing? If you have the Holy Spirit, you can do this and this and this, and oh yes, by the way, you can speak in tongues."

Traditionally, 1 Corinthians 12 has been known as the *gifts* chapter. You have probably been taught, as I have, the things Paul itemizes in verses 8 through 10 are the gifts of the Holy Spirit (something given to you totally at the discretion of the donor).

However, in verse 7, Paul calls them the manifestation of the Spirit, not gifts of the Spirit.

> *But the manifestation of the Spirit is given to every man to profit withal. (1 Corinthians 12:7 KJV)*

The word for manifestation in the Greek is *phanerosis*. Below is the Strong's definition of manifestation or *phanerosis:*

> Manifestation: Strongs 5321. phanerosis, fan-er'-o-sis; from G5319; exhibition, i.e. (fig.) expression, the extension of a bestowment:—manifestation.

As you can see, it does not mean gift nor is it translated anywhere in the New Testament as gift. Rather, it is the expression or the extension of a bestowment (gift) and is only translated manifestation in the New Testament.

The Greek word Paul uses in New Testament, when referring to a specific God-given gift, is *charisma.* It means: a divine gratuity, spiritual endowment, or free gift.

> **Gift:** Strongs 5486. charisma, khar'-is-mah; from G5483; a (divine) gratuity, i.e. deliverance (from danger or passion); (spec.) a (spiritual) endowment, i.e. (subj.) religious qualification, or (obj.) miraculous faculty:—(free) gift.

Example

*For the wages of sin is death; but the gift (**charisma**) of God is eternal life through Jesus Christ our Lord. (Romans 6:23 KJV)*

Eternal life through Jesus is a free gift (*charisma* - something given to us totally at the discretion of the donor) given to us by God and it is given to us totally at His discretion.

A gift is something you are given by someone because they want you to have it. A manifestation is the expression or extension of a gift that has been given. It is what you can do because you have received the gift. It is what someone or something does. Would you agree there is a big difference between gifts and manifestations?

Every time this Greek word *phanerosis* appears in the New Testament it is always translated manifestation and never translated gifts.

The Holy Spirit Is the Gift

The Greek word that is used throughout the New Testament when referring to the gift of the Holy Spirit is an entirely different word. It is the Greek word *dorea*, meaning a gratuity. It comes from the Greek root word *doron* which means a present, a gift, specifically a sacrifice.

Gift: Strongs 1431. dorea, do-reh-ah'; from G1435; a gratuity:—gift.
Dorea: Strongs 1435. doron, do'-ron; a present; spec. a sacrifice:—gift, offering.

Throughout the New Testament *dorea* is always translated gift and is used when referring to the gift of the Holy Spirit.

Peter on the Day of Pentecost

*Then Peter said unto them, Repent, and be baptized every one of you in the name of Jesus Christ for the remission of sins, and ye shall receive the gift (**dorea**) of the Holy Ghost. (Acts 2:38 KJV)*

Peter in Samaria: Acts 8:15-20

Now when the apostles which were at Jerusalem heard that Samaria had received the word of God, they sent unto them Peter and John: (Acts 8:14 KJV)

Who, when they were come down, prayed for them, that they might receive the Holy Ghost: (Acts 8:15 KJV)

(For as yet he was fallen upon none of them: only they were baptized in the name of the Lord Jesus.) (Acts 8:16 KJV)

Then laid they their hands on them, and they received the Holy Ghost. (Acts 8:17 KJV)

And when Simon saw that through laying on of the apostles' hands the Holy Ghost was given, he offered them money, (Acts 8:18 KJV)

Saying, give me also this power, that on whomsoever I lay hands, he may receive the Holy Ghost. (Acts 8:19 KJV)

*But Peter said unto him, Thy money perish with thee, because thou hast thought that the gift (**dorea**) of God may be purchased with money. (Acts 8:20 KJV)*

In verse 20, Peter refers to the Holy Ghost as the *dorea* of God. The Holy Spirit is the gift.

Cornelius

*And they of the circumcision which believed were astonished, as many as came with Peter, because that on the Gentiles also was poured out the gift (**dorea**) of the Holy Ghost. (Acts 10:45 KJV)*

For they heard them speak with tongues, and magnify God. (Acts 10:46 KJV)

Cornelius and his family received the gift (*dorea*) of the Holy Ghost. Clearly, the gift is the Holy Spirit. If you have the Holy Spirit, you can speak in tongues.

Paul's Use of the Word *Dorea*

Paul also used this word *dorea* exclusively when speaking of the redemptive acts of the Cross.

*But not as the offense, so also is the free gift, for if through the offense of one many be dead, much more the grace of God, and the gift (**dorea**) by grace, which is by one man, Jesus Christ, hath abounded unto many. (Romans 5:15 KJV)*

*For if by one man's offense death reigned by one; much more they which receive abundance of grace and of the gift (**dorea**) of righteousness shall reign in life by one, Jesus Christ. (Romans 5:17 KJV)*

*Where of I was made a minister, according to the gift (**dorea**) of the grace of God given unto me by the effectual working of his power. (Ephesians 3:7 KJV)*

*But unto every one of us is given grace according to the measure of the gift (**dorea**) of Christ. (Ephesians 4:7 KJV)*

*For it is impossible for those who were once enlightened, and have tasted of the heavenly gift **(dorea)**, and were made partakers of the Holy Ghost. (Hebrews 6:4 KJV)*

The word *dorea*, which means a present given at the discretion of the giver, is used exclusively throughout the New Testament when referring to the redemptive work of the Cross and receiving the Holy Spirit. It is never used when referring to the manifestations of the Holy Spirit. The manifestations of the Holy Spirit are never called *dorea* or gifts.

I can hear some of you who are students of the Word thinking, "What about Hebrews 2:4?" Let's look at it.

*God also bearing them witness, both with signs and wonders, and with divers miracles, and gifts **(merismos)** of the Holy Ghost, according to his own will? (Hebrews 2:4 KJV)*

The word gift is the Greek word *merismos* meaning a separation or distribution.

Gifts: Strongs 3311. merismos, mer-is-mos'; from G3307; a separation or distribution:—dividing asunder, gift.

The only other place in the New Testament that this word is used is Hebrews 4:12 and it is translated "dividing asunder."

*For the word of God is quick, and powerful, and sharper than any two-edged sword, piercing even to the dividing asunder **(merismos)** of soul and spirit, and of the joints and marrow, and is a discerner of the thoughts and intents of the heart. (Hebrews 4:12 KJV)*

However the translators translated the Greek word *merismos* as gifts in Hebrews 2:4, which can be misleading. A better translation would have been:

*God also bearing them witness, both with signs and wonders, and with divers miracles, and **distribution (merismos)** of the Holy Ghost, according to his own will? (Hebrews 2:4 KJV)*

At this point you are probably thinking, "I thought the Bible was the infallible Word of God and you are saying this would be better translated this way or that way. What's up with that?"

It is true; the original text of the Bible is infallible. However, the translations were filtered through the understanding and mindsets of the translators at the time of the translations. Words were used and added in accordance with their understanding or beliefs at the time. That is why each and every believer is responsible for studying and searching the Scripture that they may correctly analyze the Word of Truth (Acts 17:11 and 2 Timothy 2:15).

The Holy Spirit is the gift (the gratuity – *dorea*). He is given to you like a present wrapped up with a bow. You do not deserve it and you cannot earn it. Once you receive the gift, the *dorea,*

Lesson 3 - The Gift

the Holy Spirit, He can manifest himself in a variety of different ways in you. The manifestations (*phanerosis*) of the Holy Spirit are expressions or extensions of the gift of the Holy Spirit.

The mindset that the nine things listed in verses 8-10 of I Corinthians 12 were gifts (*dorea*) and not manifestations (*phanerosis*) would have been completely foreign to the First Century Church. Remember, Scripture can never mean to us what it did not mean to the original audience.

You are also probably asking, "Why make such a big deal over this one little word, gift?"

It is important because if we, the believer, think of this list as gifts of the Holy Spirit rather than the manifestations of the Holy Spirit, we will perceive them as something given to us totally at the discretion of the giver. This tends to create a mindset in the believer that the Holy Spirit may or may not give them to us. For example, you have probably been taught these are gifts and you may or may not have one or more of these gifts.

> *But all these worketh that one and the selfsame Spirit, dividing to every man severally as he will. (1 Corinthians 12:11 KJV)*

Verse 11 is the Scripture often used to support this line of thinking. The phrase *"dividing to every man severally as he will"* gives many people a real problem. Therefore, let's look at it in detail.

Dividing: Strongs 1244. diaireo, dee-ahee-reh'-o; from G1223 and G138; to separate, i.e. distribute:—divide.

The word dividing comes from a Greek word meaning to distribute. Paul was not painting a picture of a pie with a fixed amount of small portions being given out. Rather, the picture he was painting was more like a farmer standing in a field with a bag full of an unlimited amount of corn seed and he is distributing them as fast as he can.

Paul's point was that the Holy Spirit is not going to run out of the capability to do these things. The Holy Spirit is passing them out. Therefore, a better translation for this word *diaireo* would have been distributing.

To every: Strongs: 1538. hekastos, hek'-as-tos; as if a superlative of hekas (afar); each or every:—any, both, each (one), every (man, one, woman), particularly.

This phrase "to every" is a Greek word meaning each, each person, every, every man, everyone, every woman, any, etc.

Man is not there in the original Greek text.

Severally: Strongs: 2398. idios, id'-ee-os; of uncert. affin.; pertaining to self, i.e. one's own; by impl. private or separate:—X his acquaintance, when they were alone, apart, aside, due, his (own, proper, several), home, (her, our, thine, your) own (business), private (-ly), proper, severally, their (own).

The Greek word Paul uses for our English word severally is *idios.* It means "pertaining to self or one's own something" (you fill in the blank).

Will: Strongs: 1014. boulomahee, boo'-lom-ahee; mid. of a prim. verb; to "will," i.e. (reflex.) be willing:—be disposed, minded, intend, list (be, of own) will (-ing). Comp. G2309

This word will is a Greek word that means to be willing.

Now let's look at the word *he*. There is no second-person pronoun *he* in the Greek language. The word *he* was used by the translator to help make a complete sentence in English. It is not possible to tell who *he* was, from the Greek structure. We can only tell that there was a *he* implied.

Some translations of the Bible capitalize the word *he*. This implies it is the Holy Spirit who is willing. However, we must go beyond the language barrier to find the proper content.

The proper way to exegete a word in Scripture is to examine how the same author or others used the word in similar circumstances. With Paul, we do not have to go far. He used the term *idios,* (one's own) many times in the Book of First Corinthians.

> *Now he that planteth and he that watereth are one: and every man shall receive his own **(idios)** reward according to his own (idios) labor. (1 Corinthians 3:8 KJV)*

> *And labor, working with our own **(idios)** hands: being reviled, we bless; being persecuted, we suffer it: (1 Corinthians 4:12 KJV)*

> *Flee fornication. Every sin that a man doeth is without the body. But he that committeth fornication sinneth against his own **(idios)** body. (1 Corinthians 6:18 KJV)*

> *Nevertheless, to avoid fornication, let every man have his own wife, and let every woman have her own **(idios)** husband. (1 Corinthians 7:2 KJV)*

Consistently throughout First Corinthians and even his other writings Paul used the word *idios* when talking about the person's own something: their will, body, hand, etc.

Paul never used *idios* to describe God's will. Paul used a completely different word when referring to divine will or God's will. Therefore, I believe a more accurate translation of this phrase would be:

> *But all these worketh that one and the selfsame Spirit, distributing to each person as their own self be willing. (1 Corinthians 12:11 KJV)*

We believe the Bible to be inspired by God. It is God-breathed. Therefore, when Paul presents the list of things in verses 8 through 10 as the manifestations of the Holy Spirit, we have to believe both Paul and the Holy Spirit wanted to communicate something important to us about the Holy Spirit.

I am confident in saying that in 1 Corinthians 12 Paul is explaining to us that the manifestations of the Holy Spirit operate in accordance or partnership with the believer's *own* will, or as the person (man or woman) is willing.

If you are willing the Holy Spirit will use you to manifest Himself in many different ways in the Body of Christ for the purpose of being a blessing to others.

Lesson 3 - The Gift

In verses 12-26 Paul continues to present his case on the necessity for unity in the Church. He reminds the believer that by one Spirit they were baptized into one body, the Body of Christ. The Body of Christ has many members yet it is one body.

Then in verses 27-31 Paul gives another list of the diversity of the believers in the Church.

1 Corinthians 12:27-31

Now ye are the body of Christ, and members in particular. (1 Corinthians 12:27 KJV)

And God hath set some in the Church, first apostles, secondarily prophets, thirdly teachers, after that miracles, then gifts of healings, helps, governments, diversities of tongues. (1 Corinthians 12:28 KJV)

Are all apostles? are all prophets? are all teachers? are all workers of miracles? (1 Corinthians 12:29 KJV)

Have all the gifts of healing? do all speak with tongues? do all interpret? (1 Corinthians 12:30 KJV)

But covet earnestly the best gifts: and yet show I unto you a more excellent way. (1 Corinthians 12:31 KJV)

Notice Paul listed some of the same things he mentioned in verses 8-10, but there are some that were not listed. Again, his intention seems not to be to give a complete or exhaustive list. Did you also notice that he listed speaking in tongues at the end of the list again?

The key words in these verses are "in the Church" (verse 28).

And he gave some, apostles; and some, prophets; and some, evangelists; and some, pastors and teachers; (Ephesians 4:11 KJV)

For the perfecting of the saints, for the work of the ministry, for the edifying of the body of Christ. (Ephesians 4:12 KJV)

These different functions were placed in the Church by God, *"For the perfecting of the saints, for the work of the ministry."*

God's plan has always been to equip every believer to do the work of the ministry. The Holy Spirit wants to manifest Himself in and through every believer that the whole Body of Christ will be blessed.

Summary

Clearly the major theme of 1 Corinthians 12 is the necessity for unity in the Body of Christ. The key to accomplishing unity is the common experience of the believer with the Holy Spirit.

God made a sacrifice to give us a present. Once we receive this present, this *dorea,* the Holy Spirit, we are expected to work in cooperation with the Holy Spirit in the same way Jesus worked in cooperation with the Holy Spirit. It was through His cooperation with the Holy Spirit that Jesus knew when to spit and make mud, or say, *"Arise, take up your bed and walk,"* or *"Your sins are forgiven."*

The Holy Spirit of God, in Jesus, cooperating with Him, manifesting through His flesh, was able to affect signs and wonders, miracles, prophetic utterances, healings, etc.

The Holy Spirit causes the things that are in the heart of God to come to pass. He always works when God or someone else speaks the heart of God; it is a partnership or a working together.

When the believer receives the *dorea,* the Holy Spirit, He begins to cooperate with us and manifest in us the ability to prophesy, receive a Word of Knowledge and a Word of Wisdom, to do miracles and healings, to build faith, etc. in us for the purpose of being a blessing to others. All these things come as a result of the Holy Spirit manifesting God, Himself, in cooperation with the believer.

Our part is to develop an intimate relationship with the Holy Spirit, learn to recognize the voice of God operating on the inside of us, and respond to His leading. This is especially important in the area of healing and deliverance.

When we begin to think about this list as ways in which the Holy Spirit manifests Himself in a believer, it will dramatically change our perception of the spiritual capabilities that are within us.

The Holy Spirit is always ready to bless mankind. The Believers need only to be willing to allow the Holy Spirit to flow through them. We are to desire all the manifestations of the Spirit and actively pursue them (verse 31).

Activation Time

- *Halal* for at 2 minutes using the list of attributes of God.
- Pray in the Holy Spirit for 3 minutes.
- Activation: When I Look at You I See (This activation is designed to be used in group studies. However, if using this manual for individual study time, the reader can practice on friends and family.)
- When the manual is being used in group studies, divide the students into small groups of 4 or 5 students – the number of groups will depend on how many are in the class. Allow about 30 minutes or more for the activation.

Activation Description

This activation is an exercise in hearing or receiving words of knowledge about others from the Holy Spirit.

- Have students write their name at the top of the sheet provided at the end of this lesson, entitled "When I Look at You I See."
- Each group picks one person from their group to be a recorder.
- The recorder collects each person's sheet from their group.
- From the sheets collected, the recorder selects one sheet. For example: let's say the recorder picked Jane's sheet.
- Students pray briefly in the Holy Spirit and then complete the statement "When I look at you, Jane, I see _____."
- The recorder writes on Jane's paper what each member of the group, including themselves, says about her.

Example

One at a time the rest of the group members, including the recorder, will say, "Jane when I look at you I see a person who is really good working with children" or "I see someone who loves to enter into worship" or whatever else comes into your mind and the recorder writes it down on Jane's sheet.

> **Note:** Do not let Jane respond to anything a student says until everybody has had their turn. Once the recorder has completed Jane's paper and given it back to her, Jane is then encouraged to give feedback on the words spoken. (Were the words of knowledge correct? Is she good working with children?)

The recorder then picks another person's sheet and repeats the process until everybody in the group has been spoken to, including the recorder. (Someone else in the group will need to record for the recorder.)

Purpose of the Activation

The purpose of this activation is to help the student recognize and develop their ability to hear the voice of the Holy Spirit and at the same time be a blessing to the person receiving the words spoken. Therefore, all words spoken should be edifying and encouraging to the person who receives them. This is not the time for any corrective words.

Assignment

- Meditate on and memorize the memory verse.
- Add 5 more attributes of God to your list.
- Begin your daily prayer time by *halaling* for at least 2 minutes using your list of attributes of God.
- Pray in the Spirit a minimum of 10 minutes a day.
- Ask God for divine appointments to lead someone to the Lord and to pray for someone to receive the Holy Spirit.
- Practice hearing and receiving from the Holy Spirit by using today's activation.

Assignment Result and Comments

When I Look at You I See

Date: _____
Name: _____

When I look at you I see:

LESSON 4 - Healing in the Atonement

Memory Verses

Bless the LORD, O my soul, and forget not all his benefits: (Psalms 103:2 KJV)

Who forgiveth all thine iniquities; who healeth all thy diseases; (Psalms 103:3 KJV)

Introduction

*I*n order for a person to receive eternal life, healing, or any other blessing from God, they must be fully persuaded that it is the will of God for them. For example: the entire Christian community agrees that it is the will of God for all of mankind to be born again.

Except a man be born again, he cannot see the kingdom of God. (John 3:3 KJV)

Except a man be born of water and of the Spirit, he cannot enter into the kingdom of God. (John 3:5 KJV)

Jesus, speaking to Nicodemus, a Pharisee who came to Him by night, tells us that man cannot see (understand) or enter the Kingdom of God unless he is born again by the Spirit of God.

For God so loved the world, that he gave his only begotten Son, that whosoever believeth in him should not perish, but have everlasting life. (John 3:16 KJV)

In verse 16 Scripture makes it clear that the Father's purpose for sending Jesus, His only Son, as a sacrifice for sin was so that whosoever (any person who) believed in Him could have eternal life.

The Greek for the phrase "eternal life" is "*aionios zoe*" which means perpetual life. When you believe you are born again and you receive eternal life. You cannot do anything to earn it nor do you deserve it. It is miraculous and only comes through faith in the finished work of the Cross. It is a free gift.

Although we do not instantly go to heaven, we can experience the benefits or first fruits of that *zoe* life. Our relationship is restored with Father God instantly. We have the assurance of spending eternity in His presence but we can also experience His presence today, in this lifetime.

> *The Lord is not slack concerning his promise, as some men count slackness; but is longsuffering to us-ward, not willing that any should perish, but that all should come to repentance. (2 Peter 3:9 KJV)*

The majority of Christians would not dispute the truth that it is God's will for all mankind to come to repentance and receive eternal life.

However, there is a powerful truth that has been distorted and lost over the years: Jesus did not just die that you might have eternal life; He was also wounded that you might be physically and emotionally healed.

Unlike the first century Church, the Body of Christ today is totally divided in their belief in the area of healing and deliverance. They all agree there is no sickness and disease in heaven, but there is no agreement in today's Church as a whole concerning physical and emotional healing. Some even teach that the manifestations of the Spirit were necessary for the birthing of the early Church but they passed away with the death of the disciples. Others pray for healing then add *"if it be Thy will."* Still others say sickness and disease is God's way of teaching us.

The goal of this lesson is to fully persuade the reader that in the same way the believer can experience the first fruits of their spiritual salvation in this lifetime, the believer can also experience the first fruits of physical and emotional healing in this lifetime. After all, provision for both was made at Calvary.

Old Testament Types and Shadows

The fact that provision for our physical healing was made at the same time provision for our spiritual healing was made is hidden in plain view throughout the Scriptures. God often veiled His plans in a mystery so they could only be known by revelation of the Holy Spirit. In 1 Corinthians 2:6-8, Paul tells us why.

> *Howbeit we speak wisdom among them that are perfect: yet not the wisdom of this world, nor of the princes of this world, that come to naught: (1 Corinthians 2:6 KJV)*

> *But we speak the wisdom of God in a mystery, even the hidden wisdom, which God ordained before the world unto our glory: (1 Corinthians 2:7 KJV)*

> *Which none of the princes of this world knew: for had they known it, they would not have crucified the Lord of glory. (1 Corinthians 2:8 KJV)*

According to Paul, if Satan and the princes of this world had known God's plan of redemption they would not have crucified Jesus, the Lord of Glory. We know Satan knew the Scriptures, God's Word, because he quoted them (albeit incorrectly) to Jesus when he tempted Him in the wilderness.[1] However, because Satan did not have the Holy Spirit, there was no understanding and the truth was veiled to him. Had Satan fully understood God's plan of redemption, he would have done everything possible to prevent the crucifixion of Jesus.

To fully understand the Word of God one must have the inspiration and revelation of the Holy Spirit. Only then can we fully understand the meaning of the symbols found throughout the Bible and what they foretold. These symbols are usually referred to as types and shadows. They are symbolic of the sacrifice of Jesus.

The Old Testament is full of types and shadows of God's plan for the redemption of man. By studying these types and shadows, one can learn much about what was accomplished by Jesus' sacrifice.

Passover: Exodus 12

Four hundred years had passed since Joseph brought his family of seventy to Egypt. These descendants of Abraham had grown to over two million strong. The new king of Egypt, who did not know Joseph, viewed these Hebrews as foreigners and their numbers as a threat to his balance of power. He decided to make them slaves. The problem was, the more difficult the Pharaoh made their life, the more God blessed them.

Through a series of events Moses, a Hebrew boy, became a prince in Pharaoh's palace and then an outcast in the desert. God called him out of this wilderness to return to Egypt to lead God's people out of slavery. Through a cycle of plagues and promises made and broken, Israel was delivered from the Pharaoh's grasp.

In Exodus 12, the Bible records God's instructions of preparation for Israel's Exodus out of Egypt. In order for them to be spared from the "angel of death," a lamb with no blemishes had to be killed and the blood of the lamb was to be applied to the door post of their homes. The lamb was a sacrifice, a substitute for those who would have died in the plague. (This foreshadowed the blood of Christ, the Lamb of God, who would shed His blood for the sins of all people.) When the "death angel" saw the blood on the doorpost, he did not enter the house but passed over it.

They were also instructed to eat the lamb. Why were the Israelites required to eat the flesh of the Passover lamb for physical strength, unless we too receive physical life or strength from Christ, who is our sacrificed Passover Lamb?

The Israelites, descendants of Abraham, went into Egypt as a family. They came out of Egypt a nation set apart for God. After the crossing of the Red Sea, which was typical of our redemption, God made a covenant with Israel and His first promise was healing.

> *And said, If thou wilt diligently hearken to the voice of the LORD thy God, and wilt do that which is right in his sight, and wilt give ear to his commandments, and keep all his statutes, I will put none of these diseases upon thee, which I have brought upon the Egyptians: for I am the LORD that healeth thee. (Exodus 15:26 KJV)*

---

[1] Matthew 4

The very first covenant God made with this new nation, Israel, was revealed by and sealed with His first covenant and redemptive name, JEHOVAH-*RAPHA*, translated *"I am the LORD that healeth thee."*

> *He brought them forth also with silver and gold: and there was not one feeble person among their tribes. (Psalms 105:37 KJV)*

Scripture tells us the Israelites came out of Egypt with wealth and healing for their bodies. Healing was included in their deliverance. The blessing of healing that was revealed by His redemptive name, JEHOVAH-RAPHA, was available to all; nobody was excluded. As long as Israel worshiped and obeyed God, they enjoyed the blessing of divine health.

2 Chronicles 28-30

> *Ahaz was twenty years old when he began to reign, and he reigned sixteen years in Jerusalem: but he did not that which was right in the sight of the LORD, like David his father: (2 Chronicles 28:1 KJV)*

> *For he walked in the ways of the kings of Israel, and made also molten images for Baalim. (2 Chronicles 28:2 KJV)*

Under the reign of Ahaz the Israelites fell into idolatry. After the death of Ahaz his son Hezekiah reigned for twenty-nine years in Jerusalem.

> *Hezekiah began to reign when he was five and twenty years old, and he reigned nine and twenty years in Jerusalem. And his mother's name was Abijah, the daughter of Zechariah. (2 Chronicles 29:1 KJV)*

> *And he did that which was right in the sight of the LORD, according to all that David his father had done. (2 Chronicles 29:2 KJV)*

Hezekiah did what was right in the sight of the Lord. He cleansed the temple of all the unholy and re-established worship to God in the house of the Lord God of their fathers.

> *And Hezekiah sent to all Israel and Judah, and wrote letters also to Ephraim and Manasseh, that they should come to the house of the LORD at Jerusalem, to keep the passover unto the LORD God of Israel. (2 Chronicles 30:1 KJV)*

Hezekiah called for all of Israel to sanctify themselves and to gather in Jerusalem for Passover. He had it in his heart to make covenant with the Lord.[2]

---

[2] 2 Chronicles 29:10

2 Chronicles 30:18-20

For a multitude of the people, many from Ephraim, Manasseh, Issachar, and Zebulun, had not cleansed themselves, yet they ate the Passover otherwise than Moses directed. For Hezekiah had prayed for them, saying, May the good Lord pardon everyone (2 Chronicles 30:18 AMP)

Who sets his heart to seek and yearn for God—the Lord, the God of his fathers—even though not complying with the purification regulations of the sanctuary. (2 Chronicles 30:19 AMP)

And the Lord hearkened to Hezekiah and healed the people. (2 Chronicles 30:20 AMP)

Many of the people did not cleanse themselves as King Hezekiah had commanded, yet they ate the Passover. Hezekiah prayed that the Lord would pardon everyone whose heart was set to seek Him, even though they had not complied with the purification regulations of the sanctuary.

The Lord heard Hezekiah's prayer and healed the people. Hundreds of years after the crossing of the Red Sea God healed His people after they kept Passover. The Jewish people believed at least two absolutes about God: (1) He forgives sin and (2) He heals.

Rebellion in the Camp: Numbers 16

Two hundred and fifty leaders, famous in the congregation, men of renown, came against Moses and Aaron.

Numbers 16:1-3

Now Korah, the son of Izhar, the son of Kohath, the son of Levi, and Dathan and Abiram, the sons of Eliab, and On, the son of Peleth, sons of Reuben, took men: (Numbers 16:1 KJV)

And they rose up before Moses, with certain of the children of Israel, two hundred and fifty princes of the assembly, famous in the congregation, men of renown: (Numbers 16:2 KJV)

And they gathered themselves together against Moses and against Aaron, and said unto them, Ye take too much upon you, seeing all the congregation are holy, every one of them, and the LORD is among them: wherefore then lift ye up yourselves above the congregation of the LORD? (Numbers 16:3 KJV)

These men accused Moses and Aaron of appointing themselves as leaders over the people. Moses' response was to let the Lord confirm who He had chosen. Moses instructed all of them to fill their censer with incense and come together before the Lord the next day. When all two hundred and fifty had gathered together with their censers, the Glory of the Lord appeared to the congregation and told the congregation to separate themselves from these men.

Numbers 16:28-30

> *And Moses said, Hereby ye shall know that the LORD hath sent me to do all these works; for I have not done them of mine own mind. (Numbers 16:28 KJV)*

> *If these men die the common death of all men, or if they be visited after the visitation of all men; then the LORD hath not sent me. (Numbers 16:29 KJV)*

> *But if the LORD make a new thing, and the earth open her mouth, and swallow them up, with all that appertain unto them, and they go down quick into the pit; then ye shall understand that these men have provoked the LORD. (Numbers 16:30 KJV)*

When Moses finished speaking, the ground opened up and consumed all of them, their families, homes, and all their goods.

> *And the earth opened her mouth, and swallowed them up, and their houses, and all the men that appertained unto Korah, and all their goods. (Numbers 16:32 KJV)*

Some people never learn. Look what happened the very next day.

> *But on the morrow all the congregation of the children of Israel murmured against Moses and against Aaron, saying, Ye have killed the people of the LORD. (Numbers 16:41 KJV)*

The whole community accused Moses and Aaron of killing the Lord's people. God would have destroyed the whole congregation, but Moses interceded.

Numbers 16:44-46

> *And the LORD spoke unto Moses, saying, (Numbers 16:44 KJV)*

> *Get you up from among this congregation, that I may consume them as in a moment. And they fell upon their faces. (Numbers 16:45 KJV)*

> *And Moses said unto Aaron, Take a censer, and put fire therein from off the altar, and put on incense, and go quickly unto the congregation, and make an atonement for them: for there is wrath gone out from the LORD; the plague is begun. (Numbers 16:46 KJV)*

The sin of the people brought a plague on themselves. The word *plague* is a Hebrew word that means infliction of disease.[3] Moses instructed Aaron to make atonement for the people because the infliction of disease or plague had begun.

> *And Aaron took as Moses commanded, and ran into the midst of the congregation; and, behold, the plague was begun among the people: and he put on incense, and made an atonement for the people. (Numbers 16:47 KJV)*

> *And he stood between the dead and the living; and the plague was stayed. (Numbers 16:48 KJV)*

Aaron offered the incense and made atonement for their sin and verse 48 tells us the plague stopped. The atonement provided forgiveness of sin and healing for the body.

This state of health remained uninterrupted until nineteen years later when the people, not satisfied with God's way for them, spoke against God and against Moses.

The Brazen Serpent: Numbers 21

In Numbers 20 the children of Israel come against Moses and Aaron because they had no water. Moses was so angry with them that he hit the rock instead of speaking to the rock as instructed by God and as a result Moses was not allowed to go into the Promised Land.

In Chapter 21, God had just delivered the Canaanites into the hands of the Israelites. However, the congregation was not happy with the provision of God so they spoke against God and Moses.

Numbers 21:5-9

> *And the people spoke against God, and against Moses, Wherefore have ye brought us up out of Egypt to die in the wilderness? for there is no bread, neither is there any water; and our soul loatheth this light bread. (Numbers 21:5 KJV)*

> *And the LORD sent fiery serpents among the people, and they bit the people; and much people of Israel died. (Numbers 21:6 KJV)*

> *Therefore the people came to Moses, and said, We have sinned, for we have spoken against the LORD, and against thee; pray unto the LORD, that he take away the serpents from us. And Moses prayed for the people. (Numbers 21:7 KJV)*

> *And the LORD said unto Moses, Make thee a fiery serpent, and set it upon a pole: and it shall come to pass, that every one that is bitten, when he looketh upon it, shall live. (Numbers 21:8 KJV)*

---

[3] Strong's: H5063 *negeph neh'-ghef* From H5062; a *trip* (of the foot); figuratively an *infliction* (of disease): - plague, stumbling.

And Moses made a serpent of brass, and put it upon a pole, and it came to pass, that if a serpent had bitten any man, when he beheld the serpent of brass, he lived. (Numbers 21:9 KJV)

God sent fiery serpents among the people of Israel because of their sin. Many of them died as a result of being bit by the serpent. Again, Moses intercedes for them and God instructs Moses to make a brass serpent and put it on a pole. Anyone who looked on it lived.

When the Israelites met God's condition by confessing their sin and obeying what He had spoken through Moses, they were healed, every one of them. The beholding of the brazen serpent was a foreshadowing of Jesus being lifting up on a tree for all mankind.

Christ hath redeemed us from the curse of the law, being made a curse for us: for it is written, Cursed is every one that hangeth on a tree: (Galatians 3:13 KJV)

Sickness and disease is a part of the curse. Just as the Israelites' curse was removed by the lifting up of the brazen serpent, so is the curse of sickness and disease removed from the believer by the lifting up of Christ. There is "Healing in the Atonement!"

Isaiah 53:4-5

Prophecies concerning the Messiah (Messianic prophecies) can be found as far back as Adam and Eve, but none so fully detail the promise of healing as those of Isaiah, who lived and prophesied seven to eight hundred years before Jesus was crucified.

Surely he hath borne our griefs, and carried our sorrows: yet we did esteem him stricken, smitten of God, and afflicted. (Isaiah 53:4 KJV)

But he was wounded for our transgressions, he was bruised for our iniquities: the chastisement of our peace was upon him; and with his stripes we are healed. (Isaiah 53:5 KJV)

There are several words that need to be examined here because the full meaning is not clear in the King James translation. Let's look at the word grief in verse 4.

Grief: Strong's H2483. choliy, khol-ee'; from H2470; malady, anxiety, calamity:—disease, grief, (is) sick (-ness).

The word grief is the Hebrew word *kholee*. It comes from the root word *chalah*, which means to be weak, sick, and afflicted. This Hebrew word is used twenty-two times in the Old Testament and every place it occurs (with the exception of Isaiah 53 and in the book of Jeremiah) it is translated either sickness or disease.[4]

---

[4] Bible Research Systems, Version 6.1 Revision A, Austin, Texas, 1995

Sorrows: Strong's H4341. mak'ob, mak-obe'; sometimes mak'owb, mak-obe'; also (fem. Isa. 53 : 3) mak'obah, mak-o-baw'; from H3510; anguish or (fig.) affliction:—grief, pain, sorrow.

The word sorrow is the Hebrew word *makob*. It comes from the root word *kaab*, which means to feel pain. You can find this same Hebrew word translated as pain in Job and Jeremiah.

He is chastened also with pain upon his bed. (Job 33:19 KJV)

Take balm for her pain.[5] *(Jeremiah 51:8 KJV)*

Therefore, Isaiah 53:4 would be better translated: *"Surely he hath borne our sickness and carried our pain."*

Let's also examine the two verbs used in verse 4. The word borne is the Hebrew word *nasa*. This word is used 590 times in the Old Testament. The first time this word *nasa* is used in Scripture it is used by Cain in Genesis.

Cain said unto the Lord, My punishment is greater than I can bear.[6] *(Genesis 4:13KJV)*

Clearly, Cain is talking about suffering punishment for something he did. The same is true of its use in Leviticus 5.

If a soul sin,. . .then he shall bear his iniquity. (Leviticus 5:1 KJV)

This word *nasa* used in Isaiah 53:4 to describe the work of Jesus concerning healing is the same word used just a few verses later, in verse 12, to describe the work of Jesus concerning sin:

. . .and He bare the sin of many, and made intercession for the transgressors. (Isaiah 53:12 KJV)

This means that in the same way Jesus bore your sins, He bore your sickness.

The other verb in Isaiah 53:4 is the Hebrew word *sabal* (sometimes spelled *cabal*) which is translated as carried.

Carried: Strong's 5445. cabal, saw-bal'; a prim. root; to carry (lit. or fig.), or (reflex.) be burdensome; spec. to be gravid:—bear, be a burden, carry, strong to labor.

---

[5] Ibid

[6] Ibid

This is a good translation. Strong's gives the same translation for this word *sabal*: to carry (literally or figuratively), to be burdensome. You can see it used in Lamentations 5. Although the English word is borne, the Hebrew word is *sabal*, meaning to carry.

Our fathers have sinned. . .and we have borne their iniquities. (Lamentations 5:7 KJV)

Isaiah consistently used this Hebrew word *sabal* in chapter 53 to speak of sickness and sin. He used same Hebrew word that he used to describe the work of Jesus concerning sickness (verse 4) to describe His work concerning sin (verse 11).

. . .for he shall bear their iniquities. (Isaiah 53:11 KJV)

Iniquities: Strong's H5771. 'avon, aw-vone'; or 'avown (H2 Kings 7 : 9; Psa. 51 : 5 [H7]), aw-vone'; from H5753; perversity, i.e. (moral) evil:—fault, iniquity, mischief, punishment (of iniquity), sin.

The English word is bear, but it is the same Hebrew word *sabal* which means to carry. I like the Amplified Version of Isaiah 53:4-5.

Surely He has borne our griefs (sicknesses, weaknesses, and distresses) and carried our sorrows and pains [of punishment], yet we [ignorantly] considered Him stricken, smitten, and afflicted by God [as if with leprosy]. [See Matt. 8:17.] (Isaiah 53:4 AMP)

But He was wounded for our transgressions, He was bruised for our guilt and iniquities; the chastisement [needful to obtain] peace and well-being for us was upon Him, and with the stripes [that wounded] Him we are healed and made whole. (Isaiah 53:5 AMP)

Some say that the phrase *"we are healed"* refers to spiritual healing. The Hebrew word used for our English word healed is *rapha*. It means to mend, to cure, or to make whole.

Healed: Strong's H7495 râphâ' râphâh raw-faw', raw-faw A primitive root; properly to mend (by stitching), that is, (figuratively) to cure: - cure, (cause to) heal, physician, repair, X thoroughly, make whole. See H7503.

In the Hebrew language it is the same word for physician. You do not hire a physician to heal your spirit. Do not allow anyone to mislead you into thinking this word is referring to spiritual healing. It is clear the prophet is speaking of physical healing. Jesus is the great physician.

The writer used the same word used in Exodus when God revealed Himself as JEHOVAH *RAHPA*, the Lord that heals. Jehovah is distinctly the redemption name of Deity and means: the self-existent one who reveals himself. Jehovah has seven compound names which reveal Him as meeting every need of man from his lost state to the end, JEHOVAH *RAHPA* being one of them.

Hundreds of years before the cross the prophet Isaiah had the revelation of the coming Messiah. The only *surely* in this redemptive chapter prefaces God's provision for healing (verse 4). In this prophecy Isaiah clearly tells us that to the same extent the Messiah would take our sin, He would take our sickness and pain. If the full Gospel is to be preached it must include healing as well as forgiveness of sin. There is healing in the Atonement.

Jesus: The Fulfillment of O.T. Types

The Jews of Jesus' time were very familiar with the passage from Isaiah. In fact, they were anticipating the fulfillment of it because they knew it was a Messianic prophecy. Since they were looking for Messiah they were looking for someone who would fit Isaiah's description of the Messiah.

> *When the evening was come they brought unto Him many that were possessed with devils and He cast the spirits out with His Word and healed all that were sick. (Matthew 8:16 KJV)*

> *That it might be fulfilled which was spoken by Isaiah, the prophet, saying Himself took our infirmities and bare our sickness. (Matthew 8:17 KJV)*

Isaiah saw the full work of the Cross before it happened. Matthew identified the earthly ministry of Jesus as that which was foretold by Isaiah.[7] Jesus fit the description the Jews were looking for as the Messiah. Since Jesus fulfilled this prophesy, the linkage between salvation and healing is sealed for all eternity. You cannot separate them.

> *And, behold, they brought to him a man sick of the palsy, lying on a bed: and Jesus seeing their faith said unto the sick of the palsy; Son, be of good cheer; thy sins be forgiven thee. (Matthew 9:2 KJV)*

Wait a minute! This man was brought to Jesus with the expectation of being healed and Jesus says, *"Thy sins be forgiven thee."* What's up with that?

> *For whether is easier, to say, Thy sins be forgiven thee; or to say, Arise, and walk? (Matthew 9:5 KJV)*

---

[7] McCrossan, Dr. T.J., Bodily Healing and The Atonement, RHEMA Bible Church, Tulsa OK, 1982, 15-18 According to Dr. McCrossan, the word fulfilled is *plerothe*, the 1st Aorist passive, subjunctive, 3rd person singular of *pleroo*. It is the same word that appears in Matthew 12:17-21 where Matthew again quotes Isaiah and declares that the word foretold by the prophet in Isaiah 42:1-4 has been 'fulfilled'. The Aorist tense, which indicates momentary completed past action is also used to express future events which must certainly happen. So Matthew was saying that by these present actions of Jesus, we see that the rest of the word must certainly be fulfilled as well. Jesus also used this same word in the same tense when he (in Luke 4:21) took the Scriptures and read from Isaiah and declared that the scripture had been 'fulfilled' that day. Yet, there the work was not finished that day, but because he had started, it will be completed.

And he arose, and departed to his house. (Matthew 9:7 KJV)

Jesus made no difference in forgiving one's sins and the healing of their bodies. Why?

Wherefore, as by one man sin entered into the world, and death by sin; and so death passed upon all men, for that all have sinned. (Romans 5:12 KJV)

According to this Scripture when sin came into the earth through the sin of Adam, death spread to all men: spiritual death, separation from God, and physical death. Sin was the door for sickness, disease, poverty, and death to enter into the world, since they did not exist until after the fall of man.

Early symptoms of physical death manifest in the form of sickness and disease. As soon as they advance beyond the power of nature to restore they will result in death in every case unless removed by the power of God.

Therefore as by the offense of one judgment came upon all men to condemnation; even so by the righteousness of one the free gift came upon all men unto justification of life. (Romans 5:18 KJV)

In the same way death spread to the human race because of one man's sin, healing can spread to all people because of Jesus' righteous act. Likewise, if it is true that one man's act of disobedience brought the curse of spiritual and physical death (sickness and disease) to humanity, then it must also be true that the atoning work of Jesus Christ brought life, a restored relationship to God, and healing for physical and emotional sickness.

Some argue that Matthew 8:16-17 could not refer to the Atonement since Jesus had not yet been crucified.

And all that dwell upon the earth shall worship him, whose names are not written in the book of life of the Lamb slain from the foundation of the world. (Revelation 13:8 KJV)

Jesus was the Lamb of God who was "*slain from the foundation of the world.*" Jesus forgave sin and healed before He was crucified. Both were bestowed on the basis of His future atoning work of the Cross.

Since Jesus bore our sickness and His Atonement embraces all mankind, it would require the healing of all to fulfill the prophecy of Isaiah.

And the whole multitude sought to touch him: for there went virtue out of him, and healed them all. (Luke 6:19 KJV)

If sickness was not provided for all in redemption how did the *all* in the multitude obtain from Christ the healing that God did not provide? Throughout the New Testament we read that Jesus healed them all. The Atonement was His reason for making no exception when healing the sick.

Every sickness and disease known to man is recorded in Deuteronomy 28:15-62 as being a part of the curse of the law.

Lesson 4 - Healing In The Atonement

Christ hath redeemed us from the curse of the law, being made a curse for us: for it is written, Cursed is every one that hangeth on a tree. (Galatians 3:13 KJV)

Christ redeemed us from that self-defeating, cursed life by absorbing it completely into himself. Do you remember the Scripture that says, "Cursed is everyone who hangs on a tree"? That is what happened when Jesus was nailed to the Cross: He became a curse, and at the same time dissolved the curse. (Galatians 3:13 MSG)

Christ has redeemed us from the curse of the law. Sickness and disease are included in the curse. Therefore, He has redeemed us from sickness and disease.

Just as Aaron made atonement for the removal of the plague, the healing of the body, after 14,700 had died (Numbers 16), the Atonement of Jesus Christ has redeemed us from the *plague* of sickness and disease.

Plague: Strong's 3148. mastix, mas'-tix; prob. from the base of G3145 (through the idea of contact); a whip (lit. the Roman flagellum for criminals; fig. a disease):— plague, scourging.

Three times in the New Testament the Greek word *mastix* is translated *plagues*, meaning physical sickness.

For he had healed many; insomuch that they pressed upon him for to touch him, as many as had plagues. (Mark 3:10 KJV)

And straightway the fountain of her blood was dried up; and she felt in her body that she was healed of that plague. (Mark 5:29 KJV)

And he said unto her, Daughter, thy faith hath made thee whole; go in peace, and be whole of thy plague. (Mark 5:34 KJV)

Interestingly enough, two times in the New Testament this same word is translated *scourging*, meaning to be beaten with a Roman whip.

The chief captain commanded him to be brought into the castle, and bade that he should be examined by scourging; that he might know wherefore they cried so against him. (Acts 22:24 KJV)

And others had trial of cruel mockings and scourgings, yea, moreover of bonds and imprisonment. (Hebrews 11:36 KJV)

The *mastix* or beating with the Roman whip was for the plagues or physical sickness. Jesus took our sins to the Cross with Him and therefore the power of sin is broken. He also, by the scourging of the Roman whip, took every sickness and disease that existed. Jesus made provision for the redemption for mankind's spirit, soul, and body now, while we are still on earth. Because of the work of Calvary we can experience the first fruits of eternity: an intimate relationship with God the Father and divine health for our bodies.

The work of the Cross was a complete work. God did not deliver us from every penalty and consequence of sin, except one. Jesus Himself said, *"It is finished."*

> *When Jesus therefore had received the vinegar, he said, It is finished: and he bowed his head, and gave up the ghost. (John 19:30 KJV)*

> *Jesus said, "It is done . . . complete." . . . . (John 19:3 MSG)*

The power of sin and death died with Jesus. Whatever has power over you Jesus now has power over it.

The fact of healing being in the Atonement necessitates the continuation of His healing ministry during His exaltation (His resurrection, His sacrifice being accepted for the sins of all mankind, and Him being seated at the right hand of the Father).

If Christ is unwilling to heal as universally during His exaltation as He did during His humiliation (His rejection, His scourging and His suffering the death of a criminal of the Cross) Hebrews 13:8 would not be true.

> *Jesus Christ the same yesterday, and today, and forever. (Hebrews 13:8 KJV)*

In addition, Jesus would not be able to fulfill His promise in John 14.

John 14:12-13

> *Verily, verily, I say unto you, He that believeth on me, the works that I do shall he do also; and greater works than these shall he do; because I go unto my Father. (John 14:12 KJV)*

> *And whatsoever ye shall ask in my name, that will I do, that the Father may be glorified in the Son. (John 14:13 KJV)*

> *The person who trusts me will not only do what I'm doing but even greater things, because I, on my way to the Father, am giving you the same work to do that I've been doing. You can count on it. (John 14:12 MSG)*

> *From now on, whatever you request along the lines of who I am and what I am doing, I'll do it. That's how the Father will be seen for who he is in the Son. I mean it. (John 14:13 MSG)*

> *I assure you, most solemnly I tell you, if anyone steadfastly believes in Me, he will himself be able to do the things that I do; and he will do even greater things than these, because I go to the Father. (John 14:12 AMP)*

And I will do [I Myself will grant] whatever you ask in My Name [as presenting all that I AM], so that the Father may be glorified and extolled in (through) the Son. [See Exod. 3:14.] (John 14:13 AMP)

After Jesus' ascension, the disciples taught that it was the same work of the Cross, which was prophesied by Isaiah and reported by Matthew that was the basis for the ministry work of the believer.

Who his own self bare our sins in his own body on the tree, that we, being dead to sins, should live unto righteousness: by whose stripes ye were healed. (1 Peter 2:24 KJV)

Peter, looking back to the Cross, reminds us of what is included in our package. Notice he mentions forgiveness of sin and healing of our bodies. They were both purchased at the Cross of Calvary.

Isaiah looked forward to the Cross and said, *"By His stripes we are* (present tense) *healed."* Matthew declared the works of Jesus were what the fulfillment of that prophecy looked like. Peter looked back to the finished work of the Cross and said, *"By His stripes we were* (past tense) *healed."*

In the same way that it is God's will for all to be born again, it is His will for all to be healed.

Even so it is not the will of your Father which is in heaven, that one of these little ones should perish. (Matthew 18:14 KJV)

Beloved, I wish above all things that thou mayest prosper and be in health, even as thy soul prospereth. (3 John 1:2 KJV)

Many Christians today are sick because they have not properly discerned the complete work of the Cross; and many others have died because they did not know that healing was in the Atonement.

I Corinthians 11:28-30

But let a man examine himself, and so let him eat of that bread, and drink of that cup. (1 Corinthians 11:28 KJV)

For he that eateth and drinketh unworthily, eateth and drinketh damnation to himself, not discerning the Lord's body. (1 Corinthians 11:29 KJV)

For this cause many are weak and sickly among you, and many sleep. (1 Corinthians 11:30 KJV)

Jesus' life and ministry were both a revelation and a manifestation of the unchanging love and will God. He literally acted out the will of God for Adam's race.

For I came down from heaven, not to do mine own will, but the will of him that sent me. (John 6:38 KJV)

When Jesus healed all those who came to Him for healing He was doing and revealing the will of God the Father for our bodies.

But now hath he obtained a more excellent ministry, by how much also he is the mediator of a better covenant, which was established upon better promises. (Hebrews 8:6 KJV)

Since the New Covenant is a better covenant than the Old Covenant and is established on better promises, it must include healing.

The two things mankind lost in the Garden, our intimacy with the Father (spiritual life) and the healing of our body (physical life), have been restored to the believer. Sin and sickness have passed from mankind to Calvary. Eternal life and divine health have passed from Calvary to mankind.

Provision for healing for our bodies was made at the same time provision for the forgiveness of our sin was made through the atoning work of the Cross of Jesus Christ. They came in the same package. They both belong to every believer.

Sozo

Since healing is in the same package as our forgiveness of sin, the next logical question is, "Well, if I'm not healed, am I saved?" The answer is yes. You can be saved and still be plagued with sickness and disease.

Unfortunately, the Church world today has reduced the English word salvation to refer only to the born-again experience. Let me explain.

Marvel not that I said unto thee, Ye must be born again. (John 3:7 KJV)

For God so loved the world, that he gave his only begotten Son, that whosoever believeth in him should not perish, but have everlasting life. (John 3:16 KJV)

It is from these two verses in John that we get our concept of being born again. In verse 7 the word again is the Greek word *anothen*[8] which means "from above." The phrase for "everlasting life," in verse 16 in the Greek is *"aionios*[9] *zoe"* which means: "perpetual life."

If you believe in Jesus you are born from above and are promised eternal life. It happens instantaneously and there is nothing you can do to earn it or deserve it.

---

[8] Strongs G509 ἄνωθεν anōthen *an'-o-then* From G507; *from above*; by analogy *from the first*; by implication *anew*: - from above, again, from the beginning (very first), the top.

[9] Strongs G166 αἰώνιος aiōnios *ahee-o'-nee-os* From G165; *perpetual* (also used of past time, or past and future as well): - eternal, for ever, everlasting, world (began).

For by grace are ye saved through faith; and that not of yourselves: it is the gift of God. (Ephesians 2:8 KJV)

The word saved in this verse of Scripture is the Greek word *sozo*. Here is the definition of *sozo* from three good sources:

- **Strong's:** Deliver or protect (lit. or fig.), to heal, to preserve, to save yourself, to do well, to be made whole.
- **Septuagint:** to save, to keep safe and sound, to rescue from danger or destruction, to save one who is suffering from disease or is perishing, to make well, to heal, to restore to health, to include spiritual healing, to rescue, to bring safely forth from, to save in a technical Biblical sense, to deliver from the penalties of Messianic judgment, to save from the evils which are an obstruction of the Messianic deliverance, to make one a partner to the salvation of Christ.
- **Vine's Complete Expository Dictionary**: the material and temporal deliverance from dangerous sufferings, of the spiritual and eternal salvations granted immediately by God to those who believe in the Lord Jesus Christ, the present experiences of God's power to deliver from the bondage of sin, the future deliverance of believers at the second coming of Christ, inclusively for all the blessings bestowed by God on man in Christ.

This word *sozo* includes the born-again experience, but it means much more. Just as people cannot receive forgiveness of their sin until they know that God has made that available to them, they will not exercise faith for healing until they know it has been provided for them in that very same package.

Healing is in your *sozo*. You are entitled to it because you have been justified, born again. If you do not have it, you are being robbed.

For she said, if I may touch but his clothes, I shall be whole. (Mark 5:28 KJV)

And straightway the fountain of her blood was dried up; and she felt in her body that she was healed of that plague. (Mark 5:29 KJV)

The woman with the issue of blood believed if she could just touch Jesus' clothes she would be made whole. That word whole is the Greek word sozo. Verse 29 tells us that she was healed of that plague: the Greek word mastix meaning physical sickness, discussed earlier in this chapter.

The First Century Church had a revelation of this truth. But much was lost as the Church went through what we call the "Dark Ages." When Martin Luther began to preach that one received eternal life through faith and not by works, his focus was on eternal life alone. As a result, the entire Church world today is in total agreement concerning the forgiveness of sin being for all and being part of the Atonement. Therefore, many have received the forgiveness of their sin by faith. However where healing is concerned the Church is severely divided and many who are born again fail to appropriate the rest of the package because they do not have the same kind of confidence that healing is in the Atonement.

We can see very clearly in the Scriptures, that physical healing is included in our *sozo*. It must be received the same way one receives their spiritual salvation, by faith.

Activation Time

- Put on a praise and worship CD.
- *Halal* for 2 minutes using your attributes of God list.
- Pray in the Spirit, with passion, for 5 minutes.
- Pray a prayer of repentance for ever taking communion in an unworthy manner. If using this manual in a group setting, lead the entire group in a prayer of repentance. (See example below)
- Serve communion – The Meal that Heals.

Prayer of Repentance

Father, in the Name of Jesus, I repent for each time I have received the elements of the communion table in an unworthy fashion, either knowingly or unknowingly. I repent for all the times I took Holy Communion without understanding the fullness of the provision of the shed blood and the broken body of my Lord and Savior, Jesus Christ.

Thank You, Father, for in the Atonement, the finished work of the Cross, there is full provision for me; spirit, soul, and body. In the same way You provided for the new birth of my spirit (born-again experience), You made provision for healing in my soul (mind, will and emotions) and my body (physical healing).

Lord, may I never forget that in the taking of the juice and the bread I'm renewing my commitment to the covenant that You have chosen to enter into with me. Help me to always remember Your covenant provision of spiritual healing and physical healing. Every time I partake of the bread and the juice of the Covenant Table of Communion, may this communion meal be "The Meal That Heals" in my life. Amen!

Communion: The Meal That Heals

My pastor refers to communion as "The Meal that Heals." We have four altars at the front of our church. Every Sunday teams of three are stationed at each altar and any who are sick are invited to come forward to receive communion and prayer for healing. This is in addition to our monthly congregational taking of communion.

I have the privilege of being one of those team members who minister at these altars. One Sunday, a young lady with a cane approached the altar at which I was assigned. She told us she had scoliosis, had gone through two back fusion operations, and was still unable to walk without assistance and she was in constant pain.

We served her communion and prayed the prayer of faith over her. I watched her as she walked away. She walked away still using her cane and seemed to be very unstable. I remember saying in a very passionate voice, "God! I want to see them walk away without the cane!" Little did I know!

Testimony

Almost every Sunday a video testimony is shown of someone in our congregation whose life has been changed in some way by the power of God. I'll never forget the date, Sunday, March 15,

2009, about a month after we had prayed for this young woman. Her video testimony was shown in our morning worship service.

When she was in the sixth grade in 1988 she was diagnosed with scoliosis. In 2001 she had her second back fusion operation which left her with limited mobility on her right side. For seven years her husband had to buckle her shoe on her right side because she was unable to do so. She could not feed her children from her right side. They always had to sit to her left.

In August of 2008 she began to have other symptoms related to the fusions. Her hip would lock up on her making it difficult for her to walk. She had to start using a cane in order to do simple tasks at home, when going to the grocery store, or taking the children to the park. Eventually she had to rent a scooter and had to go through handicap lines. For all intents and purposes she was living the life of a disabled person.

She was in constant pain. Every day, on a scale from one to ten, she would start at a level five and work her way up. There were many times she would cry herself to sleep because she was in so much pain. Her orthopedic doctor began to give her a series of injections to try and determine where the pain was coming from. After two MRIs it was determined that she had osteoarthritis in her spine and hip.

On February 22, 2009, during the praise and worship service at our church, she felt encouraged by the Lord to go forward and meet Him at the communion table (The Meal that Heals). She came to the altar where I, along with two other ladies, had been assigned. We served her communion, told her to receive what God had for her, and prayed a prayer of faith over her.

After prayer, she picked up her cane and turned to walk back to her seat. According to her, she was standing so straight that when she tried to use the cane she would lose her balance. Her cane was too short! After a couple of steps she just picked up the cane and carried it. She also realized that for the first time in five years, she had no pain. When she got back to her seat her husband asked her, "Why are you taller?"

The healing continued throughout the day. When she woke up on Monday morning she jumped out of bed. She had no pain. She could stand up straight. As she stood, both of her feet pointed forward (her right foot used to be at a forty-five degree angle). Her hips were in alignment. She could twist toward both of her sides, the left and the right. To test her healing she buckled her own shoes, both of them!

JEHOVAH *RAPHA* met her that Sunday morning at the "Meal That Heals." The morning her testimony was shown she was in the sanctuary walking and praising God. No cane! No pain!

For we walk by faith, not by sight. (2 Corinthians 5:7 KJV)

As one who prays for many to receive healing, I have known this truth for a long time. However, since that day this Scripture has taken on a whole new meaning for me.

The lesson to be learned was, when praying for healing for yourself or for others, do not be discouraged or moved by what you see or do not see. If you do not see an immediate change in your condition or the condition of the other person, do not negate your prayer of faith by falling into unbelief. Continue to stand in faith until the manifestation comes.

Take and/or Serve Communion

Read 1 Corinthians 11:23-30. (This passage of Scripture is provided in the Amplified Version at the end of this lesson.)

If you are sick in your body as you take communion, release your faith to receive healing. It is your covenant right. It belongs to you.

Assignment

- Meditate on and memorize memory verses.
- Add 5 more attributes to your attributes of God list.
- Begin your daily prayer time by *halaling* for at least 2 minutes using your list of attributes of God.
- Pray in the Spirit a minimum of 15 minutes a day.
- Expect divine appointments, opportunities, to pray for someone to receive salvation and the baptism of the Holy Spirit.
- Take communion every day for a week or until your next class time and renew your commitment to God's Covenant and His provision for you. Record anything the Lord ministers to you during those times,
- If you are in need of healing, declare He is Jehovah *Rapha* over your body. Do it every day, all day, and expect a miracle. Do Not stop until the manifestation comes.

Assignment Result and Comments

Communion Scriptures

I Corinthians 11:23-30

For I received from the Lord Himself that which I passed on to you [it was given to me personally], that the Lord Jesus on the night when He was treacherously delivered up and while His betrayal was in progress took bread, (1 Corinthians 11:23 AMP)

And when He had given thanks, He broke [it] and said, Take, eat. This is My body, which is broken for you. Do this to call Me [affectionately] to remembrance. (1 Corinthians 11:24 AMP)

Similarly when supper was ended, He took the cup also, saying, This cup is the new covenant [ratified and established] in My blood. Do this, as often as you drink [it], to call Me [affectionately] to remembrance. (1 Corinthians 11:25 AMP)

For every time you eat this bread and drink this cup, you are representing and signifying and proclaiming the fact of the Lord's death until He comes [again]. (1 Corinthians 11:26 AMP)

So then whoever eats the bread or drinks the cup of the Lord in a way that is unworthy [of Him] will be guilty of [profaning and sinning against] the body and blood of the Lord. (1 Corinthians 11:27 AMP)

Let a man [thoroughly] examine himself, and [only when he has done] so should he eat of the bread and drink of the cup. (1 Corinthians 11:28 AMP)

For anyone who eats and drinks without discriminating and recognizing with due appreciation that [it is Christ's] body, eats and drinks a sentence (a verdict of judgment) upon himself. (1 Corinthians 11:29 AMP)

That [careless and unworthy participation] is the reason many of you are weak and sickly, and quite enough of you have fallen into the sleep of death. (1 Corinthians 11:30 AMP)

Seven Redemptive Names of God

Jehovah-Tsidkenu

- Meaning: The Lord My Righteousness
- Benefit: Forgiveness for Sin

Jehovah-M'kaddesh

- Meaning: The Lord Who Sanctifies
- Benefit: Forgiveness for Sin

Jehovah-Shalom

- Meaning: The Lord is Peace
- Benefit: Spirit

Jehovah-Shammah

- Meaning: The Lord is There
- Benefit: Spirit

Jehovah-Rapha

- Meaning: The Lord Who Heals
- Benefit: Soundness

Jehovah-Jireh

- Meaning: The Lord's Provision Shall be Seen
- Benefit: Success

Jehovah-Nissi

- Meaning: The Lord My Banner
- Benefit: Security

Jehovah-Rohi

- Meaning: The Lord My Shepherd
- Benefit: Security

LESSON 5 - Unbelief vs. Faith

Memory Verse

For therein is the righteousness of God revealed from faith to faith: as it is written. The just shall live by faith. (Romans 1:17 KJV)

Introduction

*I*n Lesson 4 we discussed in great detail the fact that healing is a provision of the Atonement. In the same way God provided for our deliverance from the bondage of sin, He provided for our deliverance from sickness and disease.

In the light of this truth, why is it that so many Christians suffer with sickness and disease? There are an unlimited number of reasons for this condition that we find throughout the Body of Christ. The same things that prevent an individual from accepting Christ as their Savior will prevent them from accepting Him as their Physician.

The roadblocks that hinder a person from receiving spiritual healing and physical healing are numerous and very complex. However, all roadblocks could probably fall into one or more of these four major categories: ignorance, unbelief, spiritual interference, and rejection.

As we progress through our study, we will discuss, in depth, issues that fall into each of these categories. For now, below is a brief explanation of each of them.

(1) **Ignorance:** A person just does not know that Jesus died for their sins. Before a person can be "born again" and receive "eternal life" they must be taught or exposed in some way to this truth. The same is true when coming to God for healing. They just do not know they are entitled to healing. The individual must be completely convinced that healing is available to them through the same work of the Cross.

(2) **Unbelief:** An individual must be absolutely certain of the fact that God not only *can* save but He *will* save them. Healing is no different. Each person must be convinced that his or her healing is the "will of God." It is impossible to have any real faith for healing as long as there is any doubt as to it being God's will to heal.

(3) **Spiritual Interference:** The third thing that can block one from receiving eternal salvation is spiritual or demonic interference and generational curses. The enemy interferes with a person's ability to know the truth by blinding them spiritually (2 Corinthians 4:4).

In the same way, the enemy has the ability to cause one to be physically sick or block their ability to receive their physical healing. There can be spiritual roots to some illnesses or a spiritual blockage to some healings. Sometimes a person is dealing with both.

(4) **Rejection:** What I mean by rejection is a person may believe Jesus is who the Bible says He is, but they just do not want Him. They may even believe Jesus died for their sins and that if they confess Him as Lord they will have eternal life, but they just do not want it. There are some people like that. They do not want to lose control of their lives or they have some other irrational reason. Likewise, there are those who do not really want to be healed of their sickness. As unbelievable as it seems, it is true. They do not want to lose their disability, or getting healed would bring more responsibility into their life, or some other equally ridiculous reason.

Ignorance

In our previous lesson we saw that Scripture clearly reveals that healing is in the Atonement package. We learned that through the types and shadows and the feasts of the Old Testament the people of God received healing and divine health on the basis of the future work of Calvary.

The Prophet Isaiah made it clear that to the same extent the Messiah would take our sin, He would take our sickness and pain (Isaiah 53:4-5). Matthew identified Jesus' ministry of healing and deliverance as the very work that was prophesied by Isaiah (Matthew 8:16-17). By quoting Isaiah 53 Matthew was saying that in the casting out of demons and the physical healing of the sick the promise is realized. Peter, after Jesus ascended, looking back to the Cross of Jesus, makes the connection for us today.

> *Who his own self bare our sins in his own body on the tree, that we, being dead to sins, should live unto righteousness: by whose stripes ye were healed. (1 Peter 2:24 KJV)*

The word our in this passage of Scripture is the Greek word *hemon*. The use of this word tells us Christ took the infirmities and sicknesses of the very same persons for whose sins He died.[10] Not different people or some of the people, but the very same people whose sins were forgiven.

Just as forgiveness of sins is available to all, clearly, physical healing is for all. Healing is truly in the Atonement.

The first roadblock to your ability to receive healing should, at this point, be removed. You now know that healing is available to all through the Gospel of Jesus Christ. You know that it is God's will to heal everybody, anywhere, and all the time. God heals on the basis of faith in the finished

---

[10] McCrossen, 23-24. "Again we are very sure that the 'our' of Isaiah 53:4 and Matthew 8:17 includes us today, because of the way Matthew expresses himself in the Greek: 'Himself took our infirmities.' 'Our infirmities' reads in Greek *tas astheneias hemon* (the sicknesses of us). This is consistent with 1 Corinthians 15:3 'Christ died for our sins.' 'For our sins' reads in the Greek *uper ton hamartion hemon* (for the sins of us). The same word is used in 1 Peter 2:24. The word 'our' is *hemon*. 'Who his own self bare our sins in his own body on the tree.' 'Our sins' here reads in the Greek *tas hamartias hemon* (the sins of us)."

work of the Cross, not whether we deserve it or not. Praise the Lord! Ignorance should no longer be a problem.

Unbelief

Today unbelief is a major roadblock to receiving physical healing in the Church. The Church, as a whole, is in complete agreement that the born-again experience is the will of God for all. They would never think or say that anyone is beyond eternal salvation or that it is only available to a few people.

> *The Lord is not slack concerning his promise, as some men count slackness; but is longsuffering to us-ward, not willing that any should perish, but that all should come to repentance. (2 Peter 3:9 KJV)*

Those who teach only the "salvation of the soul" part of the Gospel are laboring in the midst of almost universal acceptance of that doctrine. On the other hand, those who teach healing as part of the Atonement are laboring in the face of almost universal unbelief, in the Church as a whole, in the individual, and in the leadership (elders who pray).

> *Is any sick among you? let him call for the elders of the Church; and let them pray over him, anointing him with oil in the name of the Lord: (James 5:14 KJV)*

> *And the prayer of faith shall save the sick, and the Lord shall raise him up; and if he has committed sins, they shall be forgiven him. (James 5:15 KJV)*

John Wesley said that this method was the only process of healing in the Church until it was lost through unbelief. Unlike the first century Church, the Church today is not in one accord on the matter of healing.

James 1:6-8

> *But let him ask in faith, nothing wavering. For he that wavereth is like a wave of the sea driven with the wind and tossed. (James 1:6 KJV)*

> *For let not that man think that he shall receive any thing of the Lord. (James 1:7 KJV)*

> *A double minded man is unstable in all his ways. (James 1:8 KJV)*

The Body of Christ is in total agreement that eternal life, the born-again experience, is for everybody, everywhere, all the time. But when it comes to healing they are double-minded, which produces unbelief.

Lesson 5 - Unbelief Vs. Faith

And he that doubteth is damned if he eat, because he eateth not of faith: for whatsoever is not of faith is sin. (Romans 14:23 KJV)

Unbelief is the opposite of faith. The Scripture teaches us that anything that is not of faith is a sin. In the light of this truth, unbelief is a sin.

For the wages of sin is death; but the gift of God is eternal life through Jesus Christ our Lord. (Romans 6:23 KJV)

The wages or payment for sin is death. There was no sickness or disease in the earth until man fell into sin. Sickness and disease came as a result of sin and are the early symptoms of death.

He that committeth sin is of the devil; for the devil sinneth from the beginning. For this purpose the Son of God was manifested, that he might destroy the works of the devil. (1 John 3:8 KJV)

Scripture tells us that Jesus was manifest to destroy the works of the devil. How did He do that?

How God anointed Jesus of Nazareth with the Holy Ghost and with power: who went about doing good, and healing all that were oppressed of the devil; for God was with him. (Acts 10:38 KJV)

Jesus healed people. What kind of people did He heal? Jesus healed all who were oppressed of the devil. He saw both sin and sickness as works of the devil and at the cross He paid the price for sin and for the recompense of that sin, which is sickness and disease. It was a compete work.

Unlike the early Church, the Church of Jesus Christ today has not accepted the attitude toward sickness as revealed in the Gospel. Just as the serpent caused Eve to forget and disregard words plainly spoken to her by God he causes many Christians to forget and disregard the Word of God that plainly teaches us that our redemption from sickness was actually accomplished in the body of our crucified Lord. Therefore, the sin of unbelief has taken the place of united faith, allowing sickness and disease to be rampant in the Church. Unbelief is clearly a roadblock to receiving healing.

In Mark 9 there is the story of a father whose son was possessed and tormented by a dumb spirit. This spirit would often throw the boy into water or fire, trying to destroy him. The father had taken his son to the disciples but they were unable to deliver the boy. They brought the boy to Jesus. The father said to Jesus, *"If thou canst do anything, have compassion on us, and help us."*

Jesus said unto him, If thou canst believe, all things are possible to him that believeth. (Mark 9:23 KJV)

And straightway the father of the child cried out, and said with tears, Lord, I believe; help thou mine unbelief. (Mark 9:24 KJV)

Jesus' response was that it was not a question of His ability to heal but of the father's ability to believe. This father expressed the paradox of faith and unbelief found in God's people even today. *"Lord, I believe, help thou mine unbelief"*! We want to believe but find ourselves filled with doubt and unbelief. Just as this father asked Jesus to help his unbelief and was granted the help he needed to receive, we have the Holy Spirit to help us when we fall into unbelief.

And when he is come, he will reprove the world of sin, and of righteousness, and of judgment: (John 16:8 KJV)

Of sin, because they believe not on me; (John 16:9 KJV)

The Holy Spirit was given as our helper. He was sent to convict us of this sin of unbelief. When we confess our unbelief we can count on the Holy Spirit for deliverance. The Holy Spirit can and will free our minds of all doubt if we will keep our attention on the Word of God and rely on Him to do it.

Unbelief is wicked and unrighteous because it hinders and sets aside God's divine program which consists of all that God has promised to do in response to faith. Anything short of our having a living faith for the will and work of God to be done is unrighteousness.

Just as God's grace is stronger than sin, Christ's healing virtue is more powerful than the strength of any disease. When we set ourselves to obtain the benefits of the Atonement, we have an infinitely capable helper in the Holy Spirit. His power, when relied on, can never fail. He is always ready to execute for us the fulfillment of any provision God has given. The Holy Spirit will guide us into all truth so we might believe and the plan of God can be fulfilled.

And he did not many mighty works there because of their unbelief. (Matthew 13:58 KJV)

Clearly unbelief can hinder the plans and purposes of God from being fulfilled in the lives of believers. Even though the law of the Spirit of Life which heals our souls and bodies is much stronger than the law of sin and death it can be hindered in its fulfillment by unbelief. When unhindered by unbelief, this "law of the Spirit of Life" will win every time.

God has ordained that His plan for mankind's redemption of spirit, soul, and body can only be received through faith in the redemptive work of the cross of His Son, Jesus Christ.

Faith

Faith, not unbelief, is foundational to receiving anything from God.

But without faith it is impossible to please him: for he that cometh to God must believe that he is, and that he is a rewarder of them that diligently seek him. (Hebrews 11:6 KJV)

All who come to God must believe that He is who He says He is and that He rewards or fulfills His Word to those who sincerely seek Him. To do so is the sum total of righteousness.

For what saith the Scripture? Abraham believed God, and it was counted unto him for righteousness. (Romans 4:3 KJV)

Abraham believed God and it was counted to him as righteousness. He believed what God said and acted in accordance to what was spoken to him.

And being not weak in faith, he considered not his own body now dead, when he was about a hundred years old, neither yet the deadness of Sarah's womb: (Romans 4:19 KJV)

He staggered not at the promise of God through unbelief; but was strong in faith, giving glory to God; (Romans 4:20 KJV)

In the natural the birth of Isaac was impossible. Abraham recognized the natural circumstances but refused them as reasons for doubting the Word spoken to him by God. He refused to walk in unbelief. As a result, Abraham became known as the Father of Faith.

Know ye therefore that they which are of faith, the same are the children of Abraham. (Galatians 3:7 KJV)

Abraham is the father of all those who believe that Jesus bore our sins at the Cross of Calvary that we might, by faith, become the righteousness of God.

For he hath made him to be sin for us, who knew no sin; that we might be made the righteousness of God in him. (2 Corinthians 5:21 KJV)

It is through our faith in Christ that we are made the righteousness of God - restored to right standing with Him. Through faith our fellowship with the Father has been restored along with our ability to receive eternal life. Unbelief blocks our ability to receive eternal life and faith opens the door to receive.

For by grace are ye saved through faith; and that not of yourselves: it is the gift of God: (Ephesians 2:8 KJV)

Most of you will recognize this Scripture as one used when referring to our receiving eternal life. Well, guess what Greek word is used for the English word *saved*. It is the Greek word *sozo* which includes eternal life and physical healing.

The word gift is the Greek word *dorea* which means a sacrifice or gift. We do not deserve eternal life or healing; we cannot do anything to earn them. God, in His great love and compassion for mankind, made provision for both at Calvary. God's way of doing everything is by making promises and then fulfilling them wherever they produce faith.

What Is Faith?

Faith is the foundational basis, established by God, whereby a person can receive all that has been provided for them. It is the foundation on which all Christianity is built.

Faith is the coin of the realm of heaven. Just as when you buy something in America you use dollars, if you go to London you use pounds, in Germany you have to use *euros*, if you want something from God you have to use your faith. Faith is the only way to obtain things in the spirit realm. It is the coin of the spirit realm and must be used if a person is to receive anything from God, including healing.

> *Now faith is the substance of things hoped for, the evidence of things not seen. (Hebrews 11:1 KJV)*

The first thing this familiar verse of Scripture tells us about faith is that it is *now*. Faith is not faith if it is being expressed in future tense. Future tense is always hope, not faith. "I know God is going to heal me," is a statement of hope; not faith. "*By His stripes I am healed,*" is a statement of faith. Faith must always be expressed in present tense, in order for it to truly be faith.

The second thing we can learn about faith from this passage of Scripture is that faith is the "*substance of things hoped for.*" The Amplified Bible puts it like this:

> *NOW FAITH is the assurance (the confirmation, the title deed) of the things [we] hope for, (Hebrews 11:1 AMP)*

Faith is the assurance, confirmation, or title deed of the things you hope for. You can purchase a house, sight unseen. When the title deed is transferred into your name you own the house even though you have not seen it. Faith is the substance or our title deed to those things we desire.

> *...being the proof of things [we] do not see and the conviction of their reality [faith perceiving as real fact what is not revealed to the senses]. (Hebrews 11:1 AMP)*

Not only is faith substance, it is also evidence. Faith is the evidence of things not seen. The word evidence is a legal term that means "the documentary or oral statements and the material objects admissible as testimony in a court of law." According to Scripture faith is the tangible documentary proof of those things we do not see. Faith is perceiving as real facts those things which have not yet been revealed to the senses.

Fact vs. Promise

All that is written in the New Testament will fall into one of two categories:

(1) Promise — A promise is something that has not yet been fulfilled.
(2) Fact — A fact is a promise that has already been fulfilled.

Healing was promised in the Old Testament by the prophet Isaiah (Isaiah 53:4-5). The promise of healing was demonstrated during Jesus' earthly ministry and was fulfilled at Calvary. Later, Peter spoke of healing in the past tense or as an accomplished fact. Today healing is more than a promise. It is a promise that has been fulfilled. Healing is a fact, not a promise.

One would think that nobody would pray for a fact to be fulfilled because a fact is already fulfilled. Prayer for a fact to be fulfilled would sound something like, "Oh God would you please send the Messiah and let Him be born of a virgin, in the town of Bethlehem?" We would never even think of praying anything close to that.

It is unfortunate but many believers today do not receive their healing because they are praying for a fact to be fulfilled. Their prayer sounds something like, "God, would you please heal me?" This is treating the fact of healing as if it was only a promise and that keeps healing in the future. That is hope, not faith.

Our healing was paid for 2000 years ago at Calvary and we do not have to ask God to do it for us again. There is nothing more for God to do. He has done His part. The Captain of the Hosts came, fought, and won the battle. The victory belongs to the conquering king, King Jesus. He left the battlefield to return to headquarters and left an occupation army, the Body of Christ, in the land.

Occupy till I come. (Luke 19:13 KJV)

Jesus said we are to *"Occupy till He comes."* We are simply in charge of enforcing the victory. We do not have to re-fight or re-win the battle. We only have to enforce what has already been done.

We are not to pray and ask God to heal.

We are to command the healing that was purchased.

When you use your faith to enforce your rights it does not offend God. You are not operating in presumption. Presumption is when you assume you know what God wants without even bothering to find out what He really wants.

The Bible makes it absolutely clear that God wants his children healed here in this lifetime. Therefore, it is not presumption to enforce the known Will of God on the earth.

Therefore I say unto you, what things so ever ye desire, when ye pray, believe that ye receive them, and ye shall have them. (Mark 11:24 KJV)

Jesus said that we are to believe we receive the things we pray for at the same time we pray, without seeing or feeling them. This is the only condition that He promises, *"we shall have them."* Faith that receives must be based on the authority and truth of God's Word before the manifestation comes. Nothing else is faith.

If you are the beneficiary of the will of your rich uncle you are already wealthy the moment your uncle dies even though you have not yet seen any of the money. In the same way, everything bequeathed to us in our Lord's will and testament is already ours by virtue of the death of Jesus, who is the Testator.

Healing is already ours but it must be appropriated by faith. When we accept any contrary physical evidence over the Word of God we nullify the Word as far as we are concerned. Faith is believing what God says in the face of all contrary evidence of the natural senses. We must leave the sense realm if we are to operate in faith.

Where Is Your Faith?

Your faith is not in the cognitive processes of your head. Faith is in your heart.

(Mark 11:23 KJV). . .shall not doubt in his heart.

(Luke 24:25 KJV). . .and are slow of heart to believe.

(Acts 8:37 KJV). . .if thou believe with all thine heart.

The Greek word translated heart in each of these Scriptures is *kardia*. Figuratively speaking, it refers to your thoughts and feelings, your soul or mind.

Heart: Strong's G2588 kardia kar-dee'-ah Prolonged from a primary kar (Latin cor, "heart"); the heart, that is, (figuratively) the thoughts or feelings (mind); also (by analogy) the middle: - (+ broken-) heart (-ed).

By analogy *kardia* means the middle. Man is a three-part being: spirit, soul, and body. The soul is the middle or heart of man and that is where faith is located. The spirit of man is eternal and will live forever. However, it is the condition of the soul or heart of man that will determine where he will spend eternity.

That if thou shalt confess with thy mouth the Lord Jesus, and shalt believe in thine heart that God hath raised him from the dead, thou shalt be saved. (Romans 10:9 KJV)

We can know in our physical brain that Jesus died for our sins and healing for our bodies, but that truth must penetrate into our soul (mind) before we can receive it (that truth) as a reality in our lives. Where is your faith? It is in your heart.

How Do We Get Faith?

Scripture tells us that God has given every man the measure of faith.

God hath dealt to every man the measure of faith. (Romans 12:3 KJV)

In the New Testament there are occasions when Jesus noted different levels of faith: no faith, little faith, and great faith. This indicates there is the ability to grow in faith. Faith can only exist or grow when the will of God is known. The only way we can know the will of God is to know what He has said in His Word.

The Word: Parable of the Sower (Luke 8)

Jesus and the disciples had been going throughout every city and village preaching and demonstrating the good news of the Kingdom of God. As a result many people from every city gathered together and came to Jesus and He spoke to them the "Parable of the Sower."

Luke 8:5-8

A sower went out to sow his seed: and as he sowed, some fell by the way side; and it was trodden down, and the fowls of the air devoured it. (Luke 8:5 KJV)

And some fell upon a rock; and as soon as it was sprung up, it withered away, because it lacked moisture. (Luke 8:6 KJV)

And some fell among thorns; and the thorns sprang up with it, and choked it. And other fell on good ground, and sprang up, and bare fruit a hundredfold. And when he had said these things, he cried, He that hath ears to hear, let him hear. (Luke 8:8 KJV)

The disciples asked Jesus to explain what this parable meant.

Now the parable is this: The seed is the word of God. (Luke 8:11 KJV)

The seed is the Word of God. The Greek word for *word* in this passage of Scripture is *logos*. It refers to the spoken or written Word of God.

Those by the way side are they that hear; then cometh the devil, and taketh away the word out of their hearts, lest they should believe and be saved. (Luke 8:12 KJV)

Jesus said the devil comes to take away the word from your heart so you might not believe and be saved (*sozo*). If the devil can steal the *logos* from your heart (where it is supposed to produce faith) then he can rob you of your *sozo*. But if you have faith in your heart, then it can produce your *sozo*.

And these are they by the way side, where the word is sown; but when they have heard, Satan cometh immediately, and taketh away the word that was sown in their hearts. (Mark 4:15 KJV)

Mark's account identifies the *ground* in which the seed was sown. The ground was their hearts. The word was sown in their heart and Satan came immediately to steal that word so faith could not be birthed.

Luke 8:13-15

They on the rock are they, which, when they hear, receive the word with joy; and these have no root, which for a while believe, and in time of temptation fall away. (Luke 8:13 KJV)

And that which fell among thorns are they, which, when they have heard, go forth, and are choked with cares and riches and pleasures of this life, and bring no fruit to perfection. (Luke 8:14 KJV)

But that on the good ground are they, which in an honest and good heart, having heard the word, keep it, and bring forth fruit with patience. (Luke 8:15 KJV)

The Word of God is the foundation on which any and all faith is built. If we want our faith to grow we must fill our heart up with the Word of God, the *logos* word.

Proverbs 4:20-22

My son, attend to my words; incline thine ear unto my sayings. (Proverbs 4:20 KJV)

Let them not depart from thine eyes; keep them in the midst of thine heart. (Proverbs 4:21 KJV)

For they are life unto those that find them, and health to all their flesh. (Proverbs 4:22 KJV)

Health: Strong's H4832 marpê' *mar-pay'* From H7495; properly *curative*, that is, literally (concretely) a *medicine*, or (abstractly) a *cure*; figuratively (concretely) *deliverance*, or (abstractly) *placidity:* - ([in-]) cure (-able), healing (-lth), remedy, sound, wholesome, yielding.

The word health in verse 22 is the Greek word *marpay* which means a medicine, a cure, or deliverance. The Word of God is medicine to your flesh.

Sheep Story

A friend of mine, Rev. Cheryl Schang, in her book "Heal Them All," shares a story about one of her professors in seminary who started out in life as a farmer. He went to college in Texas where he studied agriculture. As part of his curriculum he had to take two semesters of animal husbandry which required the students to study sheep.

This professor complained saying, "Why do I have to study sheep? I'm going to be a farmer. I do not need to know about sheep. I never want anything to do with sheep." Looking back he realized that he learned more about how to be a pastor in those animal husbandry classes than he did in seminary.

Know ye that the LORD he is God: it is he that hath made us, and not we ourselves; we are his people, and the sheep of his pasture. (Psalms 100:3 KJV)

Throughout Scripture God often used sheep as an analogy when speaking of His people. Why? Well, one reason is that the human body was created to heal itself and the sheep is the only animal that, in its own body, has the capability to heal itself of every disease that a sheep can get.

However, there is a catch. You have to keep the sheep eating. If the sheep stops eating he will die. Naturally the first thing a sheep wants to do when it gets sick is to stop eating.

Likewise, what is the first thing we want to do when we get sick? Stop eating! Not only do we stop eating in the natural but we stop eating spiritually. We do not feel like being spiritual, therefore, we stop praying and we stop reading the Word of God.

Scripture tells us that the Word of God is life to us and medicine to our flesh. We are supposed to take the Word of God like medicine. If you are sick do not stop eating. Continue to feed on the Word (*logos*) of God. It is the foundation on which faith is established. The Word will produce faith in your heart and will lead you to your *sozo*.

Prayer and Fasting

Another way to increase your faith is through prayer and fasting. Remember the story of the father who brought his demon-possessed son to the disciples and they were unable to cure the boy? The father then took the boy to Jesus who rebuked the devil. The devil left the boy and the boy was cured. Later the disciples asked why they were unable to cast the devil out of the boy.

And Jesus said unto them, Because of your unbelief: for verily I say unto you, If ye have faith as a grain of mustard seed, ye shall say unto this mountain, Remove hence to yonder place; and it shall remove; and nothing shall be impossible unto you. (Matthew 17:20 KJV)

Howbeit this kind goeth not out but by prayer and fasting. (Matthew 17:21 KJV)

Jesus diagnosed their problem as unbelief (verse 20). His prescription for their unbelief was prayer and fasting (verse 21).

Prayer and fasting will change you, not God. It will cause your faith to increase. A lifestyle of prayer and fasting is essential if we are to continue to maintain and grow in our faith.

Pray in the Spirit

The 20th verse of the book of Jude gives us another source for building our faith.

But ye, beloved, building up yourselves on your most holy faith, praying in the Holy Ghost. (Jude 1:20 KJV)

Praying in the Holy Ghost means to pray in tongues, use your prayer language. When you pray in the Holy Spirit you are allowing God Himself to pray through you. Your physical man does not understand but your spiritual man (spirit and soul) is built up and faith increases.

This is why we have encouraged you to develop a daily habit of praying in the Spirit with passion. Praying in the Spirit loud enough to drown out the lying thoughts the devil put in our minds for 15-20 consecutive minutes on a daily basis can make a difference in victory or defeat when believing God for any area of your life, but especially in the area of healing.

When my husband, Charles, was diagnosed with colon cancer the devil tried to rob him of his faith by bombarding him with thoughts of fear and death. The only thing that got him through that difficult time was praying out loud in the Spirit. Praying with passion in the Spirit fills your soul, where faith resides, with the perfect will of the Father and releases His perfect will into the situation. It leaves no room for the devil's thoughts of doubt and unbelief to take root and grow. I do not fully understand exactly how it works. I just know it works. Today Charles is cancer-free.

If you want to grow in faith in any area of your life develop a lifestyle of praying daily in Holy Ghost.

Get a *Rhema* Word

So then faith cometh by hearing, and hearing by the word of God. (Romans 10:17 KJV)

The word "*word*" in this passage of Scripture is not the Greek word *logos*. It is *rhema*. The word *logos* is generally used to refer to the written Word of God and the word *rhema* is generally used to refer to the uttered, current Word of God, or what we have come to call a prophetic word.

A *rhema* word is a specific word from God concerning the current situation. It sometime comes in the form of a specific Scripture given, a Word of Knowledge, a word of wisdom, a vision, a dream, etc. Any *rhema* Word of God will always line up with the *logos* or written Word of God.

Any Christian can receive a *rhema* word from God. It is not hard. Just pray in tongues with passion, then get quiet, and listen. You will hear God speak. Use what you hear Him say as the foundation for your faith for healing or any other blessing from God. Stand firm, in faith, until the manifestation comes.

Since the Word (*logos*) of God, prayer and fasting, praying in the Spirit, and the *rhema* word are so vital to our development of faith to receive all that God has provided, they must be a priority in the life of the believer. They must be a consistent part of our daily life.

If I know that I am going to be ministering to someone, I spend additional time in these areas. Before I teach a class naturally I spend more time in the Word (*logos*), but I also get a *rhema* word from God as to what He wants me to teach, set aside a time of prayer and fasting, and spend a lot of time praying in the Spirit.

God has ordained faith to be the vehicle to take us to our destination of eternal life and healing. The *logos* word, prayer and fasting, praying in the Spirit, and a *rhema* word are the four wheels of our vehicle of faith. Remove one wheel and It is going to be a bumpy ride. We need all four of them working in our lives if we are going to successfully overcome unbelief and develop faith to receive.

Summary

Unbelief should not have any place in the life of a believer. It will rob you of the blessings of God. Unbelief will destroy your ability to receive the provisions of your covenant with the Father. Unbelief is a killer of faith.

It is through faith that you receive all your covenant provisions: eternal life, prosperity, peace, deliverance, healing, etc. If you are to receive anything from God it must be appropriated by faith.

> *But without faith it is impossible to please him: for he that cometh to God must believe that he is, and that he is a rewarder of them that diligently seek him. (Hebrews 11:6 KJV)*

The Father has given you a measure of faith. He has given you His Word to feed your faith and cause faith to grow. He gave you the Holy Spirit to build your faith. He has provided all the tools you need to successfully live the life of faith that He has called you to live.

It is the responsibility of believers to position themselves to receive all that God has provided through faith. Nurturing an intimate relationship with the Father, a daily study of His Word, and praying always in the Holy Spirit are major keys to developing a "Faith That Receives" (the topic of our next lesson).

Activation Time

- Halal for 2 minutes using your attributes of God list.
- Pray in the Spirit, with passion for 5 minutes.
- Activation – Face the Wall.

Activation Description

Number off the students in this manner: one, two, one, two, one, two, etc. until every student is either a *one* or a *two*. Tell them to remember whether they are a *one* or a *two*.

Have all the *ones* stand, come forward, and make a line around the room facing the wall. Tell them to close their eyes, pray in the Spirit, and ask God for a Word of Knowledge.

Instruct all the *twos* to go stand behind one of the *ones* and put their hand on the person's shoulder.

For Example

- Jane, who is a number one, will be standing in line facing the wall with her eyes closed.
- John, who is a number two, will go to Jane and put his hand on her shoulder.

When Jane feels John's hand on her shoulder she speaks the Word of Knowledge that God gives her. Once she has spoken the word she can then turn around to see who is standing behind her and ask whether or not the word she gave is true. Both of them can then be seated.

When everyone is seated, have the *twos* stand around the room facing the wall with their eyes closed and repeat the exercise with the *ones* touching the shoulders of the *twos*.

Purpose of Activation

The purpose of "Face the Wall" is to help the believer to develop the skill of asking and receiving a specific Word of Knowledge about another person. The development of this skill will be very useful when ministering healing to others. A Word of Knowledge will oftentimes be necessary to determine what is blocking a person from receiving their healing. In addition, it can open a person up to receive since they know the only way you could know this information is that God revealed it to you. A Word of Knowledge can raise one's faith to a level of receiving.

Assignment

- Meditate on and memorize the memory verse.
- Add 5 more attributes of God to your list.
- Begin your daily prayer time by halaling for at least 2 minutes using your list of attributes.
- Pray in the Spirit 15 minutes a day.
- Practice getting a Word of Knowledge about somebody every day.

Assignment Result and Comments:

LESSON 6 - Faith That Receives

Memory Verse

For as the body without the spirit is dead, so faith without works is dead also. (James 2:26 KJV)

Faith Acts

*I*t is not enough to just have faith. You must use faith. Faith is an act. Everybody could and should have gotten saved long before they did. But it did not happen until we believed and acted on the Word of God that was spoken to us.

In previous lessons we have discussed at length the fact that until a person knows God's will on a subject he or she has no basis for faith. Our faith must rest on the Word of God alone, which is the will of God. Once the foundation of faith has been established it must always be followed by action on the part of the believer.

Even so faith, if it hath not works, is dead, being alone. (James 2:17 KJV)

Unless faith is followed by corresponding action, it is dead. Healing is a provision of our redemptive package, but it can only be appropriated by acting in faith on the Word.

In Luke 6:10, Jesus healed a man with a withered hand.

And looking round about upon them all, he said unto the man, Stretch forth thy hand. And he did so: and his hand was restored whole as the other. (Luke 6:10 KJV)

Jesus told the man to *"stretch forth thy hand."* When the man, in obedience to the Word of God, put forth the effort to stretch out his hand divine power was released and the man's hand was restored. Although the action took place in the natural, this act of faith became a way of entrance for the supernatural to meet the man's need.

Many fail to receive healing because they believe in their circumstances and what their five senses tell them more than they believe the Word of God. Our five senses belong to the natural and cannot know, discern, or appropriate the things of God.

> *For the preaching of the Cross is to them that perish foolishness; but unto us which are saved it is the power of God. (1 Corinthians 1:18 KJV)*

The ground on which we claim the forgiveness of sins is the fact that Christ bore them in His own body on the tree. We must appropriate physical healing on the same ground; Jesus bore our sickness and disease in His body on the Cross of Calvary. The healing of both our souls and bodies is based on the unchangeable truth of Christ's finished work.

> *But let him ask in faith, nothing wavering. For he that wavereth is like a wave of the sea driven with the wind and tossed. (James 1:6 KJV)*

> *For let not that man think that he shall receive any thing of the Lord. (James 1:7 KJV)*

The believer is not to be governed by the evidence of his five natural senses. If we are to experience our covenant rights, that which is natural must be trained to function in connection with our sixth sense, faith, which is spiritual.

The purest form of worship is faith expressed as acts of obedience to His Word.

Eye of Faith

Receiving the blessings of God requires the believer to see through the "eye of faith."

> *And the LORD said unto Moses, Make thee a fiery serpent, and set it upon a pole: and it shall come to pass, that every one that is bitten, when he looketh upon it, shall live. (Numbers 21:8 KJV)*

> *And Moses made a serpent of brass, and put it upon a pole, and it came to pass, that if a serpent had bitten any man, when he beheld the serpent of brass, he lived. (Numbers 21:9 KJV)*

The word "looketh" in Hebrew is expressed in the continuous sense. It is a continuous stare, not a mere glance. Looking means to be occupied and influenced by what you are looking at. Believers are to keep their eyes on the Word of God and allow the Word alone to influence them in every area of their lives.

Looking also means attention. God told Moses that if the children of Israel would continuously keep their eyes on the fiery serpent on the pole, a type of the Cross of Jesus, they would be healed. Both forgiveness and healing were granted to the people of God by looking to the type of Calvary. If we cannot receive as much from Christ, the Antitype, we place the type on higher ground than Christ Himself and the type becomes a false prophecy.

When we keep our attention on God's Word we cause His blessings to come to us, including healing. Since the Word of God is a seed our giving attention to it puts it in good ground and keeps it there.

Satan cannot hinder the seed from doing its work as long as we keep it in good ground. He can only hinder the Word from working in us if he can get us to turn our attention away from the Word and cause us to focus on our symptoms. By being occupied with symptoms we violate the conditions of the covenant and thereby turn off the switch to God's power.

Hebrews 11:23-27

By faith Moses, when he was born, was hid three months of his parents, because they saw he was a proper child; and they were not afraid of the king's commandment. (Hebrews 11:23 KJV)

By faith Moses, when he was come to years, refused to be called the son of Pharaoh's daughter; (Hebrews 11:24 KJV)

Choosing rather to suffer affliction with the people of God, than to enjoy the pleasures of sin for a season; (Hebrews 11:25 KJV)

Esteeming the reproach of Christ greater riches than the treasures in Egypt: for he had respect unto the recompense of the reward. (Hebrews 11:26 KJV)

By faith he forsook Egypt, not fearing the wrath of the king: for he endured, as seeing him who is invisible. (Hebrews 11:27 KJV)

Moses endured the wrath of the king by seeing God Who is invisible. As far as the optic nerve or natural eye is concerned faith is the evidence of things not seen. But to the enlightened eye of faith it is the evidence of things seen. We see with the eye of faith the glorious things that are invisible to the natural eye.

The eye of faith sees God and Calvary where sin and sickness were canceled. It sees the promises of God and His faithfulness. Faith sees that the healing and health given by the work of the Cross already belong to us.

The word looking also has an element of expectation. Faith is expecting God to do what He has promised to do. Just as we look to God expecting to receive our eternal life, we must remove from our minds the slightest thought of failing to be healed.

The eye of faith refuses to see anything but what God says. Peter walked on water as long as his eyes were focused on Jesus and what He said, which was "Come." It was only when he looked at the natural circumstances (the wind and the waves) that he began to sink (Matthew 14). It is only by steadfastly refusing to see anything but God and what He says that we can have and keep healing for our bodies.

God's Word says we are healed. Once we decide to believe God for healing for our bodies we must be determined to stay focused on what He has said. My pastor puts it this way, "What we focus on is what will develop in our lives."

The body and its senses must be removed from view. The eye of faith will always refuse to see or believe anything that contradicts the Word of God.

Faith Speaks

And Jesus answering saith unto them, Have faith in God. (Mark 11:22 KJV)

For verily I say unto you, That whosoever shall say unto this mountain, Be thou removed, and be thou cast into the sea; and shall not doubt in his heart, but shall believe that those things which he saith shall come to pass; he shall have whatsoever he saith. (Mark 11:23 KJV)

The word say or says is used four times in verse 23. The word believe is only used once, indicating to me that it takes a little bit of believing and a whole lot of saying to receive the promises of God.

- The first say is the Greek word lego. What does that bring to mind? Lego building blocks? That is exactly what you should think of because that Greek word means "a set, systematic discourse. If you were building a house it would be like an architect framing up the house: putting the framework, the building blocks in place.
- The second time you see the word say it is the Greek word epo which means to command.
- The third time it is the Greek word laleo which means to speak with a loud voice.
- And the last time it is lego again.

So here is the picture Jesus was painting about how to move mountains with your faith: command it, speak it with a loud voice, and by that voice of faith you will frame your world.

Breath of God

And the LORD God formed man of the dust of the ground, and breathed into his nostrils the breath of life; and man became a living soul. (Genesis 2:7 KJV)

In the beginning God reached down, scooped up some dirt, and formed Adam. Physically Adam had everything he needed. He had a heart, he had lungs, he had everything. Even though Adam was a complete human being, he was not alive until God leaned down and breathed into Adam's nostrils. God breathed His breath into Adam and man became a living soul.

You are not alive because you have a heart, lungs and a brain. You are alive because you have the breath of God.

The spirit of God hath made me, and the breath of the Almighty hath given me life. (Job 33:4 KJV)

Job had this revelation when he said, *"The Spirit of God has made me and the breath of God gives me life."* That is why God told us that the power of life and death is in our tongue.

Death and life are in the power of the tongue: and they that love it shall eat the fruit thereof. (Proverbs 18:21 KJV)

The reason your words have power is because you speak them with the breath/Spirit of God. That's why you will have whatsoever you say. Whatever you speak will come to pass in your life someday. If you do not like what you have check what you have been saying. You will have whatsoever you say.

A good man out of the good treasure of his heart bringeth forth that which is good; and an evil man out of the evil treasure of his heart bringeth forth that which is evil: for out of the abundance of the heart his mouth speaketh. (Luke 6:45 KJV)

The Scripture teaches us that out of the abundance of our heart our mouth speaks. You do not have to talk to a person very long before their words will expose whether their heart is filled with doubt or faith. Since our heart is the ground in which faith resides and grows, we must constantly fill our heart with the Word of God so that when the trials of life come, what comes out of our mouth is faith, not doubt and unbelief.

The voice of faith will always agree with the Word of God. When we agree with and speak the Word, we have the assurance that we will receive our healing.

I will worship toward thy holy temple, and praise thy name for thy loving kindness and for thy truth: for thou hast magnified thy word above all thy name. (Psalms 138:2 KJV)

This is amazing! God has magnified His Word above His Name. One of the names of God is Omnipotent. God is all powerful. He can do anything. God, who can do anything He wants, chose to limit himself to His Word. In other words, God could change His Word but He will not. He wrote it down so we can know Him, so we can count on Him, and so we can know what is in our contract.

Have you heard people say that God might not want to heal everybody because God is sovereign? Yes! He is sovereign but He decided to limit His sovereignty to His Word. His Word-Made-Flesh (Jesus) proved, by His action, that you may all (everybody, whosoever, whatsoever, totally, thoroughly, wholly, completely) be healed.

Who his own self bare our sins in his own body on the tree, that we, being dead to sins, should live unto righteousness: by whose stripes ye were healed. (1 Peter 2:24 KJV)

We now have the evidence written right here in our contract, the Bible. God has put it in writing and that means He is committed to it. Because He said it and because He wrote it down, it is now magnified above His sovereign Name. Amazing! Healing and divine health belongs to the believer. You are entitled to the full *sozo* package.

The Word of God never loses its power. The power that was present when He first spoke those words is contained in the words, even now. God spoke and created the worlds. He said, *"Let there be light,"* and there was light. We still have light.

The words God spoke thousands of years ago are still working. When God speaks the power released by those words lives forever. If He speaks something once, those words are still alive and they still have power in them. When believing for physical healing, remove any demonic influence that may hinder you from receiving (we will discuss this in depth in a future lesson) and speak the Word of God over your body.

> *For unto us was the gospel preached, as well as unto them: but the word preached did not profit them, not being mixed with faith in them that heard it. (Hebrews 4:2 KJV)*

The Word of God spoken with the Breath of God mixed with the Faith of God will manifest the Promises of God.

Guard Your Tongue

In addition to saying the right thing you need to guard against saying the wrong thing! In Psalms, King David said,

> *Set a watch, O LORD, before my mouth; keep the door of my lips. (Psalms 141:3 KJV)*

Remember, you will have whatsoever you say, good or bad. Therefore, it is vital that you ask the Lord to put a guard on your tongue.

The next time a word that is not full of faith or that is full of negative faith wants to get in your mouth, stop it at the door. Say, "No you do not. The last time I let you in my mouth you robbed me of everything. You are not getting in my mouth." That is putting a guard on your mouth.

> *I will take heed to my ways that I sin not with my tongue; I will keep my mouth with a bridle. (Psalms 39:1 KJV)*

If I slip and say something that contradicts the Word of God, I have given the Holy Spirit permission to convict me. This allows me to quickly repent and break my agreement with those words, thereby canceling the recompense of those words before they can take root in my life.

Coyote Hunting

There was a preacher from Louisiana whose elders invited him to go coyote hunting. He was not all that excited about hunting coyotes, but he thought, "I get to dress up like Rambo so I'll give it a try."

When the pastor got into the woods with the hunters he learned that in the same way duck hunters use a duck call to attract the ducks, these coyote hunters used a coyote call to attract coyotes. Do you know what the coyote call sounded like? It made the sound of a wounded rabbit. In that instant the Lord spoke to the preacher and said, "When we whine, we attract the enemy."

Just like the coyote is attracted to a wounded rabbit, so are demons attracted to whiners. Sniff! Sniff! Sniff! LUNCH! Easy prey! Do not whine unless you want every demon in your neighborhood sniffing you out and thinking you are lunch. Sometimes we need to bind our mouths more than we need to bind the devil. We have been robbed with our own mouths.[11]

Cuban Missile Crisis (James 3:2-6)

We get it wrong nearly every time we open our mouths. If you could find someone whose speech was perfectly true, you'd have a perfect person, in perfect control of life. (James 3:2 MSG)

A bit in the mouth of a horse controls the whole horse. A small rudder on a huge ship in the hands of a skilled captain sets a course in the face of the strongest winds. A word out of your mouth may seem of no account, but it can accomplish nearly anything—or destroy it! (James 3:3 - 5A MSG)

It only takes a spark, remember, to set off a forest fire. A careless or wrongly placed word out of your mouth can do that. By our speech we can ruin the world, turn harmony to chaos, throw mud on a reputation, send the whole world up in smoke and go up in smoke with it, smoke right from the pit of hell. (James 3:5 B - 3:6 MSG)

James tells us the tongue is like the rudder on a ship. During the Cuban Missile Crisis America did not want the Russians to get any weapons into Cuba, so we set up an embargo by circling the island with our ships. If Russian ships approached the island our troops were given instructions to fire two shots. The first shot was to be over the bow of the ship, which was a warning shot. If the Russian ships did not turn back, the second shot was to take out their rudder, which would make it impossible for the Russian ship to navigate properly.

This is the same plan that Satan uses to rob us of our healing or any other blessing from God. He will fire a warning shot to scare you. If you do not back off, he will aim for your rudder, which is your mouth. If he can take out your mouth, stop you from speaking faith-filled words, he's got you. He knows the difference between defeat and victory is in your own mouth.

Words kill, words give life; they're either poison or fruit—you choose. (Proverbs 18:21 MSG)

Our words have creative power. They have the power to create death or life. The voice of faith must speak in agreement with the Word of God in order to experience the fulfillment of the plans and purposes of God in our lives. If we want to experience healing in our body, the voice of faith must always speak in agreement with the Word that says, *"by His stripes we were healed."*

And the tongue is a fire, a world of iniquity: so is the tongue among our members, that it defileth the whole body, and setteth on fire the course of nature; and it is set on fire of hell. (James 3:6 KJV)

---

[11] Schang, Rev. Cheryl, Heal Them All, Xulon Press 2005

The medical field has discovered that the speech center of the brain controls the entire central nervous system. They say if you touch one area in the brain, the arm will move. Touch another area in the brain and the leg will move. But if you touch the speech center, the entire central nervous system responds, so much so that if a person says, "I am weak," the entire body begins to prepare to be weak.

There is actually something physical that happens in your body when you speak. God built it into you and when you confess doubt, unbelief, sickness or disease, your body prepares to make that happen. When you confess faith, health and healing, or declare who God is and what He has done or what belongs to you, your body begins to prepare to receive that. You make it happen with your words.

At this point it is important to note that just quoting the Word of God does not always bring the desired result. It must be mixed with faith and acted on.

Unfortunately all of us struggle from time to time with some measure of unbelief. When people are suffering with sickness and disease in their bodies it can be very difficult to operate in faith. God in His great compassion for mankind has made provision for those who are weak in faith to receive healing through the faith of others in the Body of Christ.

The Prayer of Faith

> *Is any sick among you? Let him call for the elders of the Church; and let them pray over him, anointing him with oil in the name of the Lord: (James 5:14 KJV)*
>
> *And the prayer of faith shall save the sick, and the Lord shall raise him up; and if he has committed sins, they shall be forgiven him. (James 5:15 KJV)*
>
> *Confess your faults one to another, and pray one for another, that ye may be healed. The effectual fervent prayer of a righteous man availeth much. (James 5:16 KJV)*

In verse 14 James tells us that if any of us are sick we can call for the elders of the Church and they will do two things: (1) pray for us and (2) anoint us with oil in the name of the Lord.

Have you ever wondered why they were to anoint a person with oil? I did and through some research I learned some interesting things.

One of the things I learned is that in Biblical times every god had his own anointing oil and each god had a special formula for their oil. When a person was anointed with oil they were believed to be marked as belonging to the god whose oil was used to anoint them. This was very common in all people groups of Old Testament times.

Jehovah God also had a special formula for His anointing oil.

Exodus 30:23-25

> *Take thou also unto thee principal spices, of pure myrrh five hundred shekels, and of sweet cinnamon half so much, even two hundred and fifty shekels, and of sweet calamus two hundred and fifty shekels, (Exodus 30:23 KJV)*

And of cassia five hundred shekels, after the shekel of the sanctuary, and of oil olive anhin: (Exodus 30:24KJV)

And thou shalt make it an oil of holy ointment, an ointment compound after the art of the apothecary: it shall be an holy anointing oil. (Exodus 30:25KJV)

God forbade anyone to duplicate His formula for anointing oil.

Upon man's flesh shall it not be poured, neither shall ye make any other like it, after the composition of it: it is holy, and it shall be holy unto you. (Exodus 30:32 KJV)

God was saying, "I have my own oil and when you mark somebody with that oil, you are marking them with the mark of Jehovah God."

The oil of Jehovah God was holy and was to be used for two purposes: (1) to set those things or people who were anointed apart as holy and consecrated, and (2) to confer authority on the person who was anointed. Anointing with oil symbolized God's choice and appointment and therefore involved divine action in preparation for service.[12]

Oil was also used in everyday life in Biblical times. Along with other staples, oil was seen as an essence of life and a tangible sign of God's blessing and favor which could be lost by disobedience (Deuteronomy 11:13-17). Possession of oil was a sign of prosperity and abundance, as well as of God's good provision (Job 29:6; Joel 2:24).[13]

In the New Testament the term anointing is more often used to describe the spiritual basis of Jesus' ministry (Luke 4:18; Acts 10:38; Hebrews 1:9) and the spiritual work God performs in the lives of believers (2 Corinthians 1:21-22; 1 John 2:20-27). The emphasis is not on the act of anointing but on the Holy Spirit with whom one is anointed. Although oil had some medicinal value in the ancient world (Isaiah 1:6), the use of it in James' day is more than likely symbolic of invoking God's power.[14]

When the elders anoint you with oil they are marking you as belonging to Jehovah God. At the same time they are calling on the power of the Holy Spirit for help on your behalf. They are to do all this in the Name or authority of the Lord and it must be done in faith.

And the prayer of faith shall save the sick, and the Lord shall raise him up; and if he has committed sins, they shall be forgiven him. (James 5:15 KJV)

When the prayer of faith is prayed and the power of the Holy Spirit is invoked in the authority of Jesus Christ, the Lord will raise the sick up and forgive his or her sin if they have sinned.

Notice it is the prayer of faith which the elders pray that will save *(sozo)* the sick, not the prayer of the sick person.

---

[12] Dictionary of Biblical Imagery, InterVarsity Press, Downers Grove, Illinois, USA Leicester, England, 33

[13] Ibid, 603-604

[14] Ibid, 33 and 605

Confess your faults one to another, and pray one for another, that ye may be healed. The effectual fervent prayer of a righteous man availeth much. (James 5:16 KJV)

The elders of the Church are not the only ones who have been given the power and authority to heal in the Name of Jesus. Every believer has been given the same power and authority (Mark 16:17-18). We have the Holy Spirit and we have the Word of God (Jesus). The Word is our authority and Holy Spirit is our power. But how can confessing our faults to one another bring healing?

>**Faults:** Strong's 3900. paraptoma, par-ap'-to-mah; from G3895; a side-slip (lapse or deviation), i.e. (unintentional) error or (willful) transgression:—fall, fault, offence, sin, trespass.

The word fault is the Greek word *parapotma,* which means a side slip, unintentional error, or willful transgression. James is saying if we confess our spiritual error or sin to one another we can be healed.

All sickness and disease is indirectly the result of sin, if not directly. There was no sickness in the earth before the fall of man. But not all sickness is the direct result of one's personal sin, as was the case of the man that was born blind from birth recorded in John 9. However, one's personal sin can be the root of an illness. Remove the sin and the body can usually heal itself. (We will discuss this in depth in a future lesson.)

By letting someone help you deal with your sin they can help you get healed. Once we remove the thing that is blocking the healing it only takes a tiny amount of faith to bring the results.

Grain of Mustard Seed

>*If ye have faith as a grain of mustard seed, ye shall say unto this mountain, Remove hence to yonder place; and it shall remove; and nothing shall be impossible unto you. (Matthew 17:20 KJV)*

Jesus said all we need is faith the size of a grain of mustard seed. That is a tiny, tiny amount.

When I was first learning to use my faith for healing I prayed for some that were healed, but I also prayed for some who died. After a while, it became more and more difficult to believe God was going to heal everyone. I found myself becoming hesitant to even pray for people.

However, I just could not get away from the fact that Jesus healed them all. The more I studied the more convinced I became that it is always God's will to heal everybody, all the time. I developed an overwhelming passion to see the Body of Christ walk in the inheritance of healing that God provided at Calvary. I realized I had to find a place of faith that I could go to as a foundation for any and all healing of everybody, regardless of current circumstances or past experience.

I found that place of faith in the Lord Himself. I only need to remind myself:

- It is not about me. It is about Him and His faithfulness.
- Jesus is the Word of God and the Word teaches me that God wants to heal EVERYONE, all the time.
- God exalted His Word above His Name and He is always faithful to confirm His Word with signs following.

> The Holy Spirit is present in the believer and is the power of God that causes faith to arise and appropriate the plans and purposes of God in the earth.

In other words, I believe in His willingness and ability to accomplish the task more than I believe in the circumstances and my inability or lack of faith.

This may not sound as strong as some of the faith-filled prayers you have heard, but the times when I had very little faith for someone to be healed this little bit of faith has been enough to get them healed. I can now pray with a greater assurance of results because I have seen person after person healed from incurable diseases or traumas.

Thanksgiving

The prayer of faith can best be summed up in these two words: thank-you. The Word of God teaches us that healing is provision that was purchased for us at the Cross of Calvary. The Father has given us healing. It is written in our contract. When someone has bought you a priceless gift the only thing left for you to do is say, "Thank-you." There is power in this truth.

> *And he directed the people to sit down on the grass. Taking the five loaves and the two fish and looking up to heaven, he gave thanks and broke the loaves. Then he gave them to the disciples, and the disciples gave them to the people. (Matthew 14:19 NIV)*

When Jesus needed a miracle this is how He accomplished it. When He had to feed five thousand people with a sack lunch, He gave thanks.

> *Then they took away the stone from the place where the dead was laid. And Jesus lifted up his eyes, and said, Father, I thank thee that thou hast heard me. (John 11:41 KJV)*

One of Jesus' greatest miracles was raising Lazarus from the dead. He stood in front of the tomb of Lazarus who had been dead four days. What did He do? He turned His face towards heaven and Jesus said, *"Thank You Father, that You have heard me."* When Jesus needed a miracle He prayed a prayer of faith.

The prayer of faith is: "Thank You Father, I have the thing that You have promised and provided." He gave you healing; it is written down in your contract. The prayer of faith must include a "Thank You."

Reverend Kenneth Hagin

Something I learned many years ago from Rev. Kenneth Hagin is this: when we pray for someone we never know whether it is going to be a miracle, which is instant, or if it will be a healing, which is a process. Some people get a miracle but you cannot always count on it. But you can absolutely go to the bank with the promise of healing, which is the process of your body healing or recovering.

Kenneth Hagin said when he laid hands on people and prayed for them sometimes a miracle happened and sometimes the recovery started. For those who were in the recovery process, he would give these instructions:

- Go home tonight and get in bed and say, "Thank You, God, that Your power went into my body tonight and it is working now to effect a healing and a cure."
- When you get up tomorrow morning say, "Thank You, God, Your healing power is working in my body right now, and I will see the cure."
- When you pray over your food at noon, bow your head and say, "Thank You, God, Your healing power came into my body, and it is working even now to bring a total healing and a cure."

He told story after story of people whose healing manifested as they were thanking God.[15] One of those stories was of how one person left his meeting still in a wheelchair. For three days that man thanked God that the healing power was working in his body to bring a full recovery. On the third day he just got up out of his wheelchair and walked.

We are not guaranteed the miracle but we are guaranteed the healing.

Reverend Norvel Hayes

Reverend Norvel Hayes tells a wonderful story about declaring healing. His fifteen-year-old daughter's body was covered with forty-two warts. You know how embarrassing that would be for a fifteen-year-old girl. Reverend Hayes had a doctor remove the warts one time, but they had all come back. He was not excited about the idea of having them cut off again.

Reverend Kenneth Hagin was traveling through their town and he called the Hayes family and invited himself to stay at their house. Shortly after he arrived the daughter said to Reverend Hagin, "Please talk to my daddy about letting the doctor cut off these warts."

Reverend Hagin said, "Oh honey, I can curse those warts and they'll die." Before he had a chance to actually curse the warts Reverend Hagin got a phone call and had to leave.

A couple of days later Reverend Hayes was walking through the living room and his daughter was sitting there with her boyfriend. As he passed them he heard the Lord say, "How long are you going to let those warts stay on your daughter's body?" He thought, "Well, not another minute, I guess. My daughter is going to kill me."

He walked into the living room and said, "I curse those warts in the Name of Jesus! Wither and die!" Then he turned and walked out. The daughter was mortified. She said, "Oh Daddy, you embarrassed me so much."

From that moment on Reverend Hayes started saying, "I thank You, God, those warts are disappearing from my daughter's body; I thank You, God, they are withering up and dying even now." He said it morning, noon and night.

Finally, after two weeks the daughter confronted him. She was in tears: "Just STOP! I cannot stand it! I wake up in the morning and I hear you saying, 'Thank You, God, for taking those warts off my daughter.' I go to bed at night and I hear you saying, "Thank You, God, for removing those

---

[15] Hagin, Kenneth E., "The Healing Anointing", Rhema Bible Church, Tulsa, OK, 1997.

warts from my daughter's body. I count them every single morning and I still have every one of those forty-two warts. I cannot stand hearing you pray this anymore!"

So what do you think Reverend Hayes did? He increased his thanksgiving to hurry up the results! Every single time the thought came into his head he said, "Thank You, God, that you are removing those warts from my daughter's body. Thank You that they are going away, for they are cursed and they cannot live in her body, I praise Your Name."

One week later the daughter came home from school and she said, "Daddy, can I ask you a question? Every morning I get up and I count my warts. I have forty-two warts and It is always the same. This morning, when I got up and counted, I had thirty-four warts. Where did the other eight go?"

Reverend Hayes said, "I do not know, but the other thirty-four are going there as well!" He stepped it up another notch.

One week later she was hanging clothes up in her closet. You know how teenagers can get a big mess of clothes at the bottom of the closet? She was hanging up dresses. As she was hanging them up she was looking at her hand. In the middle of this chore, she looked at her hand and all the warts were suddenly gone. All, totally gone, permanently! They have never come back.

I have heard members of the faith movement discuss the conflict they feel declaring they are healed before the healing manifested. Is it faith or is it a lie? I never tell people to walk around saying they are healed before they see the manifestation of it. What they can say truthfully, and still have words of faith, is this: God's healing power is working in my body to bring a full recovery.

Your faith must speak. It must agree with the Word of God. Dig in your heels and do not let go. You grab hold of that Word by faith. Do not stop speaking it. Do not stop giving thanks!

No Faith

In John 11 is the story of Jesus raising Lazarus from the dead. It certainly was not Lazarus' faith that was at work, it was Jesus' faith.

In Matthew 8 we read about a Centurion soldier who asked Jesus to heal his servant. Again, it was not the servant's faith at work. In fact the servant himself never even came to Jesus. It was the Centurion who came to Jesus on behalf of his servant and the servant was healed.

I was ministering at Zion Road Healing Room one Saturday when a lady came in for prayer. She had asked a friend to come with her. This friend at first said no but at the last minute she decided to come.

I was talking to her friend while our ministry team was ministering to the other lady. I learned that this friend was not saved. She had no knowledge or faith for healing and did not know why she agreed to come to the healing room.

I also learned that she had some health issues that were causing pain in her body so I asked if we could pray for her. This was all new to her. Therefore, she was a little hesitant at first but she finally agreed. God healed her body and the pain left. As a result, she received Jesus as her Lord and Savior and she was baptized in the Holy Spirit. She came in with no faith or expectation and left healed, saved, and talking in the Holy Ghost. Praise the Lord! It was not her faith at work. It was the ministry team's faith.

Rev. Cheryl Schang

Cheryl Schang, in her book "Heal Them All," shares as story about a time when she was teaching a healing course and a girl who was raised in a denomination that did not believe in healing came to the class because a friend invited her. This girl was excited by what she saw and heard in the seminar. She saw people were getting healed in the meetings so she asked if she could bring her mother who had fibromyalgia. She warned Cheryl that her mother did not believe in healing. Cheryl's response was that it did not matter; she (Cheryl) always expected to be the one with the faith.

The next night the girl and her parents came. This was a practice night for the students and a large group of them gathered around her to practice what they had learned. Cheryl asked the lady if we could pray for her, and she agreed. The lady said that she had never prayed for herself for healing, nor had she had anyone else pray for her. She told us she did not believe she would be healed.

Cheryl told her that was fine she would still be healed because they were not going to use her faith; the team would use their own faith.

The woman was in extreme pain. She could hardly move her body. The team began to pray for a Word of Knowledge as to anything that may hinder her from receiving her healing. As they prayed, Cheryl saw that someone had done something bad to the lady when she was in her late teens. One of the students said that she saw a hand. Cheryl understood that to mean the lady thought the bad thing was the work of her own hand.

Speaking gently to the woman, Cheryl said to her, "When you were a young woman of about seventeen years old something bad happened to you and you have always thought it was your own fault." The woman started crying and admitted that this was true and she had never told anyone. She had kept the pain inside all these years. Remember, whatever you let rule your soul will eventually rule your body.

Cheryl prophesied over her that the Lord said it was not her fault. They commanded the spirit of guilt and pain to get out and then commanded her body to be healed. Within a short time the woman was completely healed. All pain was gone and she walked normally for the first time in many years. Praise God!

As believers if we are going to pray for others to be healed it is important that we are aware that those who come to us for prayer may have very little faith and some may have no faith at all. This leaves you, as the minister, as the one who needs to be able to release faith into the situation.

For years we have said to sick people, "If only you had enough faith, you could be healed." I say to you, "It does not have to be the sick person that has the faith." However, someone in the equation must pray the "prayer of faith." As ministers of healing we must depend on our own faith if we want to see them healed.

Faith is to be used to convert Biblical truth into reality. This should be characteristic of the people of God in the earth.

Lesson 6 - Faith That Receives

Activation Time

- Halal for 2 minutes using your list of attributes of God.
- Pray in the Spirit, with passion, for 5 minutes.
- Activation – Pray for those who have pain in their body.

Activation Description

Jesus took our pain so we would not have to suffer pain. Pain has no right or authority to be in the body of a born-again believer. Therefore, pain must be treated as an intruder.

Leader: Have one volunteer who has pain in some area of their body to come forward. Lay hands on them and pray the following prayer:

- In the Name of Jesus, I speak to pain. Pain you are an intruder in _____'s body. Jesus took his/her pain so he/she would not have to have pain. Therefore, as a minister of the Gospel, in the name of Jesus and by the power of the Holy Spirit, I speak to pain and command it to go now! Pain, get out!

    Have the person take a deep breath. Ask them, "Where's the pain now?" Pain should be gone; if not repeat the process. Be sure to use a firm voice. (It is not necessary to scream but you must be firm.) If the pain is still there have them repent for allowing the pain to operate in their body. Have them repeat the following prayer after you:

- I repent for allowing pain to operate in my body. I break all agreement with pain, in every word, thought, or deed.

    After the person has repented and broken their agreement with pain, then you, as the minister, command pain to go.

- Pain, _____ has broken his/her agreement with you and you no longer have authority to be in his/her body. In the Name of Jesus and by the power of the Holy Spirit, I command you to go, now! Pain, get out!

    Have the person take a deep breath. Ask them, "Where's the pain now?" Pain should be gone.

    However, if the pain still does not go then there is some issue that needs to be dealt with before the pain can be kicked out. We will deal with this in a later chapter.

    Note: Pain is usually the easiest thing to get a person set free from. However, if there is an issue that gave it a legal right to be there the pain will return unless they deal with the issue.

Group Activation:

Divide students into groups of four or five. Have them take turns kicking pain out using the same process as demonstrated by the leader. If the pain does not go have them practice getting a Word of Knowledge as to what the issue is that is allowing the pain to remain. Have the person repent and break their agreement with whatever it is. Then kick it and the pain out using the procedure demonstrated above.

> **Note:** Do not let the person being ministered to answer anything but yes or no until the process is completed and pain is gone.

Purpose of Activation

The purpose of this exercise is first of all to show how easy it is to get rid of pain and then to practice getting a Word of Knowledge concerning the issue that is giving the pain the legal right to stay in the person, if necessary.

Assignment

- ➢ Meditate on and memorize the memory verses.
- ➢ Add 5 more attributes of God to your list.
- ➢ Begin your daily prayer time by halaling for at least 3 minutes using your list of attributes.
- ➢ Pray in the Spirit 15 minutes a day.
- ➢ Pray for at least three people who have pain in their body.
- ➢ Read Psalms 139 and Romans 8:35-39 before the next class.

Assignment Results and Comments

LESSON 7 - Hindrances to Faith

Memory Verses

Then said Jesus to those Jews which believed on him, If ye continue in my word, then are ye my disciples indeed; (John 8:31 KJV)

And ye shall know the truth, and the truth shall make you free. (John 8:32 KJV)

Introduction

*I*n previous lessons we discussed at length the first two major roadblocks to healing: (1) ignorance and (2) unbelief. Hopefully, at this point you are convinced that healing is for all and are aware of the importance of faith and how it works in the life of the believer to bring healing to their body.

We have also learned that our healing and eternal salvation was provided for us through the same work of the Cross. Healing and forgiveness of sin are in the same package.

Scripture clearly reveals that the Father wills our healing. Therefore, we receive our healing the same way we received the forgiveness of our sin, by faith. Then why is it that so many seeking healing fail to receive it?

Unfortunately, a large part of the Church today, unlike the First Century Church, is not in one accord on the matter of healing, causing many Christians to be unaware of the healing power of the Gospel.

In addition, the Church of today as a whole has not accepted the attitude toward sickness as it is revealed in the Gospel and *unbelief* has taken the place of united faith causing individuals, leaders and the Church, as a whole, to be double minded concerning healing.

James 1:6-8

But let him ask in faith, nothing wavering. For he that wavereth is like a wave of the sea driven with the wind and tossed. (James 1:6 KJV)

For let not that man think that he shall receive any thing of the Lord. (James 1:7 KJV)

A double minded man is unstable in all his ways. (James 1:8 KJV)

In this lesson we will be discussing some traditions of men that can cause the believer to be double minded and hinder his/her faith for receiving healing.

Traditions of Men

The Bible clearly teaches us that:

(1) God in not the author of sickness and disease. (James 1:13-17)
(2) God wants everyone to be healed. (3 John 1:2)

Traditions of men are teachings that have found their way into the Church that are contrary to the Word of God.

But he answered and said unto them, why do ye also transgress the commandment of God by your tradition? (Matthew 15:3 KJV)

Jesus, speaking to the Jewish leaders, said the traditions of men transgress, go contrary to, or invalidate the commandment or Word of God. Unfortunately, this is the case in many of the Churches today. Many pastors/teachers have made void the healing part of the Gospel by their traditions.

Making the word of God of none effect through your tradition, which ye have delivered: and many such like things do ye. (Mark 7:13 KJV)

Again, Jesus says their traditions made the Word of God of none effect. There are teachings in the Church today concerning healing that are based on the experience and understanding of man and not on the truth of the Word of God. This makes it absolutely necessary for the one seeking healing to do as the Jews in Berea.

These were more noble than those in Thessalonica, in that they received the word with all readiness of mind, and searched the Scriptures daily, whether those things were so. (Acts 17:11 KJV)

Paul and Silas went to Berea and the Jews received the word they preached with an eager and open mind. They were teachable. However, they also searched the Scriptures daily to see if the things they heard were true or not.
We as believers must do the same. We must be responsible for searching the Scriptures and allow the Holy Spirit to expose that which is contrary to what the Word of God teaches.

The Bible never contradicts itself. If there seems to be a contradiction there is something wrong with our understanding.

Let's take a look at some of the "traditions of men" that can hinder our faith and prevent us from receiving our healing.

God Is the Author of Sickness and Disease

Those who teach that God is the author of sickness use Exodus 15:26 to support their teaching.

And said, If thou wilt diligently hearken to the voice of the LORD thy God, and wilt do that which is right in his sight, and wilt give ear to his commandments, and keep all his statutes, I will put none of these diseases upon thee, which I have brought upon the Egyptians: for I am the LORD that healeth thee. (Exodus 15:26 KJV)

First of all, we must remember that this was the Old Testament or Covenant. Because of the work of Jesus our covenant changed. We cannot look at the way God dealt with His people in the Old Covenant and say that is what we should expect today. We now have a better covenant.

Secondly, those who teach this have taken this one verse of Scripture and built a doctrine without considering the context of the Scripture. Proper exegesis of Scripture always includes the context in which the Scripture is written as one of the considerations before establishing a doctrine.

In order to discover the context we must look to see what was going on before and after it was written. This Scripture was written immediately after Passover and the crossing of the Red Sea. In Chapter 15 Moses and the children of Israel begin to declare the wonderful things God had done.

Exodus 15:23-25

And when they came to Marah, they could not drink of the waters of Marah, for they were bitter: therefore the name of it was called Marah. (Exodus 15:23 KJV)

And the people murmured against Moses, saying, What shall we drink? (Exodus 15:24 KJV)

And he cried unto the LORD; and the LORD shewed him a tree, which when he had cast into the waters, the waters were made sweet: there he made for them a statute and an ordinance, and there he proved them, (Exodus 15:25 KJV)

They came to *Marah* which means bitter. This was representative of the bitter experiences of life. The tree suggests the Cross of Calvary, which transforms the bitter things of life into something sweet.

And said, If thou wilt diligently hearken to the voice of the LORD thy God, and wilt do that which is right in his sight, and wilt give ear to his commandments, and keep all his statutes, I will put none of these diseases upon thee, which I have brought upon the Egyptians: for am the LORD that healeth thee. (Exodus 15:26 KJV)

Lesson 7 - Hindrances To Faith

It is in this context of covenant that God revealed Himself as the Lord that heals, Jehovah *Rapha*, one of His seven covenant names.

> *And they came to Elim, where were twelve wells of water, and threescore and ten palm trees: and they encamped there by the waters. (Exodus 15:27 KJV)*

Elim, with its twelve wells of water and seventy palm trees, suggests the rest and refreshment that is ours after coming to the Cross of Calvary.

The entire Book of Exodus is about the Jewish people's deliverance from Egypt and God establishing a covenant with them. They went into Egypt as twelve tribes and came out a nation set apart unto God. This verse was written in the context of God establishing a covenant with the Jews.

By studying covenants, we learn that they were not unique to the Hebrews. Covenants existed in all cultures of the time. People made covenants with each other and with their gods.

There were common elements to all covenants and without them it was not a valid covenant. Two of these elements were blessings and curses. The party offering the covenant told the other party what they could expect in the way of blessings if they honored the covenant. There was also a clause that detailed what they could expect if they broke the covenant.

> *And it shall come to pass, if thou shalt hearken diligently unto the voice of the LORD thy God, to observe and to do all his commandments which I command thee this day, that the LORD thy God will set thee on high above all nations of the earth: (Deuteronomy 28:1 KJV)*

And all these blessings shall come on thee, and overtake thee, if thou shalt hearken unto the voice of the LORD thy God. (DeuteThe counterpart to this covenant blessing, the covenant curses, is listed beginning in verse 15 and in verse 45:

> *Moreover all these curses shall come upon thee, and shall pursue thee, and overtake thee, till thou be destroyed; because thou hearkenedst not unto the voice of the LORD thy God, to keep his commandments and his statutes which he commanded thee: (Deuteronomy 28:45 KJV)*

This is standard contractual language for covenants. The covenant was not considered valid without it. Sickness, disease, and death were common curses. In covenants between men it is plain that they could not cause sickness and disease to come on another person. Therefore, typically the god that the parties served would be the one expected to fulfill the blessings and curses.

Notice it is not the covenant writer that brought the sickness and disease. Sickness and disease came because of the action of the covenant breaker.

Theologically speaking, we broke the Old Testament Covenant and the curses that were contained therein came into our lives. There was a penalty of sickness and death. But because God did not want us to suffer these things, He sent His Son to pay the penalty of the curse for us all.

> *For the wages of sin is death; but the gift of God is eternal life through Jesus Christ our Lord. (Romans 6:23 KJV)*

> *Christ hath redeemed us from the curse of the law, being made a curse for us: for it is written, Cursed is every one that hangeth on a tree: (Galatians 3:13 KJV)*

The curse for breaking the covenant was laid on Jesus. Therefore, we cannot look at Old Testament Scripture to form our doctrine of healing under the New Testament dispensation.

What about Job?

The Book of Job is also commonly used to say that God is the author of sickness and disease. In reality, a close study of Job clearly reveals that Satan, not God, is the author of sickness and disease.

> *Then satan answered the LORD, and said, Doth Job fear God for nought? (Job 1:9 KJV)*

> *Hast not thou made a hedge about him, and about his house, and about all that he hath on every side? thou hast blessed the work of his hands, and his substance is increased in the land. (Job 1:10 KJV)*

> *But put forth thine hand now, and touch all that he hath, and he will curse thee to thy face. (Job 1:11 KJV)*

Job was a godly man and therefore enjoyed the protection and prosperity of God. Satan, the accuser, implied that the only reason Job feared God was because He (God) had been so good to him.

> *And the LORD said unto Satan, Behold, all that he hath is in thy power; only upon himself put not forth thine hand. So Satan went forth from the presence of the LORD. (Job 1:12 KJV)*

It was Satan who went forth from the presence of the Lord to destroy the livestock and family of Job. Scripture clearly reveals that it was Satan who smote Job with boils.

> *So went Satan forth from the presence of the LORD, and smote Job with sore boils from the sole of his foot unto his crown. (Job 2:7 KJV)*

Even though God had given permission for Job to be tested, Satan could not just attack Job without a reason. Satan still had to find a legal way to attack Job.

> *For the thing which I greatly feared is come upon me, and that which I was afraid of is come unto me. (Job 3:25 KJV)*

By his own admission Job had great fear. The thing he feared was the *door* Satan used to put a skin disease on Job.

Today medical doctors have discovered the connection between fear and skin diseases as well as many other illnesses. Dermatologist will now tell you that certain skin conditions will get worse when you are under stress. Stress comes from fearing a particular outcome. Rev. Henry Wright mentions the same connection in his book, "A More Excellent Way."[16]

At first glance it does seem God was a bit slow to heal Job. Why the delay? Remember I said earlier that there may be a spiritual root to the illness, and/or there may be a spiritual blockage to the healing. For Job, both were true. The fear was the root of the illness. Then once he was in trouble, he created a blockage by what he said.

The story starts out with three of Job's friends trying to *comfort* him by telling him he must have sinned for such calamity to come to him. They threw out all sorts of likely causes. . . all of them wrong. Suddenly a young man named Elihu spoke up. He must have been listening all along. Elihu scolded the three friends.

> *Also against his three friends was his wrath kindled, because they had found no answer, and yet had condemned Job. (Job 32:3 KJV)*

But first, Elihu unloaded on Job.

> *Then was kindled the wrath of Elihu the son of Barachel the Buzite, of the kindred of Ram: against Job was his wrath kindled, because he justified himself rather than God. (Job 32:2 KJV)*

In his suffering Job began to justify himself rather than God. Elihu continued to accuse Job.

> *For he hath said, It profiteth a man nothing that he should delight himself with God. (Job 34:9 KJV)*

Elihu quotes Job's claim that it profits a man nothing to serve God. Job was beginning to wonder if there was any benefit to serving God. Then Elihu declares that God does not do wickedness or commit iniquity.

> *Therefore hear me, you men of understanding. Far be it from God that He should do wickedness, and from the Almighty that He should commit iniquity. (Job 34:10 AMP)*

When God finally spoke, He reproved Job and the three friends, but not Elihu. It appears that what Elihu said was true.

Job had both a spiritual root to his illness and a spiritual blockage to his healing. God promised healing to Job if he would pray for his friends. Job got himself a bit of faith, acted on that *rhema* word and was healed.

How do I know he had faith? Faith is revealed by actions

> *Even so faith, if it hath not works, is dead, being alone. (James 2:17 KJV)*

---

[16] Wright, Henry, A More Excellent Way, Pleasant Valley Publications, Thomaston, GA, 2002, 234-235.

Faith without works is non-existent. You know faith is operating when there is action. For example, as Job prayed for his friends according to the *rhema* his actions revealed his faith:

And the Lord turned the captivity of Job and restored his fortunes, when he prayed for his friends; also the Lord gave Job twice as much as he had before. [Deut. 30:1-3; Ps. 126:1, 2.] (Job 42:10 AMP)

God brought total restoration to Job. Job was seventy years old when he experienced this testing of his faith in God. After being healed and all restored, Job lived one hundred forty years. What we should learn from the Book of Job is:

(1) God is not the author of sickness and disease.
(2) Sickness and disease come from Satan.
(3) When good people suffer loss or sickness, it is not the work of God.

Sickness Brings Glory to God

There are many who believe and teach that sickness brings glory to God. If this were true, Jesus robbed the Father of His Glory when He healed them all.

Insomuch that the multitude wondered, when they saw the dumb to speak, the maimed to be whole, the lame to walk, and the blind to see: and they glorified the God of Israel. (Matthew 15:31 KJV)

And immediately he arose, took up the bed, and went forth before them all; insomuch that they were all amazed, and glorified God, saying, We never saw it on this fashion. (Mark 2:12 KJV)

Luke 13:11-13

And, behold, there was a woman which had a spirit of infirmity eighteen years, and was bowed together, and could in no wise lift up herself. (Luke 13:11 KJV)

And when Jesus saw her, he called her to him, and said unto her, Woman, thou art loosed from thine infirmity. (Luke 13:12 KJV)

And he laid his hands on her: and immediately she was made straight, and glorified God. (Luke 13:13 KJV)

According to these Scriptures it is the healing that brings the glory to God, not the sickness.

The Age of Miracles Has Passed Away

And the earth was without form, and void; and darkness was upon the face of the deep. And the Spirit of God moved upon the face of the waters. (Genesis 1:2 KJV)

It was the Holy Spirit at work in creation. It was the anointing of God, the Holy Spirit, who worked signs and wonders in the Old Testament through the prophets.

> *How God anointed Jesus of Nazareth with the Holy Ghost and with power: who went about doing good, and healing all that were oppressed of the devil; for God was with him. (Acts 10:38 KJV)*

Jesus did all His miracles by the power of the Holy Spirit. All the miracles ever wrought until the day of Pentecost were accomplished by the Holy Spirit, the Miracle Worker.

> *Know ye not that ye are the temple of God, and that the Spirit of God dwelleth in you? (1 Corinthians 3:16 KJV)*

The age in which we live is intended by God to be the most miraculous of all the dispensations. It is the age of the Miracle Worker, the Holy Spirit.

> *Verily, verily, I say unto you, He that believeth on me, the works that I do shall he do also; and greater works than these shall he do; because I go unto my Father. (John 14:12 KJV)*

It is this age that God has promised to pour out His Miracle Worker on all flesh. This is the only age the Holy Spirit would incarnate Himself in the believer.

1 Corinthians 12:7-10

> *But the manifestation of the Spirit is given to every man to profit withal. (1 Corinthians 12:7 KJV)*

> *For to one is given by the Spirit the word of wisdom; to another the word of knowledge by the same Spirit; (1 Corinthians 12:8 KJV)*

> *To another faith by the same Spirit; to another the gifts of healing by the same Spirit; (1 Corinthians 12:9 KJV)*

> *To another the working of miracles; to another prophecy; to another discerning of spirits; to another divers kinds of tongues; to another the interpretation of tongues: (1 Corinthians 12:10 KJV)*

The Holy Spirit is still manifesting Himself through us. How absurd to teach that the Holy Spirit will work miracles in every age but His own age! This present age is the age of the Holy Spirit. The age of the Spirit is that time between the first and second advent of the Lord. That's us!

At the beginning of this age the Church was in her Spirit-filled period and we are now in the lukewarm period of the same age. We are to labor to lift the true Church up to the Bible standard of the first century, not make the Bible fit the standard of the lukewarm Church of the twentieth century.

Praying "If It Be Thy Will"

Another tradition of men that is a faith destroyer, especially in the area of healing, is the practice of adding the phrase *"if it be Thy will"* to our prayers. Let's look at the Scriptures that are used to promote this way of thinking.

> *And it came to pass, when he was in a certain city, behold a man full of leprosy: who seeing Jesus fell on his face, and besought him, saying, Lord, if thou wilt, thou canst make me clean. (Luke 5:12 KJV)*

> *And he put forth his hand, and touched him, saying, I will: be thou clean. And immediately the leprosy departed from him. (Luke 5:13 KJV)*

The word clean in this passage is the Greek word *katharizo* and it means "to cleanse." It does not mean "to heal." It was never translated heal or healing in the New Testament. It was always translated "cleanse, purify, purge," etc. A good example of the way this word was used when talking about something other than leprosy is found in 1 John 1:9.

> *If we confess our sins, he is faithful and just to forgive us our sins, and to cleanse us from all unrighteousness. (1 John 1:9 KJV)*

When the man declared Jesus could cleanse him if He wished, he was making a declaration that Jesus was the Messiah and He had the power to forgive sins. It was a question about Jesus' willingness not His ability.

The "I will" of Jesus cancelled the "if " of the leper. Jesus added to the leper's faith by declaring not only His ability to cleanse the leper but His willingness to do it.

Faith for anything can only be exercised to its full potential where the will of God is known on the subject. This is especially true when seeking healing. We must be fully persuaded that is it God's will to heal everybody, every time. We must know healing is as much a part of our covenant right as forgiveness of sin.

In addition to forgiveness of sin, which is what the leper asked for, he also received healing in his body proving that healing is as much God's will as is forgiveness of sin.

No one is fully persuaded that God will do what He has promised when they add *"if it be Thy will"* to the end of their prayer.

Sickness Is God's Way of Teaching Us

Another blockage to receiving healing is the mindset that sickness is God's way of teaching us something. I cannot tell you how many times I've heard Christians say things like, "God had to put me on my back to teach me so and so."

God may take what the devil has done and turn it around for our good and His glory, but God does not put sickness and disease on us to teach us a lesson. There are God-ordained ways for believers to be trained.

The Holy Spirit Is the Teacher

First and foremost, the Bible tells us that the Holy Spirit is the Teacher.

For the Holy Ghost shall teach you in the same hour what ye ought to say. (Luke 12:12 KJV)

But the Comforter, which is the Holy Ghost, whom the Father will send in my name, he shall teach you all things, and bring all things to your remembrance, whatsoever I have said unto you. (John 14:26 KJV)

Which things also we speak, not in the words which man's wisdom teacheth, but which the Holy Ghost teacheth; comparing spiritual things with spiritual. (1 Corinthians 2:13 KJV)

The Word of God Should Teach Us

All scripture is given by inspiration of God, and is profitable for doctrine, for reproof, for correction, for instruction in righteousness: (2 Timothy 3:16 KJV)

Spiritual Leaders and Pastors Should Teach Us

And God hath set some in the Church, first apostles, secondarily prophets, thirdly teachers, after that miracles, then gifts of healings, helps, governments, diversities of tongues. (1 Corinthians 12:28 KJV)

And he gave some, apostles; and some, prophets; and some, evangelists; and some, pastors and teachers; (Ephesians 4:11 KJV)

For the perfecting of the saints, for the work of the ministry, for the edifying of the body of Christ: (Ephesians 4:12 KJV)

Whom we preach, warning every man, and teaching every man in all wisdom; that we may present every man perfect in Christ Jesus: (Colossians 1:28 KJV)

Let the word of Christ dwell in you richly in all wisdom; teaching and admonishing one another in psalms and hymns and spiritual songs, singing with grace in your hearts to the Lord. (Colossians 3:16 KJV)

If people tell me the Lord had to give them cancer in order for them to learn to trust Him, or God put them flat on their backs in bed to teach them something, it tells me that they do not know the voice of the Holy Spirit or they do not listen. They do not know the Word or search out answers from the Word in their time of need. They do not receive teaching by other believers or leaders. All of these are the God-ordained ways to be instructed by the Lord.

There is no Scripture in the Bible that says God puts sickness and disease on His people to teach them a lesson.

If You Only Have Enough Faith

We were taught for many years that, if you just had enough faith, you could be healed. There are several Scriptures that proponents of this doctrine use to make their point. I have listed only two.

Woman with the Issue of Blood

> *But Jesus turned him about, and when he saw her, he said, Daughter, be of good comfort; thy faith hath made thee whole. And the woman was made whole from that hour. (Matthew 9:22 KJV)*

The woman with the issue of blood was healed. Jesus told her that her faith had made her whole. By the way, this word whole is the Greek word *sozo* which I defined earlier. Notice that Jesus did not have to command her healing or cast anything out of her. She used her own faith and so Jesus had to do NOTHING.

Blind Man Received His Sight

> *And Jesus said unto him, Receive thy sight: thy faith hath saved thee. (Luke 18:42 KJV)*

The blind man received his sight. Jesus said, *"Receive your sight; your faith has saved you."* Jesus never ministered to this man. He did not command anything or cast out anything. He merely informed the man that his own faith had saved him. Please note the word saved here is also *sozo*.

Both of these were healed because of their faith. However many neglect to consider other Scriptures where the person was healed because of another person's faith.

The Syrophenician Woman's Daughter Healed

> *Then Jesus answered and said unto her, O woman, great is thy faith: be it unto thee even as thou wilt. And her daughter was made whole from that very hour. (Matthew 15:28 KJV)*

The daughter was healed because of her mother's faith, not her own faith.

Centurion's Servant Healed

Matthew 8:5-13

> *And when Jesus was entered into Capernaum, there came unto him a centurion, beseeching him, (Matthew 8:5 KJV)*

And saying, Lord, my servant lieth at home sick of the palsy, grievously tormented. (Matthew 8:6 KJV)

And Jesus saith unto him, I will come and heal him. (Matthew 8:7 KJV)

The centurion answered and said, Lord, I am not worthy that thou shouldest come under my roof: but speak the word only, and my servant shall be healed. (Matthew 8:8 KJV)

For I am a man under authority, having soldiers under me: and I say to this man, Go, and he goeth; and to another, Come, and he cometh; and to my servant, Do this, and he doeth it. (Matthew 8:9 KJV)

When Jesus heard it, he marveled, and said to them that followed, Verily I say unto you, I have not found so great faith, no, not in Israel. (Matthew 8:10 KJV)

And I say unto you, That many shall come from the east and west, and shall sit down with Abraham, and Isaac, and Jacob, in the kingdom of heaven. (Matthew 8:11 KJV)

But the children of the kingdom shall be cast out into outer darkness: there shall be weeping and gnashing of teeth. (Matthew 8:12 KJV)

And Jesus said unto the centurion, Go thy way; and as thou hast believed, so be it done unto thee. And his servant was healed in the selfsame hour. (Matthew 8:13 KJV)

In the story of the centurion's servant it was his master who had the faith. Jesus was ready to go to his home to minister but the centurion made it clear that was not necessary. *"Just speak a word,"* he said. You can almost hear some surprise in Jesus' voice here. He said to the centurion:

I say unto you, I have not found so great faith, no, not in Israel. (Luke 7:9 KJV)

Jesus Used His Own Faith

There were several times when Jesus had to use His own faith as the minister. Here are some examples:

- Luke 7:12-15: Jesus raised a man from the dead. In this case it does not appear that anyone involved, except Jesus, had their own faith. Certainly, the dead man did not have faith.
- John 9:1-7: Jesus healed a man that was blind from birth. The man did not ask for healing. When asked about it later, he declared that he did not even know who healed him. He referred to Jesus as a prophet. The man did not have any faith of his own.
- John 11:1-44: Jesus raised Lazarus from the dead. The dead man had no faith. The people standing around mourning had no faith. Even Lazarus' sisters had no faith because they told Jesus that if he had come earlier their brother would have recovered.

Jesus is our example. It is wonderful when others have their own faith but we cannot always count on that being the case. Therefore, it is vital that we develop our faith for ourselves and others.

Paul's Thorn

> *And lest I should be exalted above measure through the abundance of the revelations, there was given to me a thorn in the flesh, the messenger of Satan to buffet me, lest I should be exalted above measure. (2 Corinthians 12:7 KJV)*

This Scripture is responsible for another blockage to receiving the healing God has provided for His people. This Scripture has spawned many traditions of men. Was Paul's thorn in the flesh sickness or disease? Did Paul really suffer from an incurable eye disease? Is it true that God refused to heal Paul of this eye disease, even though Paul prayed repeatedly? The answer, to all these questions, is a firm NO!

The first law of proper Biblical exegesis (critical explanation or analysis, especially of a text) is that you must determine what the word or phrase meant to the original audience. In the context of their culture and their literature what would it have meant to them? We can find clues by looking at other documents of that era or other documents that might have influenced the people of that era.

The first step in this kind of analysis is to look within the document itself to see if, perhaps, other occurrences of the same word or phrase might give us clues. In this case, Paul only used this phrase once in this letter.

The next step then is to see how the writer might have used this word or phrase in other writings. Again, in this case Paul never used the phrase *"thorn in the flesh"* in any of his other writings. He did, however, use the word buffet.

> *Even unto this present hour we both hunger, and thirst, and are naked, and are buffeted, and have no certain dwelling place; (1 Corinthians 4:11 KJV)*

> *And labor, working with our own hands: being reviled, we bless; being persecuted, we suffer it: (1 Corinthians 4:12 KJV)*

> *Being defamed, we entreat: we are made as the filth of the world, and are the off scouring of all things unto this day. (1 Corinthians 4:13 KJV)*

Paul not only used the word buffet, but expanded his description to include a definition. He listed the ways in which they were buffeted and the list does not include sickness or disease.

Next, we look at what historical or cultural influences were present in Paul's life that might have caused him to use this word or phrase.

Paul was a scholar. In fact, he was trained as a Pharisee by one of the most brilliant scholars of his time, Gamaliel. Paul would have been greatly influenced in his speech and writings by his studies of the Old Testament. In fact, throughout Paul's writings he uses words found in the Old Testament. BINGO!

Paul's audience would also have been familiar with the Old Testament. Therefore, we have every reason to believe Paul would have used the term in a manner consistent with Old Testament writings.

So, let's look to the Old Testament to see how others used this word *thorn*. Remember, we are looking for the figurative use of the word, not the literal. (As far as I know, there is no one who believes that Paul had a literal thorn in his flesh.) By the way, those who try to interpret the thorn as sickness are agreeing that the thorn is figurative.

> *But if ye will not drive out the inhabitants of the land from before you; then it shall come to pass, that those which ye let remain of them shall be pricks in your eyes, and thorns in your sides, and shall vex you in the land wherein ye dwell. (Numbers 33:55 KJV)*

> *Know for a certainty that the Lord your God will no more drive out any of these nations from before you; but they shall be snares and traps unto you, and scourges in your sides, and thorns in your eyes, until ye perish from off this good land which the Lord your God hath given you. (Joshua 23:13 KJV)*

> *Wherefore I also said, I will not drive them out from before you; but they shall be as thorns in your sides, and their gods shall be a snare unto you. (Judges 2:3 KJV)*

> *But the sons of Belial shall be all of them as thorns thrust away, because they cannot be taken with hands. (2 Samuel 23:6 KJV)*

Proper Biblical exegesis dictates that a word or phrase cannot mean to us what it could never have meant to the original hearers.

Never, in the entire Bible, was the word thorn used for sickness or disease, literally or figuratively. Therefore, it could not have meant that to the hearers of Paul's words either. Figuratively this word was used to describe people, or groups of people, who were aggravating or harassing. This interpretation certainly seems to fit the life of Paul as we know it. He was beaten, thrown in jail, stoned, and left for dead. Yes, this certainly fits.

It fits the life of Paul; it fits the context of his words and it fits with all the proper elements of scholarly Biblical interpretation.

> *. . .the messenger of Satan to buffet me, lest I should be exalted above measure. (2 Corinthians 12:7 KJV)*

Paul said his thorn was a messenger of Satan (angel of the devil). This word messenger is the Greek word *angelos*. It appears 188 times in the Bible. It is translated angel 181 times and messenger the other 7 times. In all the 188 times in the entire Bible it is always used to describe a being, not a thing.[17]

Paul not only tells us that it was a being but he describes the mission of the being: to buffet him. This word buffet means to strike blow after blow.

---

[17] Bosworth, F.F., "Christ The Healer, Fleming H. Revell, a division of Baker Book House Co, Grand Rapids, MI 1973, 194.

Rotherham translates it *"that he might be buffeting me."*[18] The word *buffet* means repeated battering as when the waves buffet a boat or as when they buffeted Jesus:[19] Notice how Rotherham uses the personal pronoun *he* when translating this passage.

Likewise, Weymouth translates this as *"Satan's angel dealing blow after blow"* (Weymouth New Testament). Both of these translators chose the personal pronoun *he* when translating this verse. Buffeting was never a word used in connection with sickness. It was a word used in connection with people who are repeatedly attacked or aggravated.

> *And some began to spit on him, and to cover his face, and to buffet him, and to say unto him, Prophesy: and the servants did strike him with the palms of their hands. (Mark 14:65 KJV)*

Paul's use of the words thorn and buffet is both consistent with other New Testament writers and with Old Testament writers.

Now we come to another argument that is often used in defense of the wrong interpretation regarding Paul's sickness:

Galatians 4:13-15

> *Ye know how through infirmity of the flesh I preached the gospel unto you at the first. (Galatians 4:13 KJV)*

> *And my temptation, which was in my flesh ye despised not, nor rejected; but received me as an angel of God, even as Christ Jesus. (Galatians 4:14 KJV)*

> *Where is then the blessedness ye spake of? For I bear you record, that, if it had been possible, ye would have plucked out your own eyes, and have given them to me. (Galatians 4:15 KJV)*

At first glance it might sound like Paul had a sickness in his eyes. But we can only get to that conclusion based on our bias.

Paul spoke of his infirmity in verse 13. The Greek word for infirmity here is *asthenia,* meaning feebleness of body or mind.

Infirmity: 769. astheneia, as-then'-i-ah; from G772; feebleness (of body or mind);

Paul also said they did not despise or reject him because of the temptation which was in his flesh. The Greek word for temptation in this verse is *peirasmos;* meaning a putting to proof.

---

[18] Rotherham, Joseph Bryant, Rotherham Emphasized Bible, Grand Rapids, Michigan, Kregel Publications, 1959, 189

[19] Bosworth, 194

Lesson 7 - Hindrances To Faith

Temptation: 3986. peirasmos, pi-ras-mos'; from G3985; **a putting to proof** (by experiment [of good], experience [of evil], solicitation, discipline or provocation); by impl. adversity:—temptation, X try.

In other words, the word *temptation* refers to being proved by going through a hard time.

Scholars believe Paul was probably preaching to the Galatians just after his stoning at Antioch. (You can find the story in Acts 14:19). They stoned him and left him for dead. Now, if Paul's next preaching assignment after this was to the Galatians, no wonder he called himself feeble at the first. It would also explain his use of the word temptation or proofing. God certainly proofed or proved Paul at Antioch. His faith and his work were put to the test. This possible explanation of this feebleness also fits Paul's other statement about the thorn in the flesh, the messenger from Satan that buffeted him.

Where is then the blessedness ye spake of? For I bear you record, that, if it had been possible, ye would have plucked out your own eyes, and have given them to me. (Galatians 4:15 KJV)

This is the sole verse on which most misinterpretations are based. Consider the possibility that Paul was using this phrase in the same manner as we would say, "I know you would give me your right arm if you thought I needed it." In other words, could this have been a colloquialism?

Finally, even if we grant (and I do not) that Paul was sick in the sense of disease or illness, it is clear that it was only for a time, and he recovered. Let's assume for argument's sake that Paul had a sickness. Perhaps this is why he said in:

You know how through infirmity of the flesh I preached the Gospel unto you at the first. (Galatians 4:13)

Notice the last phrase "at the first." He does not mean he preached the Gospel "at the first," but his infirmity was "at the first." If his infirmity was "at the first," it must not have lasted. However, it is still not clear, from this passage, that he was sick at all. He was probably wounded, cut up, and bruised from the stoning, but not sick.

If you still cannot shake what you have been taught by tradition, I still say to you, "If Paul had a sickness he implied by his own choice of words that it was "at the first" and he recovered. It was not related to the buffeting which God refused to remove. That was a different issue."

The final test of one's interpretation is this: does this interpretation bring theological harmony or disharmony? Generally speaking if the interpretation brings theological disharmony it should not be considered a valid interpretation.

The suggestion that Paul had an eye disease which God refused to heal brings such theological disharmony that one would have to change the interpretation of countless verses to approach anything resembling theological harmony.

If time allowed we could fill page after page with Scriptures that would prove the theological disharmony this mindset causes. However, let us look at just one Scripture as an example of how this interpretation brings theological disharmony.

And said, If thou wilt diligently hearken to the voice of the LORD thy God, and wilt do that which is right in his sight, and wilt give ear to his commandments, and keep all his statutes, I will put none of these diseases upon thee, which I have brought upon the Egyptians: for I am the LORD that healeth thee. (Exodus 15:26 KJV)

Heal: 7495. rapha', raw-faw'; or ra-phah, raw-faw'; a prim. root; prop. to mend (by stitching), i.e. (fig.) to cure:—cure, (cause to) heal, physician, repair, X thoroughly, make whole. See H7503.

God declared himself to be Jehovah *Rapha* "the *Lord that heals you.*" Since this is one of the names of God it means God does not just DO healing — He is healing.

If God, Who is healing, refused to heal Paul then we would have to change our entire understanding of the nature and attributes of God. We could no longer say He is what His Name implies, but rather, only "sometimes" He "might" do what His Name implies. Talk about major theological disharmony!

I say the only way a person can justify the interpretation of Paul's thorn as sickness and his infirmity as an eye disease is if he or she is biased or predisposed to believe it. We cannot justify such an interpretation either from the Scriptures themselves or by applying sound Biblical exegesis.

Clearly the traditions of men have, in many cases, become a major hindrance of faith and have robbed the Church of her covenant right of physical and emotional healing.

Rejection

In addition to traditions of men rejection can be a major hindrance to our faith for healing. Just as there are those who believe Jesus is who He says He is but just do not want Him as their savior, there are those who do not want to be healed. I do not pretend to understand it, but I know it is true.

Lady Dying with Cancer/Stroke

One of the best examples of this in my experience occurred at a healing training meeting I attended. Those needing healing had been invited to this meeting where a team of student ministers would be available to pray for them. I was one of those student ministers.

A young man in his thirties brought his mother in a wheelchair to us for prayer. She had a stroke and she had cancer. She was dying. We dealt with many of the issues of her soul. Then we started commanding her body to be healed and thanking God. Nothing happened.

We went back to the beginning and looked for more spiritual issues that could be interfering with her healing. We again commanded her body to be healed. Nothing happened. We spent around three hours with this lady.

Our instructor Rev. Cheryl Schang said, "This is impossible. I know she has to be healed. It cannot be possible that she is not healed." So we checked our list of things that we knew could block healing.

(1) Ignorance? Even if she had ignorance it did not matter because we were doing the praying and we certainly were not ignorant.
(2) Unbelief? Same as ignorance it did not matter if she had unbelief because we were the ones with the faith.
(3) Spiritual Interference? We had dealt with all the issues God identified to us. We were only left with number 4.
(4) Rejection. "Is it possible she does not want healing?" we asked.

At this point Cheryl began to ask some questions. She asked the lady, "What was your life like before your illness?" The lady told us that she was very lonely because all her children had married and moved away.

Cheryl then asked, "What is your life like now that you are sick?" The lady told us that her daughter had divorced her husband to move home with her and her son had separated from his wife to help take care of her.

The next question Cheryl asked was, "What will your life be like if you get healed?" She said, "My children would leave and I would be all alone again." At that point we were all very much aware that this lady did not really want to be healed. When asked about this she admitted that it did not bother her to stay sick.

It is plain that it is God's will for all to be saved. Yet we know there are people who die without being saved. If someone does not get saved it is not God's fault. It is also the will of God for all to be healed. Yet all are not. Our free will applies just as much to our health as it does to our salvation.

This lady was dying and yet she did not really want to be healed. Again, I do not pretend to understand that mindset but sadly I know there are those who will reject the healing that is available to them.

Spiritual Interference

Spiritual Interference can be another major hindrance to our faith.

In whom the god of this world hath blinded the minds of them which believe not, lest the light of the glorious gospel of Christ, who is the image of God, should shine unto them. (2 Corinthians 4:4 KJV)

The enemy interferes with a person's ability to know the truth by blinding them spiritually. However, the truth has the ability to set a person free, spiritually speaking.

And ye shall know the truth, and the truth shall make you free. (John 8:32 KJV)

The same thing is true for healing. The enemy has the ability to cause your sickness and interfere with your healing. There are spiritual roots to some illnesses and there are spiritual blockages to some healings. Sometimes a person is dealing with both.

Unforgiveness, for example, is a major hindrance to receiving healing in the Body of Christ today.

And forgive us our debts, as we also have forgiven (left, remitted, and let go of the debts, and have given up resentment against) our debtors. (Matthew 6:12 AMP)

For if you forgive people their trespasses [their reckless and willful sins, leaving them, letting them go, and giving up resentment], your heavenly Father will also forgive you. (Matthew 6:14 AMP)

But if you do not forgive others their trespasses [their reckless and willful sins, leaving them, letting them go, and giving up resentment], neither will your Father forgive you your trespasses. (Matthew 6:15 AMP)

I like the Message translation of verses 14-15.

In prayer there is a connection between what God does and what you do. You cannot get forgiveness from God, for instance, without also forgiving others. (Matthew 6:14 MSG)

If you refuse to do your part, you cut yourself off from God's part. (Matthew 6:15 MSG)

Unforgiveness is a sin. It is often the spiritual root of lower back problems, arthritis, breast cancer, etc.

Which is simpler: to say to the paraplegic, 'I forgive your sins,' or say, 'Get up, take your stretcher, and start walking'? (Mark 2:9 MSG)

Jesus forgave the sin and the body was healed. If we are to walk free of sickness and disease, we must be willing to forgive those who have sinned against us.

We will discuss the effect of spiritual interference in depth in our next lesson. At this point, let me just say, "Whatever you let into your soul, will eventually manifest in your body!" Medical science has known about this for a long time. We in the Church are just starting to get it.

Lesson 7 - Hindrances To Faith

Activation Time

- Halal for 2 minutes using your attributes of God list.
- Pray in the Holy Spirit, with passion for 5 minutes.
- Activation – Repentance for unforgiveness.

Activation Description

You may want to provide a blank piece of paper for each student as they come into class.

Leader:

Pray, asking the Holy Spirit to reveal to each person the people they need to forgive.

- **Instruct** each person to write on a sheet of paper, everyone the Holy Spirit brings into their mind.

Demonstrate activation: Ask for a volunteer: Have him/her sit in a chair. Lead him/her in the following prayer of repentance, using his/her list of people to forgive. Have him/her repeat after you:

- Father, forgive me for allowing unforgiveness to operate in my life.

Using his/her list, have the person forgive each person for whatever it was they did to them.

- Today, _____, (example: April 1, 2009) I choose to forgive _____ (each person on their list).

There is no need for anybody else to hear them, but they do need to speak loud enough for them to hear themselves. Ask them to let you know when they are finished forgiving. Then continue.

- I repent for allowing unforgiveness to operate in my body. I break all agreement with unforgiveness, in every word, thought, or deed.

After the person has repented and broken their agreement with unforgiveness the person leading them in pray commands unforgiveness to go.

- Unforgiveness, _____ has broken his/her agreement with you. Therefore, you no longer have authority to operate in his/her body. In the Name of Jesus and by the power of the Holy Spirit, I speak to you and command you to go, now! Unforgiveness, get out!

- Have the person take a deep breath.
- Ask them to give you one word that expresses how they feel. They will usually say "light headed" or "clean" or something similar.

However, if they say they have tightness in their chest or pain in their head, the spirit of unforgiveness did not go.

- Command it to go again! Be sure to use a firm voice. (It is not necessary to scream but you must be firm.)
- Have them take a deep breath.
- Ask them again, "How do you feel?" The tightness in the chest or pain in the head should be gone.

Note: If the tightness or pain persists, there are probably other issues that need to be addressed.

Group Activation

Divide students into groups of 3-5, depending on the size of the group. Have them take turns leading each other through the prayer of repentance for unforgiveness and then kicking it out using the same process as demonstrated by the leader.

If tightness of the chest or pain in the head persists practice getting a Word of Knowledge as to what issue needs to be addressed. Have the person repent and break their agreement with whatever spirit is revealed and then kick it out, using the same process.

We will deal with this in depth in future chapters.

Assignment

- Meditate on and memorize the memory verse.
- Add 5 more attributes of God to your list.
- Begin your daily prayer time by halaling for at least 4 minutes using your list of attributes of God.
- Pray in the Spirit 15 minutes a day.
- Ask God to give you somebody to lead to the Lord, or to get filled with the Holy Spirit, or pray for their healing, or all three.
- Read Psalms 139 and Romans 8:35-39 once a day.

Assignment Result and Comments

LESSON 8 - Spiritual Interference

Memory Verse

For we wrestle not against flesh and blood, but against principalities, against powers, against the rulers of the darkness of this world, against spiritual wickedness in high places. (Ephesians 6:12 KJV)

Introduction

I wish walking in divine health was as easy as knowing and believing all the Biblical truths we have discussed so far in this manual. But there is more to be considered when seeking emotional or physical healing of our bodies.

Spiritual interference often can and does hinder Christians from receiving the healing benefits of their covenant.

Before we go any further let me make it perfectly clear that I do not believe that a Christian can be possessed by the devil or any of his demons. The word *possession* implies ownership. The Bible is very clear on the fact that Christians

But he that is joined unto the Lord is one spirit. (1 Corinthians 6:17 KJV)

As Christians our spirits belong to God. He has come to live and dwell in the spirit of the believer.

What? know ye not that your body is the temple of the Holy Ghost which is in you, which ye have of God, and ye are not your own? (1 Corinthians 6:19 KJV)

For ye are bought with a price: therefore glorify God in your body, and in your spirit, which are God's. (1 Corinthians 6:20 KJV)

We have been ransomed, bought with a price. Our spirit is one with God. Our spirit is made alive by faith in Jesus but our soul needs a house cleaning.

Derek Prince

It was Derek Prince who compared the journey of the believers' spiritual freedom to the Israelites entering the Promised Land. (Numbers 13 and 14)

God brought the Israelites out of Egypt to take them into the Promised Land. God gave them the land. It was theirs for the taking. God instructed Moses to send twelve men, one ruler from each tribe, to spy out the land and report back with their findings.

The twelve returned and reported that the land flowed with milk and honey and the fruit of the land was plentiful. But the cities were walled and there were giants in the land.

> *And Caleb stilled the people before Moses, and said, Let us go up at once, and possess it; for we are well able to overcome it. (Numbers 13:30 KJV)*

Caleb, one of the spies, declared that they were able to overcome the giants. But the others who had gone into the land with him saw things differently.

> *But the men that went up with him said, we be not able to go up against the people; for they are stronger than we. (Numbers 13:31 KJV)*

> *And there we saw the giants, the sons of Anak, which come of the giants: and we were in our own sight as grasshoppers, and so we were in their sight. (Numbers 13:33 KJV)*

All the congregation began to rebel against Moses and Aaron. All of Israel wanted to pick a new captain and return to Egypt.

> *And they said one to another, Let us make a captain, and let us return into Egypt. (Numbers 14:4 KJV)*

Only Joshua and Caleb gave the good report of victory.

Numbers 14:6-9

> *And Joshua the son of Nun, and Caleb the son of Jephunneh, which were of them that searched the land, rent their clothes: (Numbers 14:6 KJV)*

> *And they spoke unto all the company of the children of Israel, saying, The land, which we passed through to search it, is an exceeding good land. (Numbers 14:7 KJV)*

> *If the LORD delight in us, then he will bring us into this land, and give it us; a land which floweth with milk and honey. (Numbers 14:8 KJV)*

> *Only rebel not ye against the LORD, neither fear ye the people of the land; for they are bread for us: their defense is departed from them, and the LORD is with us: fear them not. (Numbers 14:9 KJV)*

Joshua and Caleb tried to assure the people that they would be victorious against their enemies but the congregation conspired to stone them. Because of their fear and unbelief the Israelites wandered in the desert for forty years after God gave the Promised Land to them. A generation of people, including Moses, died in the wilderness.

After the death of Moses God instructed Joshua to go in and possess the land that He had given them. God was with Joshua and He brought the Israelites through the Jordan River by a miracle.

> *And the priests that bore the ark of the covenant of the LORD stood firm on dry ground in the midst of Jordan, and all the Israelites passed over on dry ground, until all the people were passed clean over Jordan. (Joshua 3:17 KJV)*

Getting into the Promised Land was easy. The waters of the Jordan parted and the Israelites walked across the river on dry ground. God brought them into the Promised Land by a miracle and then He said, "You see those giants? It is your job to drive them out yourself."

When the Israelites walked away from Canaan, the Promise Land, the first time they chose by their lack of action to let the enemy live in their land, build buildings and plant crops for forty years. The enemy was quite comfortable there and was not going to leave just because the Israelites had arrived.

God gave the Israelites the strategy of war and He fought by their side but the Israelites had to take up the sword and confront the enemy themselves. Why did God make the Israelites fight? Why not another miracle?

> *Only that the generations of the children of Israel might know, to teach them war, at the least such as before knew nothing thereof; Judges 3:2 (KJV)*

God said He left the giants there to teach the Israelites how to war. God did not want His people to be victims of their enemies. If you study the battles of Ancient Israel you will find that as long as the Israelites served God they were undefeatable. By allowing the Israelites to fight the giants in the land God established a reputation among their enemies and in His people. They were not victims of their enemies.

The wiser nations were afraid to fight them which allowed the Israelites to enjoy long seasons of peace in a world where kingdoms warring against kingdoms was a regular way of life.

This is a picture of our born-again experience. In the same way God miraculously brought Israel into the Promised Land He delivered us from spiritual death (Egypt) and brought us into spiritual life (the Promised Land) by a miracle. We are justified by faith in the finished work of the Cross, an act of grace. It is instant. It is miraculous. Our spirits are born again alive unto God.

> *Therefore if any man be in Christ, he is a new creature: old things are passed away; behold, all things are become new. (2 Corinthians 5:17 KJV)*

This is a Scripture that is often quoted by those who have recently been born again when giving their personal testimony. Sometimes this being quoted can give the listener the false impression that when a person is saved, old habits, evil thoughts, lustful looks, etc. are forever gone away and everything becomes literally new in their life. We all know from experience that this is not the case. You can be born again and still have lust, fear, hate, unforgiveness, etc. operating in your life.

This Scripture is describing the believer's position in Christ not their practices. As the believer grows in Christ the desire is for our practices to increasingly correspond to our position.

As believers we come into the kingdom — the born again experience, the Promised Land. Like the Israelites there are giants occupying territories in our soul that no longer belong to them. Just as Israel had to go in and possess the land that God had already given them it is our responsibility to drive out the enemy and claim back the territory of our soul.

God gives us His strategy, His Word, and His power (the Holy Spirit) but we are to drive out the giants in our own souls.

> *For the weapons of our warfare are not carnal, but mighty through God to the pulling down of strongholds; (2 Corinthians 10:4 KJV)*

> *Casting down imaginations, and every high thing that exalteth itself against the knowledge of God, and bringing into captivity every thought to the obedience of Christ; (2 Corinthians 10:5 KJV)*

This reclaiming of our soul and cleansing it from the giants in the land is the sanctification process. We are justified by faith, miraculously. We are sanctified by the lifelong process of cleaning out our souls.

> *And be not conformed to this world: but be ye transformed by the renewing of your mind, that ye may prove what is that good, and acceptable, and perfect, will of God. (Romans 12:2 KJV)*

> *Wherefore, my beloved, as ye have always obeyed, not as in my presence only, but now much more in my absence, work out your own salvation with fear and trembling. (Philippians 2:12 KJV)*

Just as the Israelites built a reputation with their enemies with every victory we establish a reputation in the spirit world every time we experience victory over our enemy the devil.

You're in the Army Now

As Christians we are in the Kingdom of God, we are children of God, but we are also in the Army of God. The devil is the enemy of the Kingdom of God, the children of God and the Army of God. Spiritual warfare is real.

> *Be sober, be vigilant; because your adversary the devil, as a roaring lion, walketh about, seeking whom he may devour. (1 Peter 5:8 KJV)*

The devil is at enmity with God and he has declared war on all mankind. Those who do not understand that we are at war are deceived. Make no mistake you are in a war. If the devil cannot keep you from coming into the Kingdom of God he wants to render you ineffective in the kingdom.

Before the United States goes to war the Intelligence Department is instructed to identify the enemy, figure out where the enemy is located, and study how the enemy works: their capability, tactics, etc. Having compiled all this information they are then to come back and brief the leaders on their findings. With this information at their disposal leaders can determine a course of action that will ensure victory.

If you are sick or you know someone who is sick the enemy is camped in territory that no longer belongs to him. Healing and divine health is a provision of your covenant with God. In order to ensure victory, you need to identify the enemy, determine were he is located, and study how he works. . .his capability, tactics, weakness, and strengths.

It is time to enforce the provision of our covenant. It is time to go to war. But first, you need a military briefing.

Military Briefing

In earlier lessons we discussed at length that sickness and disease are the result of the fall of man. It was through sin that sickness and ultimately death came to mankind.

The Bible clearly teaches us that the devil is the author of sickness and disease. We saw in the book of Job that it was Satan who put sickness on Job.

> *The thief cometh not, but for to steal, and to kill, and to destroy: I am come that they might have life, and that they might have it more abundantly. (John 10:10 KJV)*

We only need to reflect on the violence during the hours before Jesus' crucifixion and the agony of the cross itself to understand the devil's intentions against Jesus and the Kingdom of God. Focusing on the brutal death of Jesus gives one glimpse of what the devil's intentions are toward mankind if given the opportunity.

> *When Jesus saw their faith, he said unto the sick of the palsy, Son, thy sins be forgiven thee. (Mark 2:5 KJV)*

In Jesus' time sin and sickness were seen as twins. Jesus healed a paralyzed man by saying, "*Your sins be forgiven you.*"

Even though sickness in mankind is a result of sin one should understand that not every sickness is a result of personal sin. We live in a sinful, fallen world. We have Chernobyl, acid rain, pesticides in our food, and stuff just happens. Just because you fell and broke your leg does not mean a demon tripped you. Stuff happens.

> *Or those eighteen on whom the tower in Siloam fell and killed them—do you think that they were more guilty offenders (debtors) than all the others who dwelt in Jerusalem? (Luke 13:4 AMP)*

> *I tell you, No. (Luke 13:5 AMP)*

There was a tower that fell in a town not far from where Jesus ministered. The people asked Jesus about it as though they had deserved to die for some reason. Jesus answered with words that, today, would be translated "stuff happens."

God knew stuff would happen. He also knew we would get sick and need healing.

> *Is any sick among you? let him call for the elders of the Church; and let them pray over him, anointing him with oil in the name of the Lord: (James 5:14 KJV)*
>
> *And the prayer of faith shall save the sick, and the Lord shall raise him up; and if he have committed sins, they shall be forgiven him. (James 5:15 KJV)*

Healing is in your contract. However, if you are struggling with your own faith God has made provision for that as well; go to the elders (who are supposed to have the faith for you).

When a Christian has prayed and even gone to the elders for prayer yet they are still sick something is blocking the Glory of God from being manifest. It is usually demonic interference.

Demonic and Sickness/Disease Connection

As I studied the ministry of Jesus I noticed an obvious, but often overlooked, reality. Much of the time when Jesus "healed" someone He was actually casting out a demon.

> *And, behold, there was a woman which had a spirit of infirmity eighteen years, and was bowed together, and could in no wise lift up herself. (Luke 13:11 KJV)*
>
> *And when Jesus saw her, he called her to him, and said unto her, Woman, thou art loosed from thine infirmity. (Luke 13:12 KJV)*

Jesus cast a spirit of infirmity out of this woman who had been bent over for eighteen years in order to heal her.

> *And ought not this woman, being a daughter of Abraham, whom Satan hath bound, lo, these eighteen years, be loosed from this bond on the sabbath day? (Luke 13:16 KJV)*

Also notice that verse 16 tells us that it was Satan who had bound her for those eighteen years.

There were also many other instances of Jesus healing people by casting out a demon. The following are a couple of them that come to mind.

> *And they that were vexed with unclean spirits: and they were healed. (Luke 6:18 KJV)*
>
> *And as he was yet coming, the devil threw him down, and tare him. And Jesus rebuked the unclean spirit, and healed the child, and delivered him again to his father. (Luke 9:42 KJV)*

> **Healed:** 2390. iaomai, ee-ah'-om-ahee; mid. of appar. a prim. verb; **to cure** (lit. or fig.):—heal, make whole.

The Bible uses this word *iaomai* to mean both physical healing and deliverance from a demon. You can find this same Greek word in Mark's story of the woman with the issue of blood:

> *And straightway the fountain of her blood was dried up; and she felt in her body that she was healed of that plague. (Mark 5:29 KJV)*

This word healed is the same Greek word *iaomai*. Jesus and his disciples made no distinction between curing an illness and casting out a demon. They called it all the same thing: healing.
Jesus cast out a dumb spirit and a man could speak.

> *And he was casting out a devil, and it was dumb. And it came to pass, when the devil was gone out, the dumb spake; and the people wondered. (Luke 11:14 KJV)*

It was an established belief in Biblical times that the soul was connected to the body.
I agree with the great Bible teacher Derek Prince's theological position on this issue. He said, "It is unscriptural to pray for the sick if one is not prepared also to cast out demons."[20] As we move on into the area of how to heal you will find this bit of information invaluable.

Medical Science Today

Doctors have long known this link between the soul and body existed, but most of them have not made the spiritual connection. We all know, thanks to medical science, if you allow stress in your soul you become a candidate for a heart attack. If you allow worry in your soul you may expect ulcers.

Recently doctors have discovered that if you harbor anger, bitterness, and resentment in your soul, you will get arthritis. The anger causes an over-production of a chemical. When your body cannot process the chemical fast enough the excess is stored in your joints and causes your joints to be eaten away.

> *From whom the whole body fitly joined together and compacted by that which every joint supplieth, according to the effectual working in the measure of every part, maketh increase of the body unto the edifying of itself in love. (Ephesians 4:16 KJV)*

As the Body of Christ we are supposed to be fitly joined together, each joint supplying what is needed. When we get out of joint with each other, our joints let us know it.

---

[20] Prince, Derek, They Shall Expel Demons, Chosen Books, Grand Rapids, MI, 1998, 11

Joint Pain in Mexican Lady

I can tell you story after story about people who were healed when they dealt with the issues of their soul. I went to Mexico with a friend and mentor, Rev. Cheryl Schang, to help her hold a School of Healing. During our activation time a woman asked us to pray for her to be healed. She had intense joint pain in her hips and was having trouble walking. She walked very slowly. She just hobbled along.

We tried to kick out the pain but it would not go. This is always a sign the pain in the body is connected to a pain in the soul. We prayed and God gave Cheryl a Word of Knowledge. He told Cheryl that the lady's soul was in pain because a family member, whom she should have been able to depend on, let her down. This woman was angry and refused to forgive the person.

The lady admitted the Word of Knowledge was correct. Cheryl explained to her that the pain in her hips would not leave until she dealt with the issue of unforgiveness in her soul. Unfortunately, she refused to forgive.

As we were getting ready to close the meeting the lady changed her mind. I guess the pain was so bad she was willing to do anything. Since it was late Cheryl told her to return the next day and we would pray for her. The next day she came in jumping and skipping. She followed the instructions we used in the class, repented of unforgiveness, and cast out that spirit herself! As soon as she did, the pain left and all function returned to her joints.

The soul is where sin resides. The enemy is not the owner of our souls but he can be an occupying force. It is where the enemy pitches his tent and sets up his workshop. Once established in your soul he begins to use your soul (your mind, will, and emotions) to produce harmful effects in your body.

The Agreement That Costs You Your Health

There is power in agreement. This is not a new thought to believers.

> *Again I say unto you, That if two of you shall agree on earth as touching anything that they shall ask, it shall be done for them of my Father which is in heaven. (Matthew 18:19 KJV)*

Jesus said that when two of us agree on anything on earth whatever we ask will be done for us by the Father who is in heaven. There is power in the spirit realm when we unite with the plans and purposes of God on earth. There is also power given to the enemy in the spirit realm when we unite our souls (our minds, wills, and emotions) with the plans of the enemy. In fact, agreement is the very source of demonic power in the believer.

You did not come into this world as a believer. During your life before Christ you opened the doors of your soul to the one who had plans to destroy you. You opened these doors through your thoughts, the words you spoke, and the actions you took. You formed an agreement, an alliance if you will, with the enemy. Your agreement with the enemy is what gives him power over you.

Grace of God vs. the Lie of the Enemy

The enemy is predictable. His methods rarely change. If a person is in spiritual bondage here is how it happened: the spirit came in at a vulnerable moment in that person's life. It might have been a near-death experience because they were in an accident. Maybe, as a child, their mother told them they were ugly or they would never amount to anything. These can be major junctures, or turning points in a person's life. At these moments, there are always two things coming at that person:

- There is the grace of God for the moment.
- There is the lie of the enemy.

This happens every time! The age does not matter and the circumstances do not matter. There is the grace of God that says, "You are beautiful" and there is the lie of the enemy that says, "Your mom is right, you are really ugly."

At that critical moment the person must decide what they will believe. Will they choose the grace of God or the lie of the enemy? For those who are in spiritual or physical pain I know what choice they made. They agreed with the lie of the enemy.

> **Example:** Your mother died of cancer at the age of thirty. Your thirty-year-old sister also died of cancer. Tomorrow is your thirtieth birthday and the enemy says to you, "Tomorrow you're thirty. You're going to get cancer this year and you will die before your thirty-first birthday." It is a lie! It does not have to happen to you unless you agree with the lie.

Will you agree with the grace of God that says, "By His stripes you were healed two thousand years ago?" Or will you believe the lie of the enemy, which has fear attached to it? Will you agree with the lie of the enemy and say, "I have known this all my life and now the time has come; I probably will die this year"?

If you take the lie you have just made an agreement with the enemy and it will not be long before the spirit of fear, cancer, and death set up camp in your soul and cancer will manifest in your body. That's always how the enemy gets a stronghSatan has no power over us unless he can deceive us and trick us into coming into agreement with him. It is our agreement with him that gives him power. We must not come into agreement with his lies!

Apekduomai

Many years ago, Terry Law preached a sermon on how Satan has been stripped of his power.

> *And having spoiled principalities and powers, he made a show of them openly, triumphing over them in it. (Colossians 2:15 KJV)*

The word translated spoiled is the Greek word *apekduomai*. The simple definition is: to strip. Terry Law had diligently researched this word and shared the richness of its meaning.

According to Terry the word *apekduomai* was a Roman military term. It was actually the name of a ceremony that took place after two opposing forces had engaged in a battle and one of the armies had been defeated. At the end of the battle the two generals of the two armies would meet on the battlefield. Dressed in their full military attire the captains, all other officers, and all who served with these generals would assemble on the battlefield.

Then the winning general would approach the losing general and begin to strip him of all his rank and titles. He would say, "What was yours is now mine by right of conquest. Whatever lands you hold are now mine. Whatever titles you hold are now mine. Whatever riches or servants or households you owned are now mine by right of conquest." What a sight that must have been!

General McArthur was the commander of the US forces during World War II. He was a student of military history. When we won the war against Japan he required the commander to meet him on a ship in the Pacific. There he conducted an *apekduomai*.

Colossians 2:15 tells us that on His way back to heaven Jesus stopped off in the heavens and performed an *apekduomai*. The word *triumphing* in that same verse means to shout approval and make a procession or parade. Jesus made an absolute spectacle of His enemy, Satan. I can just see and hear Jesus saying,

- "Satan you were called Lucifer, morning star; I am the Bright & Morning Star.
- You were called the anointed cherub that covers; I am the Anointed One.
- You are called that old serpent; I am the serpent lifted up in the wilderness for the healing of a nation.
- You were called an angel of light. I am the Light of the World.
- You are called the prince of this world. I am the Prince of Peace, King of Kings.
- You were one of God's prized angels. I am the Son of God."

Can't you just see all the dancing, the cheering, and shouting that must have taken place in heaven as the sound of victory and the report of this event was noised far and wide in the spirit realm?

Do not miss this point. Satan lost his power that day. He no longer has any power of his own to operate in the earth today. He was stripped of all power. The principalities have been spoiled. The only weapon Satan and his demons have is deception.

You, on the other hand, have tremendous power.

> *For verily I say unto you, That whosoever shall say unto this mountain, Be thou removed, and be thou cast into the sea; and shall not doubt in his heart, but shall believe that those things which he saith shall come to pass; he shall have whatsoever he saith. (Mark 11:23 KJV)*

Jesus said, *"You will have WHATSOEVER you say."* Words spoken have the creative power of God embedded in them to cause whatever is spoken to come to pass. If Satan can get you to agree with him then you have just given him the use of your power. It is your words and actions that will empower him.

Example: If your father was an alcoholic and his father was an alcoholic you will never become an alcoholic if you never take that first drink. In the act of taking that first drink you come into agreement with the enemy who says, "Your father was an alcoholic. Your grandfather was and you will be an alcoholic as well." Not taking a stand against these negative words is a form of agreement. Once this agreement is made, the enemy has the right and the power to pass the curse of alcoholism on to you.

Do Not Agree with the Enemy of Your Soul

Although it is true that you, as a believer, are at war it is also true that your enemy, Satan, is a defeated foe. He is only able to create bondage in your soul with your permission and cooperation.

When you come into agreement with thoughts given to you by the enemy, and/or speak words in agreement with those negative thoughts, and/or you take actions based on those thoughts, or maybe you do all three, the enemy will use those agreements to take over the rule of a part of your soul and to manifest sickness and disease in your body.

Let me say again, "I do not believe a Christian can be demon possessed." Possession is about ownership and Satan does not own you.

> *For ye are bought with a price: therefore glorify God in your body, and in your spirit, which are God's. (1 Corinthians 6:20 KJV)*

As believers, we were purchased by God. However, we can be oppressed and harassed by the enemy in the area of our soul: our mind, will and emotions. The enemy can be, and often is, camped in the territory of your soul and often times must be evicted in order for the healing to manifest.

> *Behold, I give unto you power to tread on serpents and scorpions, and over all the power of the enemy: and nothing shall by any means hurt you. (Luke 10:19 KJV)*

The word power in this verse is two different words in the Greek. The first is the Greek word that means authority. The second Greek word translated power means ability. The good news is that Jesus has given you power, authority, over all the power, ability, of the enemy.

You have authority over any giant's ability to stay encamped on any part of your Promised Land. Make no mistake! The giant will not always leave just because he no longer belongs on the land. It is your responsibility to drive him out of your Promised Land. God will work with you to give you the victory but you will have to drive the giant or enemy out.

Some left when you were born again. Some left when you got filled with the Holy Spirit. Some will leave as you study the Word of God, but some are stubborn and will refuse to leave on their own accord.

> **Example:** You may be born again but you constantly struggle with irrational fear. You've prayed, quoted Scripture, had the elders pray, and still fear rules every area of your life. This is demonic bondage and the spirit of fear must be kicked out before peace can be restored.

This kind of demonic influence, left unchecked, can affect your mind, will, and emotions, and will eventually manifest in your body as sickness and disease. Whatever you allow in your soul will eventually manifest in your body.

We will discuss this at length in the next lesson. For now, let me simply say, "You must be willing to deal with the issues of the soul in order to walk in divine health." If you are ministering to others sometimes they will need to deal with their own giants before their healing will manifest.

Activation Time

- ➢ Halal, using your attributes of God list, for 2 minutes..
- ➢ Pray in the Holy Spirit, with passion, for 5 minutes.
- ➢ Activation: Ministry Teams

Activation Description

Rejection is a major hindrance to healing in the Body of Christ. You will find this in both men and women, but more so in women. All autoimmune diseases have a link to the spirit of rejection. You must get the person delivered from rejection in order to get them healed of something like fibromyalgia or diabetes.

When dealing with a spirit of rejection extra steps are usually required.

We wrestle not against flesh and blood but against powers, principalities, rulers of darkness. (Ephesians 6:12 KJV)

There are some spirits that only have power to rule in the darkness. When exposed to the light (the truth), they lose their power to rule.

And you shall know the truth, and the truth (that you know) shall make you free. (John 8:32 KJV)

Jesus was talking to believers about the bondage that sin brings and He revealed a powerful tool for setting the captives free: truth. In John 17, Jesus as He was praying for His disciples, tells us that the "Word of God is truth."

Sanctify them through thy truth: thy word is truth. (John 17:17 KJV)

Rejection seems to be one of those spirits that can only rule in darkness. When a spirit of rejection has successfully operated in someone for a long time the result is the person begins to believe the lie that they are rejected by God as well. Therefore, you will need to deal with the lying spirit as well as the spirit of rejection, because they always travel together.

The traditional approach (repenting and renouncing) is rarely sufficient to deal with a spirit of rejection and the lies that come with it. The good news is: they are very vulnerable to the light/truth. Therefore, subjecting them to truth, the Word of God, ALWAYS works.

Leader Demonstration:

- ➢ Ask for a volunteer who has had problems with rejection.
- ➢ Instruct him/her to relax, turn all their thinking and judging off, and just listen while you speak truth to their spirits.
- ➢ Begin to speak the truths found in Psalms 139 and Romans 8:35, 38, and 39 as though it was God speaking to them. Speak to them in the first person.

For example: "I have searched you and I have known you. I have encompassed your path. Where can you go from My presence? If you ascend up into heaven, I am there. If you make your bed in hell, behold, I am there. If you take the wings of the morning, and dwell in the uttermost parts of the sea; even there shall My hand lead you and My right hand shall hold you. If you say, "Surely the darkness shall cover me;" even the night shall be light about you. How great are My thoughts toward you? If you could count them, they would be more than the grains of sand on the earth." (Psalms 139)

➢ When you hit a point where you feel the anointing of God, "dig in" at that point. Let God prophetically give you the words to expand the thought.

For example: "On those days when you made your bed in hell, when you thought I had left you and you felt all alone, I was there." When you determined to make your bed in hell, I said, "I guess we shall both sleep in hell tonight, because I will never leave you or forsake you." (Psalms 139)

"Nothing can separate you from the unconditional love I have for you. No tribulation, distress, persecution, famine, nakedness, peril, sword is able to change My love for you. Neither death, not life, nor angels, nor principalities, nor powers, nor things present, nor things to come, nor height, nor depth, nor any other creature, shall be able to separate you from the love of God, which is in Christ Jesus our Lord." (Romans 8:35, 38, 39)

➢ Use your own words to talk about how God created them as individuals with unique voice-prints and God can pick out their voices among the millions.
➢ Gently weave in the Gospel message since it is the power of God unto salvation (sozo – the whole package which includes deliverance).
➢ Speak about the awesome price God paid through Jesus so they could have access to God; the love of God that knew no price too great to bring them back into fellowship.

After about five minutes of speaking these truths, you will be able to see the truth has done its job. The person probably will be crying and you will sense they are ready to reject the lie they have believed for so long. You will find that it is now easy to dislodge. The truth has set them free!

➢ Gently lead him/her through a prayer of repentance for believing the lie that they were rejected by God. Have him/her break their agreement with a lying spirit. Tell him/her to relax and then you command that spirit to go. Have him/her take a deep breath. (Follow procedure covered during Lesson 7 activation.)
➢ Again gently lead him/her through a prayer of repentance for allowing the spirit of rejection to operate in their lives. Have him/her break their agreement with the spirit of rejection. Tell him/her to relax. Then you kick out the spirit of rejection. Have him/her take a deep breath. (Follow procedure covered during Lesson 7 activation.)
➢ If you want to be good at healing, you must learn how to deal with this spirit.

Divide class into groups of two and have them minister to each other using Psalm 139 and Romans 8:35, 38, & 39 to deal with the issue of rejection.

Assignment

- Meditate on and memorize the memory verse.
- Add 5 more attributes of God to your list.
- Begin your daily prayer time by halaling for at least 5 minutes using your list of attributes.
- Pray in the Spirit 15 minutes a day.
- Practice declaring the truths found in Psalms 139 & Romans 8:35, 38,
- Speak out Psalm 139 in the first person. (A guideline is provided at the end of this lesson.)
- Ask God for a divine appointment to minister to somebody who struggles with rejection.

Assignment Results and Comments

Psalms 139 & Romans 8:35, 38, 39

I have searched you and I know you.

I know your sitting down and your rising up.

I understand your thoughts while they are yet afar off.

I have sifted you and searched out your path.

I am acquainted with all your ways.

I am before you and behind you.

I have laid my hand on your head.

My knowledge of you is high above you and you cannot reach it.

My thoughts of you are so numerous, they are as the grains of sand on the earth and you could never count them.

You're not a mistake for I formed you in your mother's womb.

You are fearfully and wonderfully made.

I had an image of you long before I formed you in your mother's womb and I wrote a book about your days. I have a plan and purpose for your life.

I will never leave you or forsake you.

Nothing can separate you from My love; not tribulation, or distress, or persecution, or famine, or nakedness, or peril, or sword.

You cannot flee from My presence.

My Spirit is with you no matter where you go.

If you ascend into heaven I am there and when you make your bed in hell, I am there.

My love for you is unconditional.

I so wanted to spend eternity with you, I sent My only Son, Jesus, to die on the Cross just for you.

LESSON 9 - Heal the Sick

Memory Verses

And as you go, preach, saying, The kingdom of heaven is at hand. (Matthew 10:7 KJV)

Heal the sick, cleanse the lepers, raise the dead, cast out devils: freely ye have received, freely give. (Matthew 10:8 KJV)

Introduction

*I*n Matthew 10, Jesus chose twelve disciples and sent them out to the lost sheep of the house of Israel. His instructions to them were to preach the Kingdom of Heaven is at hand, heal the sick, cleanse the lepers, raise the dead, and cast out devils.

Did you notice Jesus did not tell us to pray and ask Him or Father God to heal the sick? They have already done their part. Jesus said, *"Heal the sick."* We have the delegated authority of Jesus, the Word of God, and the power of the Holy Spirit to heal the sick, cleanse the lepers, raise the dead, and cast out devils.

In Matthew 28 the disciples were instructed by Jesus to teach all nations to observe all the things He had commanded them to do.

Go ye therefore, and teach all nations, baptizing them in the name of the Father, and of the Son, and of the Holy Ghost: (Matthew 28:19 KJV)

Teaching them to observe all things whatsoever I have commanded you: and, lo, I am with you always, even unto the end of the world. Amen. (Matthew 28:20 KJV)

We are to do the things Jesus taught the disciples to do. We have a mandate from Him to preach the Kingdom and to heal the sick, cleanse the lepers, raise the dead, and cast out devils. That's the full Gospel.

There is no sickness and disease in the Kingdom of Heaven. As believers, we are to declare and enforce His will and His Kingdom rule in the earth. Therefore, there is a need for the Body of Christ to know how to receive and how to minister healing and deliverance to others.

Diversity in Methods

Just as there is diversity in the Godhead there are many different methods of ministering healing and deliverance.

Benny Hinn creates an atmosphere in his crusades through praise and worship for the Holy Spirit to manifest. When a person is touched by the Holy Spirit in their body they are asked to come forward and testify as to what God has done. He then prays for them.

Bill Johnson usually travels with a team of students who are training under his ministry. He lines the students up in front of the congregation and they speak out words of knowledge as to the physical needs of people in the audience. He has those who are suffering with the conditions spoken by the students stand. The students then go to the people, lay hands on them, and minister healing.

The God Squad goes to people on the streets. God gives them words of knowledge and they simply pray the Prayer of Faith.

Cal Pierce, founder of Healing Rooms in Spokane, Washington trains people to minister in teams of two or three people. People come to the Healing Rooms and receive ministry from these teams. He also has a program to train and release people to open healing rooms in their city.

These are all valid methods of ministering healing and deliverance. They are not the only valid methods. I mentioned only a few just to make my point of the diversity that we see in healing ministries. I'm sure you can think of others as well.

Although the practical application or method may vary there is a common thread I have seen in every successful healing ministry. That common thread is dependence on the Holy Spirit. This is the example Jesus gave us during His earthly ministry. Remember?

> *Then said Jesus unto them, When ye have lifted up the Son of man, then shall ye know that I am he, and that I do nothing of myself; but as my Father hath taught me, I speak these things. (John 8:28 KJV)*

Jesus stripped Himself of His divinity, clothed Himself in flesh and became our example of how man, filled with the Holy Spirit, is to live his life on earth. Every miracle He performed during His earthly ministry, He did as the Son of Man empowered by the Holy Spirit.

The method of ministering healing and deliverance we will be discussing in this chapter is one of the many that are available to us as believers. It is meant to be a guideline or starting place for ministry. However, it should never be considered the one and only way to minister healing.

As discussed in an earlier lesson if we are to see the lame walk, the blind see, raise the dead, and cast out devils, we too must develop an intimate relationship with the miracle worker, the Holy Spirit. Our first responsibility in ministry is to minister to the Lord. We must spend time in His Word and in His presence. All other ministry is to flow out of our daily relationship with Him.

As we continue with our study, please remember that no practical application or method of ministry is to ever replace our dependence on the Holy Spirit.

Ministering Healing and Deliverance

In an earlier lesson we learned that Jesus never separated healing and deliverance. We saw that He often cast out demons when, in the natural, it appeared that what the person needed was healing.

> *And, behold, there was a woman which had a spirit of infirmity eighteen years, and was bowed together, and could in no wise lift up herself. (Luke 13:11 KJV)*

If you are going to pray for the sick to be healed you must be willing to cast out devils. There is no such thing as a Healing Ministry void of ministering deliverance, not if you want to see them all healed.

The Church, as a whole, has avoided the ministry of casting out devils because deliverance is not always a pretty sight. When Jesus cast out a demon there was often a big uproar and it was often messy. The demon would throw the person to the ground or there would be some attempt of violence. Jesus seemed to allow this behavior.

Have you ever wondered why Jesus allowed that kind of behavior? I have. As I meditated on this I remembered that He had not yet been to the Cross. There was a power struggle still going on in the spirit realm: the kingdom of darkness against the kingdom of Light. Jesus' goal was to establish His kingdom on earth and demonstrate His superiority in the spirit realm. Casting out devils was a demonstration of His power over the devil and his kingdom.

I also noticed that most of Jesus' ministry was public and to unbelievers. Casting out of demons was a public display of His power over anything that had power over God's people and a sign and wonder toWhen I first began ministering healing/deliverance it was what I called "on-the-job training." It was early in my walk with God. I had no formal training. My pastor was not teaching it from the pulpit. God just kept bringing people to me who needed deliverance.

All I knew was Jesus commanded them to go and they went, even though it was not always pretty. I want to tell you it was not much different for me at first. I have been grabbed, scratched, people threatened to hit me, they vomited, fell on the floor, etc. Not a pretty sight! When we finished, they were exhausted and so was I.

For years I went to every healing conference and healing class that was available to me. The methods and results seemed to be the same. After a few years I began to shy away from praying for deliverance for anybody. I would pray and believe God for healing, but deliverance I left to somebody else.

I came to a point in my life when I began to seek God for His perfect will in my life. I realized that my heart's passion was in the area of healing. As I refocused on ministering healing, God began to show me that if I wanted to see them all healed I had to be willing to minister deliverance.

I began to pray, "Okay Lord, I'm willing to be used in ministering healing and deliverance. If there is a better way than I have experienced in the past, please show me." Once I made that commitment, I was reminded of:

> *And having spoiled principalities and powers, he made a show of them openly, triumphing over them in it. (Colossians 2:15 KJV)*

Jesus defeated the devil on the Cross of Calvary. There is no longer a power struggle going on between the kingdom of darkness and the Kingdom of Light. The victory is already won on earth and in the spirit realm. The devil is already defeated and he knows it!

Matthew 28:18-20

And Jesus came and spake unto them, saying, All power is given unto me in heaven and in earth. (Matthew 28:18 KJV)

Go ye therefore, and teach all nations, baptizing them in the name of the Father, and of the Son, and of the Holy Ghost: (Matthew 28:19 KJV)

Teaching them to observe all things whatsoever I have commanded you: and, lo, I am with you always, even unto the end of the world. Amen. (Matthew 28:20 KJV)

The word power in verse 18 is a Greek word that means authority.

My prayer became, "Okay God! All authority has been given to Jesus in heaven and in earth and He has delegated that authority to the believer. I'm a believer. I have authority over the enemy and his tactics. There must be a way to minister deliverance without allowing the enemy to manifest during the process." God is so faithful!

It was not long after praying that prayer that I found myself in a healing training class with Rev. Cheryl Schang who was of the same opinion. God had given her a vision, a picture, to help her relate to what was happening in the spirit realm.

She saw an ugly demon with long claws. As soon as the person agreed with the demon, the demon gained the legal right to sink his claws into the person. This made it very difficult to dislodge him.

When the person renounced the words or actions that formed the agreement the demon lost his grip. The demon was still there hoping the person would change his or her mind so he could grab hold again. However, once the demon let go it was easy to say, "Be gone." The demon would leave with no pain or fuss. It was as if the person became slippery and there were no claws for the demon to use to grab them.

Words or actions form an agreement that allows the demon to attach itself. Undoing that agreement by renouncing the words or actions removes the legal right for the demon to hold on.

Since I changed my method of ministering deliverance it has gotten much easier. It works and the person does not go through so much pain. They are refreshed rather than worn out and there are fewer manifestations. Usually people will just cough, burp, or yawn as the demons go.

By design, the following method is most effective for one-on-one ministry. It not only sets the person free and heals their body; the process teaches them how they got in the condition they're in and how to stay free once delivered. However, with a little modification I have used this process successfully when ministering to a crowd as well.

Before we go any further, let me say that although there is healing for the unbeliever, which we will discuss at length in a future lesson, we do not normally do deliverance on the unsaved. The process we will be discussing is for use when ministering to believers.

The Process

I love it when I pray for a person and the manifestation of healing comes instantly. However, if the healing does not come when I pray, I know there is a good chance that something is blocking the manifestation of the Glory of God, the healing/deliverance in that person's life.

> *Insomuch that the multitude wondered, when they saw the dumb to speak, the maimed to be whole, the lame to walk, and the blind to see: and they glorified the God of Israel. (Matthew 15:31 KJV)*

When they saw the healing, the people glorified God. Healing is what brings glory to God, not sickness. If the healing does not come instantly something is blocking the Glory of God. When someone is in bondage emotionally, spiritually, and physically, the question we need to ask is: "What is blocking God's glory in this person?"

Think for a moment. If a person could have the full Glory of God displayed in them what would it look like? What would it look like on this person? What would be true about them? They would have victory, confidence, and freedom. If you are ministering to someone and they do not display victory, confidence, and freedom in their life, then the glory is blocked.

> **For example:** The spirit of rejection is easily recognized in a person. I can usually sense the "I'm not worthy" feeling coming from them. They usually seem closed and withdrawn. I know that's not how Jesus acted and I always use Him as my model.

> *Hereafter I will not talk much with you: for the prince of this world cometh, and hath nothing in me. (John 14:30 KJV)*

Jesus was the only one who lived His life completely free of bondage. So when I see something that does not match the model, I zero in on that place. What is the thing that is causing that discrepancy?

The following process is a method of determining what is blocking the healing from being manifested and how to deal with those issues.

- ➤ Identify the enemy.
- ➤ Repent, renounce, and break your agreement.
- ➤ Cast the enemy out.
- ➤ Command the body.
- ➤ Thanksgiving.

Identify the Enemy

The first step to healing and deliverance is to identify the real enemy. One must never assume that every problem a person has is because of spiritual interference. Sometimes, it is just one's lack of self-control or laziness or habitual negative thought patterns.

Romans 6:12-14

> *Let not sin therefore reign in your mortal body, that ye should obey it in the lusts thereof. (Romans 6:12 KJV)*

> *Neither yield ye your members as instruments of unrighteousness unto sin: but yield yourselves unto God, as those that are alive from the dead, and your members as instruments of righteousness unto God. (Romans 6:13 KJV)*

> *For sin shall not have dominion over you: for ye are not under the law, but under grace. (Romans 6:14 KJV)*

Each person is in charge of governing their own soul: their mind, will, and emotions. This can be very difficult at times, because each day is filled with new challenges for our souls. Will I lose my temper today? Will I get out of bed at 6:00 A.M. and pray? Will I go one more day without a drink? Sin is to no longer have dominion or rule over the believer.

> *For the weapons of our warfare are not carnal, but mighty through God to the pulling down of strongholds; (2 Corinthians 10:4 KJV)*

> *Casting down imaginations, and every high thing that exalteth itself against the knowledge of God, and bringing into captivity every thought to the obedience of Christ; (2 Corinthians 10:5 KJV)*

The imagination and thought pattern of an individual opens the door for the enemy to operate in their life. The believer must learn to cast down any imagination or thought that is contrary to the Word of God and replace those thoughts with the truth found in the Word of God.

> *Finally, brethren, whatsoever things are true, whatsoever things are honest, whatsoever things are just, whatsoever things are pure, whatsoever things are lovely, whatsoever things are of good report; if there be any virtue, and if there be any praise, think on these things. (Philippians 4:8 KJV)*

The battle is real and the battlefield is in the mind, will, and emotions, the soul, of the individual. The good news is we have not been left to our own ability or will power. We have been given the Holy Spirit and as we yield to Him, we receive power to control our thought life and overcome any sin in our lives.

> *Submit yourselves therefore to God. Resist the devil, and he will flee from you. (James 4:7 KJV)*

Unfortunately, there are those who are only looking for a quick fix. They are not willing to fight the good fight of faith. They just want somebody to pray, wave a magic wand over them and make everything right. They are not willing to do their part. They are not willing to submit to the Word of God nor are they willing to resist the devil. They allow their imagination and thought patterns to run wild and wonder why their life is such a mess.

> *But be ye doers of the word, and not hearers only, deceiving your own selves. (James 1:22 KJV)*

Sometimes the individual needs to close the door they opened that is allowing the enemy to operate in their life by simply doing what the Word of God says to do.

Then there are those who are very diligent in their walk with the Lord and are still in a battle with the one who wishes to destroy their soul. They are still struggling with obsessions, anxiety, anger, fear, alcoholism, depression, lust, rejection and all kinds of sickness and disease. They have been prayed for over and over again and have done all they know to do, but they still do not have the victory. This is usually an indication that there is spiritual interference of some kind.

Once it has been determined there is a spiritual issue that needs to be addressed, it is time to focus on discovering the specific spiritual issue that is blocking the manifestation of the Glory of God in that person.

If you are praying for someone at the altar, you may only have a few minutes to get a Word of Knowledge, cast out a spirit, command the healing and thank God for the recovery. I have prayed for people at the altar under these conditions and many have been healed. However, many times the things that have brought people into bondage have built up over decades and it often takes a little more time to get them healed.

When I agree to pray for someone's healing, I am always committed to spending whatever time it takes to get a breakthrough. If the total healing does not come I will stay until something changes to indicate that the healing process has begun.

The Interview

Always allow some time for the person to describe what is going on in their particular situation. Many times God has already revealed to the person issues that need to be addressed. They come with their list. I love it. It makes my job a lot easier. Others come and they do not have a clue what the issues are. They may not even be aware that they have any issues.

Being a good listener is vital during this time. Ask questions and pay close attention to their response to those questions. Listen and look for clues that will help to diagnose the problem. Remember you are looking to identify any possible demonic activity and their entry points.

> **For example:** If fear is the issue when was the first time the person remembers experiencing overwhelming fear? What was going on in the person's life at that time?

When dealing with the demonic, the enemy can be spotted by doing the following:

➢ Look and listen for things that seem to be in control of the person to whom you are ministering. Identify any life-controlling issues or patterns.

> **For example:** I have met people who despise themselves for looking at pornography, but they cannot stop. I have met people who said, "I really, really wanted to

go to the party, but I could not face the possibility that people would not find me likable." When I hear these things I know I am dealing with something that has control over the person. I know if I say to them, "Just use your willpower" I will do more damage than good. They usually have really tried but their willpower hasn't worked. Something is controlling them.

➢ Listen to the words they speak. They will help you identify how the enemy has gained power. They will also reveal what kind of spirit is operating.

For example: A spirit of unbelief says, "You know I really do not believe this process is even going to work. I'm not really sure God wants me delivered. I know I seem really out of control to the point that I have to be drugged, but I am not sure I have a demon." Talk about a spirit of unbelief!

A spirit of rejection says, "I am so lonely. No one really likes me, my friends just put up with me, and God probably just puts up with me too!" It is a demon when the person says they never really believed they were important to anybody or never believed they would amount to anything or never believed they could succeed in anything.

It is also important to note that identifying the spirits at work in a person's life by listening and observing the person never negates the need for praying and asking God for a Word of Knowledge.

Word of Knowledge

A Word of Knowledge can be a major key to a person receiving their healing. It can open up an otherwise skeptical person to receive. As the person talks listen to them but at the same time listen to the Holy Spirit. The Holy Spirit will give you a picture or a word about when or where the enemy has a grip.

When God reveals something to you that they know there is no way you could know unless He told you it can cause the person's faith to rise to a level of receiving.

The interview may reveal many mental and emotional issues that the person needs to deal with. When physical healing is needed you are trying to identify the why, where, and when the enemy gained a stronghold in the person's life. You are looking for that specific thing that is blocking the Glory of God from being manifest.

A Word of Knowledge not only gives you a place to start, it often helps to pinpoint the event or time in the person's life that opened the door for the enemy.

For example: The Lord may say to you, "At the age of twelve his/her family moved from Ohio to Florida because his/her three year old brother got pneumonia every winter because the weather was bad in Ohio. That same year after moving and taking a farm job in Florida, his/her father died as a result of a farming accident. He/she has always blamed the younger brother for the father's death and he/she has never forgiven the younger brother."

He may say all that to you but in my experience that would be a rare occurrence. Usually, a Word of Knowledge is just that: "A" word.

For example: Normally, I would hear the number twelve. That's it! Just the number twelve! I would then ask the Lord, "Are talking about his/her age or did something happen about twelve years ago?"

It is alright to ask God questions! Once I believe that He is talking about his/her age, I ask God, "What happened to him/her at the age of twelve?" Sometime He may tell me but often times all I get is: silence.

It is alright to ask the person you are praying for questions, too. So I say to him/her, "Did anything traumatic happen to you when you were about 12 years old?" The person responds, "We moved from Ohio to Florida because of my younger brother's health and my father was killed in a farming accident shortly after that." Bingo!

By asking him/her questions about how he/she felt having their lives, as they knew it, disrupted you will probably find that he/she had some resentment toward the younger brother. After all, it was because of him that he/she had to leave all their friends and start all over in a new school. If they had not moved to Florida because of him maybe their father would still be alive. Blame, bitterness, anger, and unforgiveness will eventually manifest as sickness and disease in the physical body if left unchecked. These issues must be dealt with before healing can come.

When you are praying for someone and hear a Word of Knowledge from the Lord always assume God knows what He is talking about. Always assume that the Word of Knowledge is correct even if the person cannot or will not confirm it.

You will find that most people discount things that they did before they got saved. It is important that you ask the question this way, "At any time in your life have you been involved in or have you experienced _____?" (Fill in the blank with the appropriate issue or spirit.)

When the Holy Spirit puts His finger on an issue it is always for the purpose of restoration. Remember these are God's people, He loves them, and wants to see them set free from their bondage. Make it easy for them to open up. Make sure there is no judging or condemning tone in your voice.

Once they open up they usually want to tell you all the gory details. If the story is graphic (sexual or violent) do not let them tell you all the details. It will create a mental image in your mind that you will have to fight off and can hinder you from getting a clear Word of Knowledge concerning their situation. Tell the person you do not need to know the whole story.

If you are trying to get a person free of all bondage then deal with whatever comes up. If a physical healing is necessary, you may or may not have to deal with all the issues revealed by God. You are looking for the specific issue that is blocking them from receiving God's best for their lives.

Make a list

If you have the luxury of an hour or more, as the person speaks, make a list of the potential spirits that could be operating. Pray for the discernment and ask questions. The circumstances and experience will determine what questions need to be asked.

Some spirits travel in groups. Therefore, add to your list what I call collateral spirits. That is, if one spirit is revealed list all the spirits that normally travel with it.

> **For example:** lust always comes attached to a spirit of divination. If a person has ever been involved in the occult, you have to cast out all the sexual spirits too.

> A spirit of doubt attaches to a lying spirit.

Review your list with them. They may be surprised to see what you have put on the list. Let them know you will no doubt cast out some spirits that are not there, but it does no harm to cast out a spirit that is not there. My training has been when in doubt, cast it out.

Repent, Renounce, and Break Your Agreement

Having identified the enemy use the list you made and have them repent, renounce, and break agreement with each spirit on the list. Be led by the Holy Spirit as to where to start and the order to follow.

Sometimes it seems hard for a person to accept the fact they should repent when they are the real victims.

> **For example:** An adult who was raped by her father as a child may understand why they need to forgive the father but why does she need to repent of anything since it was not her fault? First of all, she will need to repent for allowing unforgiveness to operate in her life. Second, she will more than likely need to renounce the lie of the enemy that said her mother or even God did not take care of her. She will need to repent for receiving this lie. The fact that believing a lie is a sin can be a revelation to some people. (Eve believed the lie of the enemy.)

In any case, you are not having the person repent for the sin unless they have never repented for the sin. If you are dealing with Christians, this is rarely the case. If they have repented, God has forgiven the sin.

There is a difference between repenting for the sin and the kind of repentance you are asking them to do. You are taking them down to a very deep level, a legalistic level, because demons are very legalistic. They are dealing with the legal right for the demon to stay in their soul.

> **For example:** A person who tried to commit suicide has more than likely repented over and over again. The problem is: they stopped there. They need to repent for receiving the lie of the enemy that said suicide was the solution to their problem and for believing it was the only way out instead of looking to God for a solution to their problem.

They made an agreement with the lie of the enemy. They probably even spoke words like, "I hate myself. I wish I were dead." They will repeat their actions if they do not get to the root of the matter. Trying to commit suicide was a sin, but the root sin was swallowing the lie of the enemy that it was the only solution to their problem.

People who need healing and deliverance were faced with a choice at a time of offense or trauma in their life. At that moment there were two options available to them.

➢ The grace of God.
➢ The lie of the enemy.

At a critical moment, the person reached out and took the lie. I know they reached out and took the lie from the hand of the enemy of their God because they are in need of healing from some disease or deliverance. They are in bondage. Their emotions are messed up. They are taking seven kinds of drugs to try to handle their problems and manage their demons. They are in need of healing/deliverance because they believed a lie and made agreement with the enemy.

The enemy uses words that may sound familiar. "Ooh, your grandfather had this, your father had this, and you will get it too." He comes along to deceive you and the lie comes at you at some tender moment. When the person accepts the lie of the enemy he or she forms an agreement with the spirit by speaking words or taking actions in agreement with the lie.

Sometimes people remember the first time they agreed with the lie of the enemy. Often they were a child or a teenager. When they learn they swallowed a lie and that is how Satan got in they often say, "That's not fair."

Well hello! Satan is not fair and he has no code of ethics. If he can get you at five years old, that's even better. One of Satan's best plans is to keep you ignorant. His mission is to steal, kill, and destroy. Of course it is not fair. That's why we have a champion named Jesus!

Do not agree with the enemy. When this agreement is made the power to bring it to pass is released and the person is now battling sickness and disease in their body. They must repent of opening the door to this thing, inviting it in, receiving the lie, and coming into agreement with it. Get them to renounce their words and action and break their agreement with that spirit.

> **For example:** I repent for opening the door to the spirit of fear and giving it access to my life by believing the lie of the enemy. I repent for letting this spirit have control over my life and using me for its own purposes. I renounce any words I have spoken or actions I have taken in agreement with it. I break my agreement with the spirit of fear.

The repentance then is centered on removing the legal right for the spirit to operate and rule in the person's life.

You can minister deliverance to a person without any repenting or renouncing. Just be aware there will most likely be a demonic manifestation, just as there was when Jesus did it.

If the person is unwilling to repent I know I have authority and the demons have to go, but without their repentance I also know it could be messy. I have had people throw up or say, "Oh, that hurts, that hurts!" I've been grabbed, scratched, and all sorts of things. In addition, if they do not want to be free enough to repent chances are they will not be willing to do what they need to do to keep the demon out. Getting a person free is the easy part. The hard part is keeping it out.

I have now decided that if some people do not want to be free enough to repent, they can just keep all their demons.

There is an exception. When people are demon possessed, their minds are so gone that they cannot even agree with you and they cannot participate. In that case, bind the mind-controlling spirit. You can kick it out without their agreement and without their permission because you have the same Holy Spirit Jesus had.

Here is the problem. The spirits will be back, probably within 24-48 hours. You have only a small amount of time to teach the person how to resist the enemy so they can stay free.

When people take part in their own deliverance by repenting and renouncing their agreement, not only is the deliverance easy, you are teaching them how to stay free.

Remit the Sin and Break the Recompense

Whose so ever sins ye remit, they are remitted unto them; and whose so ever sins ye retain, they are retained. (John 20:23 KJV)

We know spirits attach to sin but I have found spirits will attach to the lie that the sins are not forgiven. Use the authority that Jesus gave the believers whom He sent out. At some point in the process quote the Scripture, and look the person square in the eye and say,

> ➤ "Based on your repentance, I use the authority delegated to me by Jesus and I declare those sins remitted."

Obviously, only God forgives sin. According to the dictionary the word remit means to transmit the payment, to refrain from exacting a tax or penalty, to cancel, to pardon or forgive, to restore to a former condition or position; to refer to another court for further consideration or action. So, we have the authority to declare these things done on earth because the Lord has already done them in heaven and earth.

> ➤ Declare this to them, "You are eternally separated from these sins, and they can no longer be held to your account. I forbid the enemy from extracting a penalty from you based on these prior bad acts. I break the recompense of these past sins and declare you will no longer eat the fruit of them."

I have found this declaration of sins remitted to be an extremely powerful deliverance tool. I have seen people delivered the moment I speak these words.

Do not stop there. The enemy must be cast out.

Cast the Enemy Out

Scripture gives us two different terms that Jesus used when dealing with evil spirits: rebuke and cast out. To rebuke means to forbid and cast out means to eject.

Once the legal rights are broken through the person's repenting and renouncing, take the list and, one by one, cast out the spirits.

During the casting-out process, stand to the side of the person and keep your eyes open. As the one doing the ministering you need to be aware of what is going on with the person at all times.

It is important that you remember you are not praying or asking the spirits to leave. You are commanding them to go and they must leave. You are the one in authority. Speak with a firm voice. Spirits only know what is in your heart or mind when you speak or take some action. Therefore, speak in a manner that is meant to convey a strong knowledge that you know they must go. Screaming at demons is not necessary. Just be firm.

- In the Name of Jesus of Nazareth Who came in the flesh and by the power of the Holy Spirit, I speak to the spirit of fear and command you to get out now. Get out!
- Instruct the person to take a deep breath and exhale after each spirit that you command to go. (Coughing and yawning are normal occurrences as the spirits are expelled. NO hyperventilating allowed.)
- Periodically check with the person to see if there is any tightness in the chest or pain in the head. If they are experiencing any discomfort, the spirit did not leave. Command it to go again! Remember to be firm. (The spirit of death may cause discomfort in the stomach area.

If the demon is not going out, one of two things is happening:

- The person did not mean their repentance or
- The spirit is hanging on to another spirit.

   For example: the spirit of suicide might be attached to a spirit of abortion. Both are murdering spirits.

- When you have completed casting out all the spirits on your list ask the person how they feel? A good response is "I feel lighter or even light headed."

After you are finished casting out, review the list. Deal with any spirit you overlooked. At this time also break any word curses, generational curses or ungodly soul ties that have been revealed.

Healing and deliverance is simple. We are simply undoing what the person did to bring the bondage. We are identifying and removing that thing that is blocking the Glory of God from being manifested in the person's life.

When the unclean spirit is gone out of a man, he walketh through dry places, seeking rest; and finding none, he saith, I will return unto my house whence I came out. (Luke 11:24 KJV)

Scripture teaches us that when unclean spirits are cast out they will return and try to get back in. However, the person should notice a difference once the spirit has been cast out. The spirits will seem to be on the outside speaking in, rather than on the inside speaking out. This is the time for them to use the term rebuke. They must forbid them entrance.

And when he cometh, he findeth it swept and garnished. (Luke 11:25 KJV)

> *Then goeth he, and taketh to him seven other spirits more wicked than himself; and they enter in, and dwell there: and the last state of that man is worse than the first. (Luke 11:26 KJV)*

Jesus had every weapon of the universe at His disposal and His weapon of choice, when Satan came to tempt Him (John 4), was the Word of God, the same weapon we have. If possible, you should give them the Word of the Lord that is the opposite of the lies the enemy has told them. If you uproot and cast out fear fill the empty place with power, love, and a sound mind.

> *For God hath not given us the spirit of fear; but of power, and of love, and of a sound mind. (2 Timothy 1:7 KJV)*

If they use these Scriptures on an ongoing basis, the enemy will flee and they will stay free.

> *Submit yourselves therefore to God. Resist the devil, and he will flee from you. (James 4:7 KJV)*

Command the Body

Once you are satisfied that all the necessary issues have been addressed and the person is free, it is time to command the body. It is time to speak and declare healing to the body. When commanding the body, be as specific as possible.

> **For example:** If the cause of the disease is a chemical imbalance, command the body to produce the proper amount to allow the body to function the way God created it to function.

Nurses and doctors have a working knowledge of how the body functions and how the body is affected by disease. This kind of knowledge can be very beneficial when commanding the body. I have a friend who is a nurse and I love to minister with her. I have learned so much from her in this area.

If you do not have the luxury of ministering with a nurse or doctor, ask the person. There is a very good chance that their doctor has explained in detail how their disease has affected their body.

However, details are not necessary.

> **For example:** If they have a heart problem simply command the heart to function the way it was created to function.

You will learn ways to be more specific as you go. The idea is to command the body to function as it was originally intended to function.

Thanksgiving

You are never finished with the healing session until you have given thanks. The Bible teaches us that there is a specific and unique power in thanksgiving.

It is a good thing to give thanks unto the LORD, and to sing praises unto thy name, O most High. (Psalms 92:1 KJV)

It is good or beneficial to give thanks to the Lord.

In everything give thanks: for this is the will of God in Christ Jesus concerning you. (1 Thessalonians 5:18 KJV)

In everything give thanks. Notice it did not say *for* everything give thanks. Everything is not from God. Sickness is a work of the enemy. Therefore, we are not to thank God for the sickness. But we are to thank Him in midst of it and in spite of the sickness.

Thou preparest a table before me in the presence of mine enemies: thou anointest my head with oil; my cup runneth over. (Psalms 23:5 KJV)

In the middle of a problem is where you want to give thanks. It will cause the situation to turn around. I have experienced breakthroughs in almost every area of my life through thanksgiving. So in spite of the problem, in spite of the sickness, give thanks. Thanksgiving will also protect your healing once you receive it.

The Old Testament priests and prophets seemed to have a revelation of the power of thanksgiving.

David: I Chronicles 16

When David brought the ark into Jerusalem he had a praise and thanksgiving service. He specifically appointed certain Levites to minister before the ark of the Lord. They were to record, thank, and praise the Lord God of Israel. David knew it was important to not only take territory but to protect the territory the Lord gave them. He knew praise was his offensive weapon and thanksgiving was his defensive weapon.

Hezekiah: 2 Chronicles 31

One of the first things Hezekiah did when he became king was to re-institute the activity of thanking and praising God twice a day. When he did, the nation of Israel experienced revival.

Daniel: Daniel 6

Daniel's custom was to pray (praise and thank God) three times a day. The other princes of the kingdom were jealous and conspired against Daniel. They persuaded the king to make a new law forbidding requests to be made to anyone except the king. When Daniel knew the decree had been signed he continued to pray to God even though he knew it would more than likely cost him his life. You know the rest of the story. Daniel was thrown into the lion's den. However, the mouths of the lions were shut and Daniel's life was spared. Remember, when you are thanking God lions cannot chew on you.

Paul

Paul picks up on this revelation in the New Testament.

> *Continue in prayer, and watch in the same with thanksgiving; (Colossians 4:2 KJV)*

The word watch means to be vigilant, to rise, to stay awake, to give strict attention to, to be cautious. It also means to take heed lest through laziness some destructive calamity overtake you.

I have seen people use their faith to receive things, even healing, but they are unable to keep it. They are often robbed of that which God blessed them with before they have had time to enjoy it. Thanksgiving is a form of watching over that which God has given.

Jesus

Jesus also had a revelation of the power of thanksgiving. When He needed a miracle, He gave thanks.

> *And Jesus took the loaves; and when he had given thanks, he distributed to the disciples, and the disciples to them that were set down; and likewise of the fishes as much as they would. (John 6:11 KJV)*

Before Jesus fed the five thousand He gave thanks.

> *Then they took away the stone from the place where the dead was laid. And Jesus lifted up his eyes, and said, Father, I thank thee that thou hast heard me. (John 11:41 KJV)*

Before Jesus raised Lazarus from the dead He gave thanks. Jesus thanked His Father that He, the Father, had heard Him, Jesus. Jesus thanked His Father for their intimacy and constant communication.

> *And if we know that he hear us, whatsoever we ask, we know that we have the petitions that we desired of him. (1 John 5:15 KJV)*

If we know the Father hears us then we have what we desire of Him. This verse had not been written in Jesus' time. But Jesus received all things from the Father and knew that since the Father always heard Him, He had what He desired of the Father.

Thanksgiving was Jesus' prayer of faith. He put His faith in the promise of the Father and expressed thanks for the promise, which He knew would bring the results. If you really believe you have what is promised what is there left to do but give thanks?

Thanksgiving is part of the process for getting a person healed. It is the prayer of faith. I am not asking you to do the old faith thing and just confess, confess, confess. I am asking you to thank Him for what you know to be true, not what you hope might be true.

Prayer: "Thank You Father! You are faithful to Your Word. Thank You Father! Your Word and Holy Spirit are at work in me, bringing healing and total restoration to every area of my body. Thank you Jesus! You did not just die that I could life eternally with You, You were wounded that I could be healed and walk in divine health in this lifetime. I declare that you are my Great Physician and by Your stripes I am healed."

Never forget thanksgiving when praying for healing.

I know all this sounds like a lot of work. It is certainly much longer than what Jesus did. I believe the better we get at hearing the *rhema* Word of God, the easier and quicker healings will come. Hearing the *rhema* Word of God was a skill that Jesus perfected. Jesus never even spoke a word unless He heard the Father say it.

Staying Free

Before closing the session instruct the person on how to stay free. Getting a person free is actually the easy part. The challenge is staying free. A person must engage in the fight of if they are going to stay free from demonic oppression and if they are going to maintain their healing.

Participating in their healing and/or deliverance helps them to become aware of their thoughts and actions that opened the door for the enemy to manifest in their bodies.

Give them a copy of "How to Keep Your Healing" which is provided for you at the end of this lesson.

Activation Time

- Halal, using your attributes of God list, for 2 minutes..
- Pray in the Holy Spirit, with passion, for 5 minutes.
- Activation: Ministry Teams

Activation Description

Divide students into ministry teams of three.

- Student #1 will receive ministry.
- Student #2 will minister to Student #1 using the healing process described in this manual. (Lesson 9)
- Student #3 intercedes and records any issues, revealed by the Holy Spirit during the interview, that need to be addressed. This list will be used by Student #2 during the repenting, breaking agreement, and casting out part of the process.

Instruct the students to rotate until each of them has received ministry, has recorded the issues, and has ministered using the healing process. (See Ministry Guideline)

Assignment

- Meditate on and memorize the memory verses.
- Add 5 more attributes of God to your list.
- Begin your daily prayer time by halaling for at least 5 minutes using your list of attributes.
- Pray in the Spirit 15 minutes a day.
- Ask God for a divine appointment with somebody who needs healing and/or deliverance.

Lesson 9 - Heal The Sick

Assignment Result and Comments

Ministry Guidelines

Identify the enemy:

- ➤ The interview – What do they want God to do for them?
- ➤ Word of Knowledge – Looking for the specific issue that is blocking healing/deliverance.
- ➤ Make a list – Issues to be dealt with.

Repent, Renounce, and Break Your Agreement:

Have the person repeat after you:

- ➤ I repent for allowing the spirit of _____ to operate in my life.
- ➤ I renounce every thought, word spoken, and action taken in the agreement with _____.
- ➤ I break all agreement with _____.

Remit the sin and break the recompense:

Declare the following to them:

- ➤ Based on your repentance, I use the authority delegated to me by Jesus and declare that those sins are remitted. (John 20:23)
- ➤ I further declare that you are eternally separated from these sins and they can no longer be held to your account. I forbid the enemy from extracting a penalty against you based on these prior bad acts. I break the recompense of these past sins and declare that you will no longer eat the fruit of them.

Cast the enemy out:

- ➤ In the name of Jesus of Nazareth, who came in the flesh and by the power of Holy Spirit, I speak to the spirit of _____ and command you to go! Now! Get out!
- ➤ Have them take a deep breath and exhale after each spirit you command to go.
- ➤ Periodically check with the person to see if there is any tightness in chest or head.

Command the body:

- ➤ Command the body to line up with the Word of God and be healed – function the way God intended it to function.

Thanksgiving:

- ➤ Thank God for the healing
- ➤ Partial manifestation: Have the person repeat after you.

Prayer: Thank You God! You are faithful to Your Word. Thank You God! Your Word and Holy Spirit are at work in me bringing total restoration to every area of my body. Thank You Jesus! You did not just die that I could live eternally, but you were wounded that I could be healed in this lifetime. I declare, "You are the Great Physician and by Your stripes I am healed."

How to Keep Your Healing/Deliverance

➤ Give them a copy

How to Keep Your Healing/Deliverance

Your deliverance is not complete - yet

(1) Evil spirits will seek to return. Jesus did not command them to go into the pit or hell, etc. (Matthew 12:43-45)
(2) When Satan tempted Jesus, he planned to renew his attacks on Jesus at an opportune time. (Luke 4:13)
(3) When the old thoughts or feelings return, you MUST resist and rebuke the spirit.(James 4:7)

Some reasons why deliverance may not be realized

(1) Evil spirits will seek to return. Jesus did not command them to go into the pit or hell, etc. (Matthew 12:43-45)
(2) Lack of true repentance. Repentance means a change of attitude and behavior. In the Bible the word for repentance is *Teshuva* which means to TURN from sin and return to God.
(3) Failure to confess sins. (1 John 1:9; James 5:16)
(4) Failure to forgive others. (Mark 11:25-26; Matthew 18:21-35)
(5) Failure to break with the occult. (Acts 19:13-19)
(6) Unwillingness to be completely honest with God.

Requirements to keep your healing/deliverance

(1) Yield every area of your life to the Lordship of Christ. (John 1:11-12; Matthew 7:21-23)
(2) Be continuously filled with the Holy Spirit. (Ephesians 5:18; Romans 8:13)
(3) Live by the Word of God. (Luke 11:13; Matthew 4:4,7,10; Ephesians 6:17; Psalms 1:2; Psalms 119:48)
(4) Put on the whole armor of God by living the life that equips you. (Ephesians 6:10-18)
(5) Cultivate a renewed mind. (Romans 8:26-27; 2 Corinthians 10:3-5; Romans 8:5-7; Colossians 3:1-2)
(6) Pray in the Spirit. (Romans 8:26-27)
(7) Practice praise. (Isaiah 61:3; Isaiah 60:18; Hebrews 13:15)
(8) Cultivating right relationships. (Matthew 18:15-20; 1 John 1:7, 2:9-11)
(9) Develop a strong dynamic faith. (Romans 10:17; Mark 4:24)
(10) Practice confessing the Word of God. (Hebrews 3:1, 4:14, 10:23)
(11) Seek to obey the Lord in every area of your life. If you fail in any area, make your confession immediately. (1 John 1:9)
(12) Make Jesus Christ central in your life. (John 12:31-32)
(13) Learn to know how to crucify the flesh and resist the devil. (Romans 6:6, 6:11)
(14) Avoid those people who become a bad influence on your life. (James 4:4)

(15) Submit to the Lord and to one another in love and humility. (James 4:7, 1 Peter 5:5-6)
(16) Maintain a daily prayer life. (Matthew 6:9-13)
(17) Use your weapons of defense. (2 Corinthians 10:3-5; Ephesians 6:13-18)
(18) Use your weapons of attack: the Word, the Blood, the Name of Jesus, prayer, praise, and a positive faith confession.
(19) Maintain a disciplined life. (Romans 12:1-2; 1 Corinthians 9:27)
(20) Fast regularly to keep the cutting edge in your life. (Matthew 6:16-18)

The renewed mind, praise, and thanksgiving are absolutely essential to keeping your healing.

Common Issues and Spirits

Victim of Violence or Abuse: hatred, murder, fear, anger, death, rage, retaliation, resentment, suicide, abortion.

Fear: traumatic experience, phobias, hysteria, near death experience (this should be tailored to the actual event that caused the trauma.)

Rejection: self-hatred, fear of man, fear of failure, lying spirit, insecurity, inferiority, self-pity, loneliness, inadequacy, ineptness, shyness, persecution, paranoid, despair, depression, defeatism, hopelessness, discouragement can manifest as opposite spirits of: pride, judging, criticism, faultfinding, arrogance.

The Occult /Witchcraft:

- Divination: in all forms including Ouija boards, tarot cards, transcendental meditation, crystal balls, palm reading, horoscopes, psychics, etc. (you will find something in this category if they tell you they have a problem hearing the voice of God.)
- Sorcery: (the acts of the occult) idolatry, manipulation, magic, incantation, charms, fetishes, drugs, deception, control, word curses, covenants.
- Rebellion: (parents, teacher, boss, spouse) self-will, stubbornness, disobedience, pride.

Sexual Sin and Soul Ties: pornography, homosexuality, rape, incest, bondage, bestiality, prostitution, fantasy, masturbation, molestation, adultery, fornication, bondage, lust (whenever you find a spirit of lust, you will find a spirit of witchcraft. In fact, I usually ask about the occult question first and if they answer yes to anything in that category, I tell them that I also know that they fight a spirit of lust because these two hang out together. This takes the pressure off them to admit a spirit of lust.)

Generational Curses: alcohol, drugs, or any addiction such as gambling, health problems, learning problems, fears, poverty, gluttony, compulsive, mental illness, adultery, "bad luck."

False Religions/cults: worship of Mary for Catholics, Islam, Buddhism, Taoism, Hinduism, Shintoism, Confucianism, Jehovah's Witness, Christian Science, Rosicrucianism, Mormonism, Bahaism, etc. This category would also include anything they put before God, including Masons, cults, secret societies such as sororities or fraternities where they swore oaths.

Unforgiveness: Go all the way back to childhood, parents, teachers, and anyone who might have embarrassed them or let them down. This could even include a parent who died early and "left" them.

LESSON 10 - Dealing with Issues

Memory Verse

Finally, brethren, whatsoever things are true, whatsoever things are honest, whatsoever things are just, whatsoever things are pure, whatsoever things are lovely, whatsoever things are of good report; if there be any virtue, and if there be any praise, think on these things. (Philippians 4:8 KJV)

Introduction

Let me say again: I do not believe that a Christian can be demon possessed. In fact, in America the demon possessed person is rare. However, both sinner and believer can be oppressed in the area of their soul: their mind, will, and emotions.

As sinners we had demonic activity in the area of our souls. Some of us had more than others. But the good news is these demonic forces leave, at different times, triggered by certain events in our Christian life.

Salvation

A large number of these demonic forces leave when a person receives Christ as their Lord and Savior. They cannot hang on beyond the truth of the Gospel.

Baptism

Other demonic forces leave at baptism. The Rabbis of the Old Testament believed that running (living) water had the ability to separate a person from demonic forces. Before a woman could marry she had to dip in living water to be spiritually purified. It was called a *mikvah* and it was believed to separate her from all the demons of her childhood or generations. This would let her come to the marriage spiritually clean.

In ancient Israel all the men over the age of thirty had to perform the same type of ritual before the High Holy Days. This was so they did not take demons into the Temple with them.[21] In fact, this is what John the Baptist was doing. He was cleansing the men during the time of *Teshuva* which came before the Day of Atonement.

There is scriptural basis for this belief. Numbers 19 talks about the water of separation. If a man touched something dead, he had to be cleansed by the water of separation. It was believed that spirits pass at death and they could transfer to the person who touched the dead body. There are various Scriptures that talk about a person having to wash with water after certain actions so that they would be ceremonially clean.[22]

In this way Scripture instructs that a ceremony of water has the power to separate one from uncleanness. When you are baptized, we believe, by faith, anything connected with your old life, including demonic powers, is put to death in your life and you are raised to a new life in Christ.

Why then does it appear that some of the demons survive the water? It is because we take them back, through agreement.

> **For example:** If you had a spirit of addiction operating in your life before baptism, the power of that spirit to operate in your life is broken when your old life is buried with Christ. However, the voice of your former captor sounds so familiar, you soon speak words and take actions in agreement with the enemy and you return to bondage just as quickly as you left it. Sometimes the spirit and his buddies return so quickly that you're not even aware of the fact they left.

When the unclean spirit is gone out of a man, he walketh through dry places, seeking rest, and findeth none. (Matthew 12:43 KJV)

Then he saith, I will return into my house from whence I came out; and when he is come, he findeth it empty, swept, and garnished. (Matthew 12:44 KJV)

Then goeth he, and taketh with himself seven other spirits more wicked than himself, and they enter in and dwell there: and the last state of that man is worse than the first. Even so shall it be also unto this wicked generation. (Matthew 12:45 KJV)

The problem is rarely getting free; it is staying free. This is why after you are born again you should attend a good Bible-believing Church.

Exposure to the Word of God

And ye shall know the truth, and the truth shall make you free. (John 8:32 KJV)

Sanctify them through thy truth: thy word is truth. (John 17:17 KJV)

---

[21] Berthelson, Lou., "Holiness for these Awesome Days" Destiny Image Publishers, Shippensburg PA, 1991, 85-86

[22] Leviticus 11, 15, 17, 22

Lesson 10 - Dealing With Issues

How can truth, the Word of God, set a person free? In the spirit realm, when you know the truth, you walk in the light. When the rulers of darkness are exposed to that light, they lose their power to rule in your life.

Submit yourselves therefore to God. Resist the devil, and he will flee from you. (James 4:7 KJV)

As you submit yourself to God's Word the enemy will flee. Believers need to be exposed to as much truth as possible in order to ensure their freedom.

Deliverance

Those spirits that hang on beyond the truth of the Gospel, baptism, and exposure to the Word of God do so because the agreement with them has not been broken even though the person is born again.

How can this happen? The person continues to speak words or to take actions in agreement with the spirit which constantly reinforces the hold that the spirit has on them. A stronghold is established in the person's soul and the spirit becomes what we call a "strongman spirit." This means the spirit becomes the most powerful, longest resident, or most firmly entrenched spirit in the person's life. In one person it may be fear or in another it may be rejection.

For the weapons of our warfare are not carnal, but mighty through God to the pulling down of strong holds; (2 Corinthians 10:4 KJV)

Casting down imaginations, and every high thing that exalteth itself against the knowledge of God, and bringing into captivity every thought to the obedience of Christ; (2 Corinthians 10:5 KJV)

First, God tells us that our weapons can pull down strongholds; then He goes on in the next verse to tell us what makes up a stronghold. From this passage it is plain to see strongholds are made up of imaginations and thoughts. Strongholds are in a person's mind.

If strongholds are things we think inside our heads then it only makes sense that the stronghold can be broken if we deal with the thinking. Thoughts become knowledge and knowledge becomes actions. To break the strongholds we renounce the words and actions that formed them. The agreement being broken, the spirits can easily be cast out.

Remember, these children of God have fallen into a trap and are victims, hostages of the enemy. The bondage of the enemy blocks the Kingdom of God from manifesting in their lives. They are God's creation. They have been bought with a price and He wants to be glorified in His people. God wants His children free and He wants us healed.

Once the spirits that are at work in a person's life are cast out we can command healing of the body and expect healing to manifest, or the very least the healing process to begin. The remainder of this lesson addresses suggested guidelines in dealing with a few common issues that hinder the believer in receiving their healing.

Unforgiveness

The Bible says that we must forgive in order to be forgiven.

For if ye forgive men their trespasses, your heavenly Father will also forgive you: (Matthew 6:14 KJV)

But if ye forgive not men their trespasses, neither will your Father forgive your trespasses. (Matthew 6:15 KJV)

We discussed ministering to those with unforgiveness issues in detail in Lesson 7. Therefore, please refer to Lesson 7 concerning dealing with unforgiveness.

However, let me say that surprisingly unforgiveness is a big issue in the Body of Christ. This is partly because most Christians do not understand how events that occurred even before they got saved can influence their life today. And partly it is because daily life presents us with opportunities to come in agreement with unforgiveness, thereby opening the door for a variety of demonic activity in their lives.

Perhaps another reason is that it is difficult for some to understand why they need to forgive when it is not them who did anything wrong. We must help them understand that, by holding onto unforgiveness not only are they holding the person in bondage but they are also putting themselves in bondage, making it impossible for them to receive from the Father. It is only in the releasing of unforgiveness that God can minister to either of these individuals.

Remind the person that forgiving the one who abused or raped them is not saying that what they did was right. You are asking them to repent not for the act that was committed against them but for allowing unforgiveness to operate in their life when God has said they are to forgive.

Then said Jesus, Father, forgive them; for they know not what they do. And they parted his raiment, and cast lots. (Luke 23:34 KJV)

Jesus was sinless. He did not deserve the death of the Cross. But as He hung on that cross He said, *"Father, forgive them for they know not what they do."* Wow! He's our example.

Then came Peter to him, and said, Lord, how oft shall my brother sin against me, and I forgive him? till seven times? (Matthew 18:21 KJV)

Jesus saith unto him, I say not unto thee, Until seven times: but, Until seventy times seven. (Matthew 18:22 KJV)

Jesus tells us that no matter how many times somebody has mistreated, rejected, or spoken evil of us, we are to forgive. This was not a suggestion. It was a commandment.

Pray and ask the Holy Spirit to reveal to the person anybody that they need to forgive. He/she needs to verbally forgive each person the Holy Spirit brings to their mind.

For example: Have them say, "Father I choose to forgive: my mother for not being there when I needed her, my father for the verbal abuse . . ."

It is not necessary for them to speak loud enough for you to hear clearly, but it is important that they declare the forgiveness so they can hear themselves speaking. Ask them to let you know when they are finished. Give them all the time they need to respond to the Holy Spirit is guidance. Then lead them in a prayer of repentance for allowing unforgiveness to operate in their life, have them break all agreement with unforgiveness, and kick it out.

Depression/Rejection

Depression/Rejection is another issue that is very prevalent in the Body of Christ. Events of the past can be at the root of current depression in a person. As it is with unforgiveness, opportunities for one to be depressed occur on a daily basis.

When dealing with depression you may also have to deal with rejection, self-hatred, fear of man, fear of failure, lying spirit, insecurity, inferiority, self-pity, loneliness, inadequacy, ineptness, shyness, persecution, paranoid, despair, defeatism, hopelessness, discouragement can manifest as opposite spirits of: pride, judging, criticism, fault-finding, arrogance, etc. It is not necessary to memorize all of these spirits. Just be led by the Holy Spirit and deal with any of them that comes to mind.

Remember, depression and rejection thrives in darkness. Therefore, before and during the process of deliverance (repenting, renouncing, etc.) it is always helpful to sow light, the Word of God, into the person. Declaring what the Word of God says always dispels darkness. The darkness will lose its grip and can easily be cast out. (See Lesson 8)

Abuse/Violence

Abuse most often is thought to refer to sexual abuse. Although it can refer to sexual abuse there are other forms of abuse. Those who have been victims of any kind of abuse are prime candidates for the operation of other kinds of spiritual activity in their lives.

In deliverance ministry we have discovered spirits like to nest together. Have you wondered where the term kindred spirits comes from? Kindred spirits are spirits that are similar and like to hang out together. The spirit of abuse and the spirit of violence seem to be kindred spirits. Where you find one you usually find the other.

In addition, the spirit of hatred, spirits of murder, anger, death, rage, retaliation, resentment, and suicide can all be attached to a spirit of abuse or violence. One gets in and holds the door open for its buddies.

When you find one of these spirits look to see what else might be attached to it. You can ask questions like, "Did you ever think about murdering anybody? Do you lose your temper? Do you fly into a fit of rage?" If the answer is yes to these kinds of questions you know there are kindred spirits present.

You can also tell which demons are operating by the thoughts the person has. If they are having thoughts of suicide they may or may not have a demon but for sure there is a spirit of suicide hanging around trying to get the person to agree with it. Never leave a person with the possibility of a spirit of suicide operating in their life. When in doubt, cast it out. If it is not there, there is no harm done.

Fear

And he said, I heard thy voice in the garden, and I was afraid, because I was naked; and I hid myself. (Genesis 3:10 KJV)

Fear is the first negative emotion to be recorded as the result of Adam's disobedience in the garden.

For God hath not given us the spirit of fear; but of power, and of love, and of a sound mind. (2 Timothy 1:7 KJV)

Fear is not from God. It came to mankind as the result of Adam believing the lie of Satan rather than the Word of God. An acronym for the word fear is **f**alse **e**vidence **a**ppearing **r**eal. The lies of the enemy of God appeared more real to Adam than the truth of God's Word. He came into agreement with the lie of the devil.

Fear can come in at any point, but a common point of entry is any traumatic experience.

For example: Maybe when they were in the first grade they gave the wrong answer and the teacher made fun of them in front of the whole class.

Near-death experiences are a huge entry point. If a person almost died as a result of a car accident it is possible for a spirit of death and/or a fear of death to come in at that point. All it takes is for the person to say something like, "I should have died" and the door is opened to fear.

The event produces fears, phobias, and hysteria. Usually when there is fear of one type it holds open the door for other fears as well. If they have a fear of death they may also have a fear of insufficiency or fear of failure or claustrophobia. When left unchecked fear will manifest in a variety of different diseases in the physical body. Therefore, many times fear must be dealt with before healing of the body can manifest.

Be led by the Holy Spirit and deal with each fear. Use the process previously discussed in this manual. Instruct them to repent for allowing the fear, whatever the type might be, to operate in their life, have them break their agreement with fear and cast it out. Then command the body to be healed and give thanks.

Sexual Sins

The entry point for a sexual sin is almost always pornography. This entry point is so common that I do not ask people, "Have you have you ever looked at pornography?" Instead, I was taught to ask them, "At what age did you first encounter pornography?"

The age is not the real issue. However, the question takes the focus off of the fact that they are or at least at some point have been involved with pornography and focuses on when it first happened. This seems to make it easier for them to admit their involvement with pornography.

Lesson 10 - Dealing With Issues

Notice that also I used the word encounter. The use of the word encounter takes the blame off them.

For example: Maybe a friend gave them the magazine and by the time they opened the pages to see what it was the image had already registered. The enemy will replay those images in the person's mind until they are in total bondage to pornography. Given the opportunity the person will eventually act out any number of perverted sex acts.

Pornography is an entry point for the spirit of lust. That spirit of lust says to the person, "Wouldn't you like to try what you saw?" And when the person does it says to that person, "You know, now, that's not enough. Wouldn't you like to try something else and something else and something else?" Once the spirit of lust gains entrance and develops as a stronghold it will hold the door open for other spirits such as adultery, fornication, sexual perversion, sThese spirits can lie dormant for many years. Then one day they rise up and the person finds themselves with major sexual addictions and they become involved in a variety of sexual sins. The person ends up in total sexual bondage.

People who come for deliverance are shocked when they learn that looking at pornography at the age of fifteen allowed the spirit of adultery to have access to them and now their marriage is a mess. They often say, "My marriage is a wreck. My life is down the tubes. Why didn't somebody tell me?"

In addition to pornography another common entry point for sexual sin is child abuse. Again, always take the focus off any possible personal blame when ministering to those who have been victims of child abuse. It will make it easier for people to ease into a discussion of the sexual issues if you soften it in this way.

When ministering to those with sexual issues it is an absolute necessity that the ministers not have any judgmental spirit operating in them. Remember, these people are victims of a demonic plot to entrap them.

As I mentioned before, spirits travel in groups: one gaining entry and then holding the door open for others. Therefore, if you deal with a spirit of lust you will need to address the spirit of witchcraft and rebellion. They always hang out together.

Obviously, unforgiveness will need to be dealt with as well.

Soul Ties

Our soul consists of our mind, will, and emotions. Soul ties are created when a person becomes emotionally one with another person or has sex with someone. There are natural, good, and holy soul ties that were created by God.

Therefore shall a man leave his father and his mother, and shall cleave unto his wife: and they shall be one flesh. (Genesis 2:24 KJV)

The intimate relationship between a man and a woman in the marriage setting creates Godly sexual soul ties. Likewise, the emotional soul ties that exist in a family between brothers, sisters, mother, and father are God-created soul ties.

Unfortunately we are capable, with our free will, of polluting the godly soul ties and of creating soul ties that were never of God.

> **For example:** When a mother becomes over dependant and controlling in her relationship with her son ungodly soul ties can develop.
>
> Kids pricking their fingers and mixing their blood to become blood sisters or blood brothers can also be an unholy alliance.
>
> Any sex act outside the covenant relationship of marriage between a man and woman creates ungodly soul ties.

Let's say a young man looks at Playboy Magazine. It causes him to seek the opportunity to try what he has seen. What you focus on always develops in your life. Given the opportunity, the young man commits fornication, which is sex outside of marriage, opening the door for all sort of demonic activity and sexual perversion in his life.

Later in life he marries and becomes one flesh with his mate. However, they are really struggling in developing their God-ordained intimate relationship. Why?

The bad news is: you bring all your soul ties, good or bad, into any new relationship, even the God-ordained marriage relationship. No matter how the soul tie was made, demons can pass along the lines of ungodly soul ties. This young man brought a lot of spiritual garbage into his marriage relationship. His wife is exposed to all his spiritual garbage and she can be unknowingly repelled by it.

In Genesis 34 we find the story of Shechem, who raped Dinah, Jacob's daughter.

> *And his soul clave unto Dinah the daughter of Jacob, and he loved the damsel, and spake kindly unto the damsel. (Genesis 34:3 KJV)*

The Scripture says, "*And his soul clave unto Dinah. . .*" The word clave is the Hebrew word *dabaq* which means to cling or adhere to. When soul ties are created each person gets a piece of the other person's soul.

> **For example:** Imagine two colored pieces of construction paper glued together, one yellow and one purple. After the glue has dried, if you try to separate them, little pieces of yellow paper will end up on the purple and vice versa. (This is a good visual – demonstrate when possible.)

It is the same in the spirit realm. If you make a soul tie with someone, the person is walking around with a piece of your soul.

One way of creating or receiving soul ties that is often overlooked is through blood transfusions.

> *For the life of the flesh is in the blood. (Leviticus 17:11 KJV)*

The word for *life* in this verse is the Hebrew word *nephesh*. It comes from the word *naphash* which means to breathe. The word *nephesh* is most often translated *soul*.

*God breathed life into man and man became a living soul **(nephesh)**.(Genesis 2:7 KJV)*

*Shechem's soul **(nephesh)** clung to Dinah. (Genesis 34:3 KJV)*

So the verse in Leviticus 17:11 could have appropriately been translated, "*The soul is in the blood.*" For this reason, when breaking soul ties, break the soul ties that might have come as a result of blood transfusions.

Breaking Soul Ties

It is important to break any and all emotional and sexual unholy soul ties, regardless of how they were made.

> **Example:** Rev. Cheryl Shang tells this story about a woman who started having dreams of having sex with other men years after she was married. These men were not men she recognized. She would wake up feeling so sinful and dirty. She would repent in case there was anything in her that could be causing this. During the day she had no problems with her thoughts. She was completely in love with, devoted to, and faithful to her husband. Why the dreams?
>
> She told a friend about this and the friend recommended she pray before going to sleep. This did not change anything. Then she visited a prophetic conference. A prophet gave her a word that she needed to break her soul ties. She broke all her soul ties and the dreams stopped that same day. She has never had one since. Those people were out there sinning with a piece of her soul clinging to them and it was affecting her.

Breaking these soul ties will stop the flow of demonic activity. This is good but not complete. There are still people walking around out there with pieces of your soul clinging to them. You need to release the parts of the souls that have clung to you and call back the parts of your soul that have clung to another. Then ask God to make you whole again.

> **Prayer example:** In the Name of Jesus, and by the power of the Holy Spirit, I break every unholy alliance or soul tie I have made with my body or that have come to me as a result of sharing blood. I release the part of other's souls that have clung to me and I call back any part of my soul that has clung to others. God, I ask that you make me whole again.

I have had people say that they feel whole for the first time, in a very long time, after praying this prayer.

Generational Curses

Generational curses are very common among believers. When an issue is repeated from generation to generation it is a generational curse. If a person tells you poverty, alcoholism, or heavy use of tobacco runs in their families, it is a spirit of addiction that has come down the generational lines. Ever wonder why when people stop smoking they usually gain weight? They traded one addiction for another. Instead of tobacco, they are now addicted to food. The spirit of addiction just changed clothes. You must also deal with the spirit of addiction.

A generational spirit is a familiar spirit. It is a spirit that hangs around you during your lifetime. It knows all about you. It knows your favorite color and what you ate for breakfast.

Familiar spirits like to hang around families. When your father dies that spirit tries to come to you. It knows you. It knows your family and wants to stick around. However, spirits cannot just jump on you. There has to be a door that is open. You open that door with your agreement. Remember, an agreement is formed by words or actions.

Every male in your family may have been an alcoholic but you will never be one unless you take a drink. Every woman in your family may have died at the age of forty from breast cancer but you won't unless you enter into an agreement with the spirits that caused it.

When doing deliverance for generational issues, have the person repent for agreeing with the familiar spirits and renounce their words or actions that opened the door and then kick it out.

Freemasons

Freemasonry is another cause of illness that falls in the generational curses category. Ron Campbell has written an excellent book on the subject. What you will read next comes from his book, "Free from Freemasonry."

A part of the secret rights of the Free Masons is to swear oaths and speak curses. Some of these curses are outright curses, and some are veiled ones.

> **For example:** one of the rituals every member must perform is to put on a blindfold and say, "I have long been in darkness and I now seek to be brought into the light."

These are unthinkable words for a believer to say! When people make the declaration, with the breath of God, that they are in darkness the power is there to bring that to pass. An agreement is made that is not of God and a door is created in the spirit realm.

There is also a ritual that involves putting a cable tow around the throat, chest, and stomach. Then the man swears oaths such as, "If I ever divulge Masonic secrets, I will have my throat cut from ear to ear, my heart torn out, be disemboweled, and my body cut in two." As a result we find members of the Free Masons have a higher rate of throat disorders, heart and respiratory diseases and chronic stomach problems.

The families of Free Masons also have a higher rate of some plagues than the general population. These include:

> ➢ Poverty: perpetual financial insufficiency, fearful of not having enough, even with lots of money in the bank.

- Barrenness and impotency, together with miscarriages and female-related problems.
- Divorce and other breakdown of family relationships.
- Chronic sickness: heart problems, cancer, respiratory problems, allergies, throat ailments, strokes, and attacks of the mind.
- Defeat and failure: unrealized potential
- Mental illness: torment and confusion
- Traumas: always putting out fires
- Accident prone
- Premature and violent death

When you are praying for healing and you suspect or you get a word relating to a curse from the Free Mason spirit, you should follow the procedure described earlier. Repent, renounce, and cast out.

False Religion/Idolatry

Another common stronghold is false religions or idolatry, the worship of something other than God. This might be praying to saints and Mary, being a part of the Masons, being a part of a secret society, or joining fraternities and sororities where you took a pledge or made an oath. I have never heard of a sorority or fraternity that did not have something in the oath that could be a potential problem. Even saying you pledge your oath to the sorority or fraternity may take your allegiance away from God.

Breaking Covenant

Another unsuspected cause of illness can be found in 1 Corinthians 11:29-30.

For he that eateth and drinketh unworthily, eateth and drinketh damnation to himself, not discerning the Lord's body. (1 Corinthians 11:29 KJV)

For this cause many are weak and sickly among you, and many sleep. (1 Corinthians 11:30 KJV)

Paul is speaking here about what we have come to call communion. Jesus said, *"This is my body which is broken for you. This cup is the New Testament* (covenant) *in my blood."* This was the ancient language of covenant. Jesus was signaling the disciples that they were making blood covenant with Him.

A blood covenant was an all-encompassing oath. There were always two elements to entering into a blood covenant: blessings and curses. Without these two elements it was not a legitimate blood covenant.

When we make covenant with Jesus, He makes covenant with us. He lays down His individual life as well as His right to withhold any good thing from us. If we are walking in a covenant relationship with the Lord we can ask for good things with confidence. He cannot deny us any good and perfect thing.

In return, we are to lay down our individual lives and through the observance of the blood covenant we call communion we make a pledge not to deny Him any good thing He desires of us. When we refuse that which He requires of us we break covenant with Him.

Jesus declared, in verse 30, that the curse of breaking this covenant is sickness and death. God does not take sickness and put it on us at that point. The sickness will come because we invite it in with our actions. We open the door by our agreement with the enemy to not honor our commitment to God.

To reverse the effects of this curse follow the process mentioned earlier. Repent, renounce, and cancel that curse.

> **Prayer example:** By the power of the Holy Spirit, I repent for breaking covenant with the Lord. I break the power of the curse for breaking covenant. I command this curse to fall to the ground and bear no fruit in my life."

Summary

The connection between the body and the soul is a well-documented medical fact. Whatever you allow in your soul will eventually manifest in your body. If you worry you get ulcers. Stress can cause a heart attack. The list of spiritual issues that are at the root of disease is unending. The truth is we are still discovering connections all the time.

I have given you only a few examples and guidelines on how to deal with them. Some of these examples are common issues and some not so common. No matter what the issue is the main key to success in any deliverance session is hearing from God.

> *Trust in the LORD with all thine heart; and lean not unto thine own understanding.*
> *(Proverbs 3:5 KJV)*

Regardless of how you have ministered to a person with the same issue before you must always be sensitive to the Holy Spirit. A Word of Knowledge from God always trumps any understanding, training, guideline, or experience you have. When you are looking for the name of the spirit, emotion, or the trigger event, you can safely assume every single time that when the Lord puts His finger on something it is a factor in the healing.

After the issue is identified it is still important to allow the Holy Spirit to lead you in the deliverance process: the repentance, breaking of agreement, casting out of spirits, commanding the body, and even the thanksgiving for their healing. The study, training, and experience you have are important in that they give the Holy Spirit truths to use as He leads you. However, you should always be open if He leads in a new or different way.

This is why it is important to develop a lifestyle of Bible study, praying, and spending time in His presence. The more sensitive you become to recognizing His voice, the more successful you will become when ministering deliverance.

Word of warning: NEVER recommend that someone stop taking their medicine or go against doctor's orders. That is practicing medicine without a license and in the U.S. that will get you into trouble. If the person asks you about medication tell them they should ask God and get advice from their doctor. If the healing has started to manifest to the point they do not need medication tests will confirm it.

Activation Time

- Halal, using your attributes of God list, for 2 minutes..
- Pray in the Holy Spirit, with passion, for 5 minutes.
- Activation: Ministry Teams

Activation Description

Divide students into ministry teams of three.

- Student #1 will receive ministry.
- Student #2 will minister to Student #1 using the healing process described in this manual. (Lesson 9)
- Student #3 intercedes and records any issues, revealed by the Holy Spirit during the interview, that need to be addressed. This list will be used by Student #2 during the repenting, breaking agreement, and casting out part of the process.

Instruct the students to rotate until each of them has received ministry, has recorded the issues, and has ministered using the healing process.

Assignment

- Meditate on and memorize the memory verse.
- Add 5 more attributes of God to your list.
- Begin your daily prayer time by halaling for at least 5 minutes using your list of attributes.
- Pray in the Spirit 15 minutes a day.
- Ask God for a divine appointment with somebody who needs healing and/or deliverance.

Assignment Results and Comments

Common Illnesses and Demonic Roots

This is a sample list of illnesses and common demonic roots. It is designed to help you to begin to see how the spirit, soul and body are linked together. **Please do not let this list be a replacement for the *rhema* word.**

- ADD: attention deficit disorder. Double mindedness and self-rejection, also deaf and dumb spirit
- Addictions: reduced serotonin levels. Low self-esteem and those things that accompany it.
- Alcoholism: and other chemical additions – can be an allergy. Usually a generational familiar spirit.
- Arthritis: (inflammation of the joints) – bitterness and anger. Not being jointly fit together with the rest of the body.
- Autoimmune Diseases: the immune system mistakenly attacks self, targeting the cells, tissues, and organs of a person's own body. Most autoimmune diseases strike women more often than men; in particular, they affect women of working age and during their childbearing years. The spiritual implications are astonishing. As we attack ourselves spiritually the body eventually agrees and starts attacking itself physically. This includes diseases such as MS, diabetes, lupus, psoriasis, etc. The roots of these diseases are often rejection, self-hatred, and guilt.
- Back/Spine problems: spiritual alignment. Usually out of alignment with spiritual authorities. Doctors who deal with the back will tell you that a misalignment of the spine will cause inflammation or disease in various organs. We have heard of people receiving improved eyesight, restored hearing, and even improved bladder control, when the issues of the spine were corrected. Can also be a demon of scoliosis, sciatica, etc.
- Cancer (cells in rebellion): caused by spirits of rebellion and regret. Curse it at the root. Look for rebellious behavior. Cast out spirit of cancer and rebellion or regret. Command both of the anti-oncogenes to be present and functional.[23]
- Breast Cancer: conflict and resentment between females.
- Liver Cancer: fornication, adultery, and/or pornography (Proverbs 7:21-23).
- Hodgkin's: (cancer of lymph) bitterness and rejection from father.
- Leukemia: (cancer of the blood) bitterness and rejection from father.
- Cholesterol: often found in people who are angry with themselves.
- Endometriosis: can be caused by abortion – interruption in hormone cycle.
- Fibromyalgia: often found in healthy females who tend to be stressed, tense, depressed, anxious, striving, driven, a perfectionist. Deal with the spirit of fear and striving, also rejection and self-hatred.
- Gallstones: anger and resentment.
- Headaches: witchcraft and/or guilt.

---

[23] Wright, 138

- Manic Depression: inherited mental disease caused by a continual underproduction of serotonin as a result of a defect on the 27th lower right-hand side of the X chromosome.[24] Also spirit of depression.
- Obsessive Compulsive Disorder (reduction in serotonin levels): Fear of man, fear of failure, fear of abandonment, fear of rejection, control spirit.
- Osteoporosis (bone deterioration): envy and jealousy results in rottenness of the bones (Proverbs 14:30)
- Ovarian and Breast Cysts: relationship problems with mother or sister. Unresolved issues involving a breach, no fellowship.
- Paranoid Schizophrenia (malfunction of two neurotransmitters): result in over-secretion of nor epinephrine and over-secretion of dopamine and serotonin. Two competing demons of rebellion and self-rejection.
- Skin eruptions (rashes, humps, bumps, hives, and shingles): anxiety, stress, and fear, usually coupled with self-rejection.
- Vein problems: root is anger, rage and resentment – can be internalized.
- Viruses: It is a life form that is capable of self-action. Consider viruses to be Spirits of Infirmity.

The purpose of this list is to give the reader a picture of the relationship that exists between body and soul and is not meant to be conclusive. No list should negate the importance of receiving a Word of Knowledge from God and/or the leading of the Holy Spirit. Being led by the Holy Spirit is the major key if we are to follow Jesus' example a

---

[24] Wright, 58

LESSON 11 - Healing for the Unbeliever

Memory Verses

In those days came John the Baptist, preaching in the wilderness of Judea, (Matthew 3:1 KJV)

And saying, Repent ye: for the kingdom of heaven is at hand. (Matthew 3:2 KJV)

Kingdom of God Has Come to You

This was the message John the Baptist preached (Memory Verses). After John was thrown into prison the Bible tells us that Jesus began to preach the same message.

From that time Jesus began to preach, and to say, Repent: for the kingdom of heaven is at hand. (Matthew 4:17 KJV)

When Jesus sent the disciples out, He instructed them to preach the same message and then to demonstrate the power of God through signs and wonders, healings and deliverances.

And as ye go, preach, saying, the kingdom of heaven is at hand. (Matthew 10:7 KJV)

Heal the sick, cleanse the lepers, raise the dead, cast out devils: freely ye have received, freely give. (Matthew 10:8 KJV)

When He sent out the seventy they were to heal the sick and preach the same message.

And heal the sick that are therein, and say unto them, the kingdom of God is come nigh unto you. (Luke 10:9 KJV)

This kingdom message was an integral part of the work and earthly ministry of Jesus.

But if I with the finger of God cast out devils, no doubt the kingdom of God is come upon you. (Luke 11:20 KJV)

The phrase *"finger of God"* was very familiar to the Jewish people of Jesus' day. The first time that phrase was used in the Bible was in the book of Exodus.

Then the magicians said unto Pharaoh, This is the finger of God: and Pharaoh's heart was hardened, and he hearkened not unto them; as the LORD had said. (Exodus 8:19 KJV)

Moses had gone before Pharaoh demanding the release of God's people. He performed many signs and wonders but the magicians were matching Moses, sign for sign, wonder for wonder, until he reached a certain level and the magicians could no longer duplicate what Moses was able to do.

At that point the magicians said, "We cannot do this. This must be the Finger of God." This was a phrase that meant this power you see is more powerful than any power on earth. When Moses confronted the demonic forces of the magicians and he proved that he had power over them it was a type of casting out devils.

The Exodus was a defining moment in Jewish history. When Jesus used the phrase *"finger of God"* the Jewish mindset would have automatically flashed back to this time in their history.

The Exodus was about the delivering power of God and the making of a nation, a people set apart unto God. When the descendants first went into Egypt they were only tribes of kinsmen. The slavery, Moses' confrontation with Pharaoh, Passover, leaving with the silver and gold, not a feeble one among them, parting of the Red Sea, and the giving of the Ten Commandments on Mt. Sinai were all part of the Exodus. The result was that under the mighty hand of God they came out of Egypt a nation. They became the nation known as Israel, a people set apart by God.

Jesus' life, ministry, and death were the fulfillment of the prophetic picture of the Exodus. The atonement for sin was accomplished in His death. He made it possible for all mankind to enter the Kingdom of God by faith in the work of the Cross. Jesus' shed blood paid the price and made it possible for God to have a people set apart unto Him.

This first part of this Kingdom message, the delivering power of God and the fact that it had come to you, the individual, was the focus of Jesus' life and earthly ministry.

Up until the time of Jesus the Jewish people had no concept of salvation for the individual. There was a sacrifice for sin, which was necessary because they were sinful men, born in a sinful world, and separated from God. There was also a trespass offering for those sins one personally committed. Therefore, they had the concept of sin and separation from God but in the Jewish mindset there was no salvation apart from the nation of Israel. Once a year, on the Day of Atonement, the High Priest would go into the Holy of Holies, offer a sacrifice and make Atonement for all of Israel. Their only concept of salvation was one of national holiness and righteousness before God.

At the time of Jesus' earthly ministry there were two priestly sects: the Sadducees and Pharisees. The Sadducees were pretty much in charge of the temple and the Pharisees where considered the teachers, the Rabbis. The Sadducees believed God was only in the temple; it did not matter that the Ark of the Covenant had not been there for a long time. They still said God is in the temple and if you want to get to God you have got to go through us.

Jesus comes on the scene, takes God out of the temple, and takes Him to where the people live. The Kingdom message was: no longer do you have to go to the temple to find God nor do you have to go through anybody. God cares about you personally and He has come to you right here on the streets where you live to meet your need. To the Jewish mindset this was a radical concept.

The Jews were looking for the Messiah to come who would be like unto the Prophet Moses. The Sermon on the Mount was figuratively a picture of Jesus sitting in the Seat of Moses, outside the temple, interpreting the Torah. The healings, miracles, casting out of devils, signs and wonders were all proof that the finger or power of God was present to touch the individual.

When Jesus used the phrase "the finger of God" the hidden message was that He was the Messiah. The signs and wonders, the healings, and the miracles Jesus preformed were proof that He was who He claimed to be.

The Messianic Miracles

Now when John had heard in the prison the works of Christ, he sent two of his disciples, (Matthew 11:2 KJV)

And said unto him, Art thou he that should come, or do we look for another? (Matthew 11:3 KJV)

From prison John the Baptist sent two disciples to Jesus and asked, *"Are you the one?"* Are you the Messiah?

Jesus answered and said unto them, Go and show John again those things which ye do hear and see: (Matthew 11:4 KJV)

The blind receive their sight, and the lame walk, the lepers are cleansed, and the deaf hear, the dead are raised up, and the poor have the gospel preached to them. (Matthew 11:5 KJV)

Jesus' response to John was that the miracles He performed proved that He was the Jewish Messiah.

A Messianic Rabbi and scholar, Arnold Fruchtenbaum, made a significant discovery while studying at a library of old and rare books in Israel. He found evidence that the Rabbis prior to the first century decided they should have a process, a test if you will, for identifying Messiah.[25]

The Rabbis of the First Century were looking for a miracle-working Messiah. According to rabbinic tradition there were certain types of miracles that no human was able to perform and therefore some Jews believed only the Messiah would be able to perform them. It seems there were four miracles that the Jews believed were reserved for Messiah only.

---

[25] Fruchtenbaum, Arnold, Radio Manuscript No. 035, The Life of the Messiah, Ariel Ministries, Tustin, CA

Lesson 11 - Healing For The Unbeliever

With this in mind it is easy to understand that the performance of the following four miracles were not random acts of compassion by Jesus. There were performed with a purpose in mind. They were designed to validate that Jesus was the Messiah, the Son of the living God.

Healing of a Jewish Leper

The first Messianic miracle was the healing of a Jewish leper. Why?

The Rabbis had been given a process for curing many diseases, but not leprosy. It appeared there was no human cure for leprosy. The word leprosy means strike of God, or stroke of God, or a person associated with sin.

Generally under the Mosaic Law one could become ceremonially unclean or defiled by touching a dead human body, a dead animal body, or a live unclean animal body, such as a pig. But the only type of living human capable of causing defilement was a leper."[26]

Now here is a curious thing. Leviticus Chapters 13 and 14 give detailed instructions on what the Rabbis were supposed to do when a Jewish leper got healed. These chapters in Leviticus offer a beautiful prophetic picture of Messiah.

Once healed, a leper was to come to the temple and present himself. The priest was then to make an offering of two birds; one would be killed as the sacrifice and the other was to be dipped in the blood of the dead bird. The priest would then sprinkle the blood upon the one to be purified of leprosy and let the living bird go free. This is a prophetic picture of the redemption from sin that we would all experience through the Blood of Messiah.

For the next seven days they were to intensively investigate the situation to determine three things.

> ➤ Was the person really a leper?
> ➤ If indeed he was a real leper was he actually cured of his leprosy?
> ➤ If he was truly cured of his leprosy what were the circumstances of the healing?[27]

On the eighth day, there was to be a complex offering. The cleansed leper was to bring two lambs without blemish and they were to be offered for trespass and sin. Some of the blood was applied to the person being cleansed and then he was to be anointed with oil.

From the time these two chapters in Leviticus were written down until the time of Jesus no Jewish leper had been healed. Miriam sinned against her leader Moses and was struck with leprosy. She was Jewish and was healed but that was before the Levitical law was given. Naaman had leprosy and was healed. But he was a Syrian.[28]

The Hebrew mind always associated leprosy with sin so it was only natural to think that only Messiah could heal a leper because it would mean that he had power to forgive sins.

---

[26] Fruchtenbaum

[27] Fruchtenbaum

[28] 2 Kings 5

And it came to pass, when he was in a certain city, behold a man full of leprosy: who seeing Jesus fell on his face, and besought him, saying, Lord, if thou wilt, thou canst make me clean. (Luke 5:12 KJV)

According to this Scripture there was no doubt the man had leprosy. It says he was a man *"full of leprosy."* It is interesting to me that when the man approached Jesus he did not ask to be healed, cured, or any of the other words we associate with healing. He asked to be made clean.

The word clean in this passage is the Greek word *katharizo* and it means to cleanse. It does not mean to heal. It was never translated heal or healing in the New Testament. It was always translated cleanse, purify, purge, etc. Throughout the New Testament, this word cleanse is consistently used to speak of spiritual cleansing (forgiveness of sin), not healing.

A good example of the way this word was used when talking about something other than leprosy is found in 1 John 1:9:

If we confess our sins, he is faithful and just to forgive us our sins, and to cleanse us from all unrighteousness. (1 John 1:9 KJV)

When the man declared Jesus could cleanse him if He wished he was making a declaration that Jesus was the Messiah and He had the power to forgive sins. The leper believed Jesus could forgive his sin. His lack of knowledge of God caused him to question whether or not Jesus was willing to do so.

And he put forth his hand, and touched him, saying, I will: be thou clean. And immediately the leprosy departed from him. (Luke 5:13 KJV)

Jesus forgave the man's sins (cleansed him) and the leprosy disappeared. Jesus had fulfilled the first Messianic miracle. He healed a Jewish leper.

And he charged him to tell no man: but go, and show thyself to the priest, and offer for thy cleansing, according as Moses commanded, for a testimony unto them. (Luke 5:14 KJV)

Jesus healed the Jewish leper and what instruction did He give to the man? "Go and show yourself to the priest and offer the offering that was commanded by Moses." The healing of this Jewish leper triggered the first use of Leviticus 13 and 14. It also set into motion the process whereby the Jewish priest and leaders would be forced to acknowledge Him as Messiah.

The Rabbis were seeking four signs or proofs of Messiah. Once the first sign occurred an observation phase would begin. During this phase of observation they would send a delegation from the Sanhedrin to observe the person who had performed the Messianic sign or miracle.

This delegation was not to ask any questions, only to watch and listen. They would then report back to the Sanhedrin as to whether or not this was a significant movement. If it was not nothing further was required. If it was significant then the second phase of the investigation would begin.

When Jesus healed the Jewish leper the observation phase of the investigation was triggered. The next place we find Jesus was in Capernaum. He was teaching and from the Scriptures it appears that there was a Rabbi convention in town. They came from everywhere: Samaria, Judea, and Galilee. They all gathered at Capernaum to observe this man who had healed a Jewish leper.

The place was so crowded that a man who was paralyzed had to be lowered through the roof to get to Jesus.

> *And when they could not come nigh unto him for the press, they uncovered the roof where he was: and when they had broken it up, they let down the bed wherein the sick of the palsy lay. (Mark 2:4 KJV)*

It was in this setting that Jesus did something that He had never done before.

> *When Jesus saw their faith, he said unto the sick of the palsy, Son, thy sins be forgiven thee. (Mark 2:5 KJV)*

Can't you just hear the gasps when Jesus said, "thy sins be forgiven thee"? Remember they weren't allowed to ask any questions during this observation phase.

> *And immediately when Jesus perceived in his spirit that they so reasoned within themselves, he said unto them, why reason ye these things in your hearts? (Mark 2:8 KJV)*

> *Whether is it easier to say to the sick of the palsy, Thy sins be forgiven thee; or to say, Arise, and take up thy bed, and walk? (Mark 2:9 KJV)*

Jesus was letting them know that the same power that causes the lame to walk also forgives sins and He had the power to forgive sins. Either way, the man got up and walked.

Needless to say the report went back to the Sanhedrin that this was a significant movement. The second phase of the investigation was the interrogation phase. From this point on in Jesus' ministry you will see the Jewish leaders following Him everywhere He goes constantly challenging both Jesus and His disciples.

Healing of a Man Blind from Birth

The second Messianic miracle was the healing of a man who was blind from birth.

> *Since the beginning of time it has never been heard that anyone opened the eyes of a man born blind. (John 9:32 AMP)*

Nobody in history who was born blind had ever been known to receive their sight. Anyone born blind was considered to have been created unfinished. Therefore, the Jews associated this miracle with the Creator since the one who healed such a person would have to create sight in the blind. Surely, only the Messiah could do this.

John, Chapter 9, records the story of Jesus and His disciples passing by a man who was blind from birth.

And his disciples asked him, saying, Master, who did sin, this man, or his parents, that he was born blind? (John 9:2 KJV)

Jesus answered, neither hath this man sinned, nor his parents: but that the works of God should be made manifest in him. (John 9:3 KJV)

This is a good place to point out that not every sickness and disease is the result of personal sin. Sometimes sickness is simply the result of the fact we live in a fallen world. This is another reason why knowing and hearing the voice of God is a major key when ministering healing and deliverance. That's how Jesus knew whether to cast out a demon or make mud; He did only what He heard the Father say.

As long as I am in the world, I am the light of the world. (John 9:5 KJV)

When he had thus spoken, he spat on the ground, and made clay of the spittle, and he anointed the eyes of the blind man with the clay. (John 9:6 KJV)

During ancient times spit was considered to have healing virtue. Jesus spits in the dirt, made a clay paste, and put the clay on the man's eyes. In doing so Jesus was equating Himself with the Creator. Remember, God created man from the dust of the earth.

And said unto him, Go, wash in the pool of Siloam, (which is by interpretation, Sent.) He went his way therefore, and washed, and came seeing. (John 9:7 KJV)

Jesus got the blind man's faith involved by telling him to go and wash in the pool of Siloam. The man did so and he returned seeing.

A man that is called Jesus made clay, and anointed mine eyes, and said unto me, Go to the pool of Siloam, and wash: and I went and washed, and I received sight. (John 9:11 KJV)

This was not a case of sight being restored. This was a man who had never seen, a man who was seemingly created unfinished. Jesus finished the act of creation and the man could see for the first time in his life. It did not take long for the news to reach the Pharisees.

They brought to the Pharisees him that aforetime was blind. (John 9:13 KJV)

Immediately the Pharisees began to investigate this second Messianic miracle. It was obvious that the man could see. However, the interrogation phase required that they determine whether or not the person had really been blind from birth. If so, they wanted to know every detail of the circumstances of the healing. The leaders returned to debate with the man who had been blind and was now healed.

Then again the Pharisees also asked him how he had received his sight. He said unto them, He put clay upon mine eyes, and I washed, and do see. (John 9:15 KJV)

Lesson 11 - Healing For The Unbeliever

The man's testimony caused division among the Pharisees. Some said Jesus could not be from God because He healed on the Sabbath. Others said, *"If He is not from God, how could do this miracle?"* (verse 16)

They say unto the blind man again, What sayest thou of him, that he hath opened thine eyes? He said, He is a prophet. (John 9:17 KJV)

The man who was healed declared that Jesus was a prophet. Many still refused to believe a miracle had been performed so they called for his parents.

John 9:19-21

And they asked them, saying, is this your son, who ye say was born blind? How then doth he now see? (John 9:19 KJV)

His parents answered them and said, we know that this is our son, and that he was born blind. (John 9:20 KJV)

But by what means he now seeth, we know not; or who hath opened his eyes, we know not: he is of age; ask him: he shall speak for himself. (John 9:21 KJV)

The parents confirmed he was their son who was born bind. However, they were afraid to answer about how he was healed.

These words spake his parents, because they feared the Jews: for the Jews had agreed already, that if any man did confess that he was Christ, he should be put out of the synagogue. (John 9:22 KJV)

The Jewish leaders had already decided that if any man would acknowledge Jesus as the Messiah they would be put out of the synagogue. Because of this, the parents simply said their son was old enough to speak for himself.

Then again called they the man that was blind, and said unto him, Give God the praise: we know that this man is a sinner. (John 9:24 KJV)

He answered and said, whether he be a sinner or no, I know not: one thing I know, that, whereas I was blind, now I see. (John 9:25 KJV)

If this man were not of God, he could do nothing. (John 9:33 KJV)

As a result of his testimony the man who was healed was kicked out of the synagogue.

John 9:35-37

Jesus heard that they had cast him out; and when he had found him, he said unto him, dost thou believe on the Son of God? (John 9:35 KJV)

He answered and said, Who is he, Lord, that I might believe on him? (John 9:36 KJV)

And Jesus said unto him, Thou hast both seen him, and it is he that talketh with thee. (John 9:37 KJV)

And he said, Lord, I believe. And he worshiped him.(John 9:38 KJV)

This miracle was a declaration that Jesus was the Son of God, the Messiah. In demonstration of the power of God, the Gospel was preached and a man was drawn to God.

Casting Out of a Dumb Spirit

The third Messianic miracle was the casting out of a dumb spirit. The Rabbis had a rabbinical formula for casting out demons. They would ask the demon its name then using their name they would cast the demon out. Even Jesus did it this way when He healed the Gadarene demonic.

And he asked him, What is thy name? And he answered, saying, My name is Legion: for we are many. (Mark 5:9 KJV)

The problem with a dumb spirit is that it cannot speak. Therefore, the spirit cannot tell you its name. The casting out of a dumb spirit would require one to get their information from a source other than the demon. This implies the need to be God or at least hear from God. Therefore, the Jews believed only Messiah could cast out a dumb spirit.

And one of the multitude answered and said, Master, I have brought unto thee my son, which hath a dumb spirit; (Mark 9:17 KJV)

And wheresoever he taketh him, he teareth him: and he foameth, and gnasheth with his teeth, and pineth away: and I spake to thy disciples that they should cast him out; and they could not. (Mark 9:18 KJV)

It was a dumb spirit that the disciples were unable to cast out.

Mark 9:25-27

When Jesus saw that the people came running together, he rebuked the foul spirit, saying unto him, Thou dumb and deaf spirit, I charge thee, come out of him, and enter no more into him. (Mark 9:25 KJV)

And the spirit cried, and rent him sore, and came out of him: and he was as one dead; insomuch that many said, He is dead. (Mark 9:26 KJV)

But Jesus took him by the hand, and lifted him up; and he arose. (Mark 9:27 KJV)

Jesus did what the Rabbis could not do. He cast out a dumb spirit.

Then the eyes of the blind shall be opened, and the ears of the deaf shall be unstopped. (Isaiah 35:5 KJV)

Then shall the lame man leap as a hart, and the tongue of the dumb sing: for in the wilderness shall waters break out, and streams in the desert. (Isaiah 35:6 KJV)

The performance of this miracle by Jesus fulfilled this well-known Messianic prophecy of the prophet Isaiah and seemingly, again, validated that Jesus was who He claimed Himself to be: the Messiah.

A Fourth-Day Man, Raised from the Dead

The fourth Messianic miracle was the raising of the man who had been dead for more than three days. Other prophets, Elijah and Elisha for example, had raised people from the dead. Therefore, in itself, the raising of the dead was not considered to be a Messianic miracle.

However, nobody had ever been raised from the dead after being dead for more than three days. The Rabbis believed that the soul hung around the body for those three days hoping a prophet would come along and raise the person up so the soul could return to its body.

On the third day the body begins to decay. At that time Jewish tradition tells us, the Rabbis believed the soul gave up and departed. For this reason the Jews believed only Messiah could raise a "fourth-day man."

Lazarus was a fourth-day man. The story is recorded John 11. Martha sends a messenger to Jesus who was in another city, saying that the one who Jesus loved, Lazarus, was sick.

When he had heard therefore that he was sick, he abode two days still in the same place where he was. (John 11:6 KJV)

At first glance this bothered me that Jesus waited two days before going to Bethany. One would think that if Jesus really loved these three friends He would have dropped everything and hurried to their home. It appeared that Jesus hung around waiting for His friend, Lazarus, to die so He could do a spectacular miracle. What was with that? I was really glad when, after further study, I found that not to be the case.

Then said Jesus unto them plainly, Lazarus is dead. (John 11:14 KJV)

Jesus did not wait for Lazarus to die. He knew Lazarus was dead before He left to go to Bethany. The messenger that came from Martha took a day to get to where Jesus was; he delivered the message that Lazarus was sick. Jesus waited two more days, or a total of three days. On the next day Jesus went to Bethany. This is now the fourth day.

> *Then when Jesus came, he found that he had lain in the grave four days already. (John 11:17 KJV)*

According to verse 17, Lazarus had been buried four days by the time Jesus arrived. That would mean Lazarus died before the messenger even reached Jesus. Jesus, who heard from God, knew his friend was already dead by the time He received the message. Jesus was not waiting for Lazarus to die. He just waited for him to become a fourth-day man.

> *Then they took away the stone from the place where the dead was laid. And Jesus lifted up his eyes, and said, Father, I thank thee that thou hast heard me. (John 11:41 KJV)*

At the tomb of Lazarus Jesus was facing His most impressive and defining miracle, the raising from the dead of a fourth-day man. He looks toward heaven and says, *"Father, I thank thee that thou hast heard me."* The word for Father that Jesus used was not the word the Rabbis normally used when referring to Father God. He used the personal, intimate term "Abba." He was calling God "Daddy." Jesus was saying, "Thank you Daddy that we have constant, intimate communication."

> *And I knew that thou hearest me always: but because of the people which standby I said it, that they may believe that thou hast sent me. (John 11:42 KJV)*

> *And when he thus had spoken, he cried with a loud voice, Lazarus, come forth. (John 11:43 KJV)*

Jesus raised a fourth-day man. The key to His ability to do what others could not was His constant communication with the Father.

The entire earthly ministry of Jesus was the fulfillment of Father God's divine plan and purpose. It is true they were all acts of compassion but not even one act was random.

It was not by chance that Jesus performed a lot of the same kind of miracles that the Old Testament prophets did.

> **For example:** Abraham, a prophet, performed the first healing. Elijah and Elisha reproduced food and also raised people from the dead. Elisha healed a leper, although it was not a Jewish leper. (Jesus was the first and only one to heal a Jewish leper.)

These healings and miracles established Jesus as a prophet in the sense that a prophet is one who hears from God. They exhibited a power that was greater than any power on earth through the healings, deliverances, miracles, signs and wonders. Jesus proved His ability to forgive sins by the fact that He had the power to heal and deliver. He performed the tasks of Messiah.

Jesus performed the miracles to prove He had power over everything that has power over mankind and that He was indeed the Messiah.

It is in these Messianic miracles that we see the example of Jesus integrating the message and the power of the message. He not only declared that He was the Messiah, but the demonstration of the power of God operating in His life confirmed that He was who He claimed to be.

Paul and those who followed after Jesus carried on the pattern He had set before them. Their mission was the same as Jesus' mission: to prove He was the Messiah. Their message and demonstration of the power of the message was the same.

> *For the kingdom of God is not in word, but in power. (1 Corinthians 4:20 KJV)*

Paul makes it clear that the power of God, signs and wonders, miracles, and healings, are to be a part of the Gospel message. According to him the faith of the believer should not rest on words but in a demonstration of power.

> *And my speech and my preaching was not with enticing words of man's wisdom, but in demonstration of the Spirit and of power. (1 Corinthians 2:4 KJV)*

> *That your faith should not stand in the wisdom of men, but in the power of God. (1 Corinthians 2:5 KJV)*

In Romans 15, Paul went as far as to imply that the Gospel is not fully preached without signs and wonders.

> *Through mighty signs and wonders, by the power of the Spirit of God; so that from Jerusalem, and round about unto Illyricum, I have fully preached the gospel of Christ. (Romans 15:19 KJV)*

The early Church carried on the pattern of demonstrating the power of God, meeting people's most basic human needs in order to attract them to the Gospel message. They preached the same message Jesus preached; Jesus has power over anything that has power over you and the Kingdom of God has come to you, the individual.

Their mission was the same as Jesus' mission: to prove Jesus was the Messiah. They used the demonstration of signs and wonders to fulfill this mission.

Our Mission

Should the Church of our day have as a part of its function the demonstration of the power of God? For too long the Church as a whole has preach a Gospel void of the demonstration of power.

This power message is not an old message without relevance for today. The Apostle Paul's words on this point leave little room for any doubt that it is time to train the leaders of today's Church in the power message — the fullness of the Gospel.

The demonstration of God's power through signs, wonders, miracles, and healings were the tools Jesus used as proof that He was who He claimed to be.

As thou hast sent me into the world, even so have I also sent them into the world. (John 17:18 KJV)

Jesus Himself said that as the Father had sent Him into the world He, Jesus, sent His disciples into the world.

How God anointed Jesus of Nazareth with the Holy Ghost and with power: who went about doing good, and healing all that were oppressed of the devil; for God was with him. (Acts 10:38 KJV)

Jesus stripped himself of His divine attributes, came to earth in human flesh, and demonstrated how man anointed with the Holy Spirit was to function on earth. None of His earthly ministry was done as the Son of God. Although He was God He accomplished His earthly ministry as the son of man anointed by the Holy Spirit.

Jesus stripped himself of His divine attributes and clothed himself in human flesh. He demonstrated how a man or woman anointed with the Holy Spirit was to live on earth.

And, being assembled together with them, He commanded them that they should not depart from Jerusalem, but wait for the promise of the Father, which, saith he, ye have heard of me. (Acts 1:4 KJV)

For John truly baptized with water; but ye shall be baptized with the Holy Ghost not many days hence. (Acts 1:5 KJV)

But ye shall receive power, after that the Holy Ghost is come upon you: and ye shall be witnesses unto me both in Jerusalem, and in all Judea, and in Samaria, and unto the uttermost part of the earth. (Acts 1:8 KJV)

Before Jesus ascended into heaven He instructed the disciples to go to Jerusalem and wait until they received the Holy Spirit. After receiving the Holy Spirit the disciples displayed the same kind of power as Jesus.

Insomuch that they brought forth the sick into the streets, and laid them on beds and couches, that at the least the shadow of Peter passing by might overshadow some of them. (Acts 5:15 KJV)

There came also a multitude out of the cities round about unto Jerusalem, bringing sick folks, and them which were vexed with unclean spirits: and they were healed every one. (Acts 5:16 KJV)

The New Testament is filled with acts of miracles by the disciples who were anointed with the Holy Spirit. As God sent Jesus, Jesus sent His disciples.

Matthew 28:18-20

And Jesus came and spake unto them, saying, All power is given unto me in heaven and in earth. (Matthew 28:18 KJV)

Go ye therefore, and teach all nations, baptizing them in the name of the Father, and of the Son, and of the Holy Ghost; (Matthew 28:19 KJV)

Teaching them to observe all things whatsoever I have commanded you: and, lo, I am with you always, even unto the end of the world. Amen. (Matthew 28:20 KJV)

Jesus instructed His disciples to teach all nations to observe all the things He commanded them to do.

I do shall he do also; and greater works than these Verily, verily, I say unto you, He that believeth on me, the works that shall he do; because I go unto my Father. (John 14:12 KJV)

And whatsoever ye shall ask in my name, that will I do, that the Father may be glorified in the Son. (John 14:13 KJV)

Jesus said *"He that believeth on Me"* (that's you and me) *"the works I do shall he do also."* Jesus is still our example. As believers, disciples of Jesus, we are to demonstrate the power of God on earth.

What? Know ye not that your body is the temple of the Holy Ghost which is in you, which ye have of God, and ye are not your own? (1 Corinthians 6:19 KJV)

As believers we are temples of the Holy Ghost, the same Holy Spirit as Jesus. The Holy Spirit is the power. The Holy Spirit is not a thing. He is not a force. He is the third person of the Godhead and is the embodiment of the power of God. The Holy Spirit works in conjunction with the Will of God to perform the desire of God.

And the earth was without form, and void; and darkness was upon the face of the deep. And the Spirit of God moved upon the face of the waters. (Genesis 1:2 KJV)

And God said, Let there be light: and there was light. (Genesis 1:3 KJV)

In the beginning God spoke the earth into existence. The Hebrew word for spirit in the phrase "Spirit of God" is *ruwach*. The Hebrew word for breath is the same word *ruwach*. God spoke, released His breath, and the Spirit performed it. When God speaks His will His breath/spirit is released and there is power present to bring the desires of God to pass.

The power that was present in the person of Jesus during His earthly ministry and at his death, the power of the Holy Spirit, is also present in the one who is a witness of those events. When a witness testifies of those events, the same creative power is present to save, heal, and set the captives free.

Jesus died for mankind. He offers us His righteousness, which cannot be earned, in exchange for our sins.

> *For He hath made him to be sin for us, who knew no sin; that we might be made the righteousness of God in him. (2 Corinthians 5:21 KJV)*

When the truth of this spiritual reality is retold and an individual believes and declares this same spiritual reality, the same power that was at the original event of the crucifixion is released to set free, to save, and to heal that person.

> *That if thou shalt confess with thy mouth the Lord Jesus, and shalt believe in thine heart that God hath raised him from the dead, thou shalt be saved. (Romans 10:9 KJV)*

> *For with the heart man believeth unto righteousness; and with the mouth confession is made unto salvation. (Romans 10:10 KJV)*

The word for saved is the Greek *sozo* which means saved, healed, delivered, and made whole. The power that was present at Jesus' death, burial and resurrection was so great that it can still produce eternal life, healing, and deliverance in a person today. This is a mysterious spiritual reality that cannot be explained with charts and graphs. Yet it is the foundation of our faith. It is the mystery of the Gospel.

> *But if the Spirit of him that raised up Jesus from the dead dwell in you, he that raised up Christ from the dead shall also quicken your mortal bodies by his Spirit that dwelleth in you. (Romans 8:11 KJV)*

It is important that you get this point. The believer has the same Holy Spirit Jesus had and the same Spirit that raised Him from the dead operating in their life today. Not a different Holy Spirit, the same Holy Spirit. The Holy Spirit is the power of God.

When a representative of God speaks or declares the Word of God the power to bring that Word to pass is released. The Bible has numerous examples of prophetic words that were spoken by a prophet of God that have come to pass. One example is:

> *And Elijah the Tishbite, who was of the inhabitants of Gilead, said unto Ahab, As the LORD God of Israel liveth, before whom I stand, there shall not be dew nor rain these years, but according to my word. (1 Kings 17:1 KJV)*

The prophet Elijah declared, "There will not be rain except by my word" and there was no rain. The demonstration of the supernatural power of God caused the king to believe there was a power operating that could not be explained with logical or reason.

Likewise, it is the demonstration of the power of God that will open the hearts of the unbeliever to the preaching of the Gospel.

For example: I had the privilege of going to Ethiopia on a medical mission trip. In addition to ministering medically to the people we encouraged all who came to the medical clinic to also go through the prayer room, especially those with issues that the volunteer medical staff could not help.

I was in charge of the prayer room. The majority of those who came to our prayer room were not Christians. They were almost all from other religious backgrounds. As they sat before us we told them that God had sent us to Ethiopia to tell them that He loved them and He had not forsaken them. Then we asked them what it was they wanted God to do for them.

We saw legs and arms grow out, blind eyes opened, deaf ears opened, the cripple walk without any assistance, chronic pain gone, deliverance from depression, fear, and many other oppressions of the enemy.

After prayer we told them that it was not any of the team members that healed them. It was Jesus. Then we asked them if they would like to know Him personally. Because they experienced the healing power of God in their body their hearts were open to the Gospel message. In the five days that the prayer room was open hundreds received Jesus as their Messiah, their Lord and Savior.

We were able to plug these new converts into a Church that had been established as the result of a similar trip this group made to Ethiopia the year before. This made it possible for the new converts to have the opportunity to be established in the ways of the Lord.

Members of this Church and some of those who were healed the year before volunteered in the prayer room and in other areas of clinic.

Unfortunately, in many Churches of our day the Word of God is preached but they deny the power of God. Therefore, hundreds or even thousands of people get saved and yet our Churches do not experience a growth equal to the salvation rate. Their faith rested on the enticing words of man void of the power of God. Because of this many fall away from the faith when someone comes along with equally good sounding words.

According to the Apostle Paul the faith of the believer was never meant to rest on words, but rather on power. We must preach the full Gospel. The true Gospel must include the power message.

Whether is easier, to say, Thy sins be forgiven thee; or to say, Rise up and walk? (Luke 5:23 KJV)

But that ye may know that the Son of man hath power upon earth to forgive sins, (he said unto the sick of the palsy,) I say unto thee, Arise, and take up thy couch, and go into thine house. (Luke 5:24 KJV)

Jesus healed and delivered to prove He had power to forgive sins. This is why healing should be used in evangelism. It proves to the unbeliever that God is who you say He is and Jesus is who you say He is. It proves God does have the power to forgive their sins because He heals their body.

Our mission is to prove in a tangible, personal way that Jesus is the Messiah. When we preach the Gospel there should be signs and wonders for unbelievers. Our message must be the same one that Jesus and the disciples after Him preached; it must be a message of power.

Whatever has power over you, such as cancer, Jesus has power over it and He comes to you personally. You do not have to find Him because he has found you. He is the only Son of God. He died that you might have life and He was wounded that you may be healed.

The same miracles that Jesus did, even the Messianic miracles, have been delegated to us.

Verily, verily, I say unto you, He that believeth on me, the works that I do shall he do also; and greater works than these shall he do; because I go unto my Father. (John 14:12 KJV)

Summary

We have the Holy Spirit, the third person of the Godhead, the power of the Almighty God living on the inside of us. Knowing God wants to heal everyone, including the un-believer, the believer can release the Faith of God and be willing to give the Holy Spirit the opportunity to manifest Himself through us.

We can lay hand on believers and unbelievers and expect to see blind eyes open, deaf ears open, demons flee and even the dead rise. God wants to be glorified in the Son, the Son wants to bring glory to the Father, and the Holy Spirit wants the glory of the Father to be revealed in the Son. When you bring healing and deliverance, using the Name of Jesus, you are glorifying God in the Son.

Just as it is the Father's will for all to be saved, it is His will for all to be healed. The Atonement gives the believer the assurance of his or her right to be healed. In Matthew 15, Jesus called healing and deliverance "the children's bread." Mark 16 promises the sick will recover. For the believer this is not always a miracle but a proWe see the miracle more frequently when ministering to unbelievers. The miracle, a power demonstration, is the proof that Jesus is who He claims to be. The healing of the body proves He has the power to forgive sin and set the soul free. That is the message that is in a miracle. It is designed to draw the unbeliever to God. When this message is taken to the unbeliever God shows up every time.

If we are going to reach the world, the unbeliever of our day, with the message that Jesus is the Messiah of every nation, it will not be done in the words or wisdom of man but through the demonstration of the power of God.

My prayer is that this study has helped the student to:

➢ develop a closer relationship with the Father;
➢ increase their knowledge of God's will concerning healing and deliverance;
➢ increase their awareness of the power that resides on the inside of them;
➢ increase their ability to hear the voice of God;
➢ raise their awareness of who they are in God and who He is in them, and

> establish a biblical foundation on which to receive healing and deliverance for themselves and to minister healing/deliverance to those they come into contact with on a daily basis.

Special Note: All the manifestations of the Holy Spirit are to operate by LOVE.

Love Chapter

I Corinthians 13:1-8

IF I [can] speak in the tongues of men and [even] of angels, but have not love (that reasoning, intentional, spiritual devotion such as is inspired by God's love for and in us), I am only a noisy gong or a clanging cymbal. (1Corinthians 13:1 AMP)

And if I have prophetic powers (the gift of interpreting the divine will and purpose), and understand all the secret truths and mysteries and possess all knowledge, and if I have [sufficient] faith so that I can remove mountains, but have not love (God's love in me) I am nothing (a useless nobody). (1 Corinthians 13:2 AMP)

Even if I dole out all that I have [to the poor in providing] food, and if I surrender my body to be burned or in order that I may glory, but have not love (God's love in me), I gain nothing. (1 Corinthians 13:3 AMP)

Love endures long and is patient and kind; love never is envious nor boils over with jealousy, is not boastful or vainglorious, does not display itself haughtily. (1 Corinthians 13:4 AMP)

It is not conceited (arrogant and inflated with pride); it is not rude (unmannerly) and does not act unbecomingly. Love (God's love in us) does not insist on its own rights or its own way, for it is not self-seeking; it is not touchy or fretful or resentful; it takes no account of the evil done to it [it pays no attention to a suffered wrong]. (1 Corinthians 13:5 AMP)

It does not rejoice at injustice and unrighteousness, but rejoices when right and truth prevail. (1 Corinthians 13:6 AMP)

Love bears up under anything and everything that comes, is ever ready to believe the best of every person, its hopes are fadeless under all circumstances, and it endures everything [without weakening]. (1 Corinthians 13:7 AMP)

Love never fails [never fades out or becomes obsolete or comes to an end]. As for prophecy (the gift of interpreting the divine will and purpose), it will be fulfilled and pass away; as for tongues, they will be destroyed and cease; as for knowledge, it will pass away [it will lose its value and be superseded by truth]. (1 Corinthians 13:8 AMP)

Activation Time

- Halal, using your attributes of God list, for 2 minutes.
- Pray in the Holy Spirit, with passion, for 5 minutes.
- Activation: Ministry Teams

Activation Description

Divide students into ministry teams of three.

- Student #1 will receive ministry.
- Student #2 will minister to Student #1 using the healing process described in this manual. (Lesson 9)
- Student #3 intercedes and records any issues, revealed by the Holy Spirit during the interview, that need to be addressed. This list will be used by Student #2 during the repenting, breaking agreement, and casting out part of the process.

Instruct the students to rotate until each of them has received ministry, has recorded the issues, and has ministered using the healing process.

Assignment

- Meditate on and memorize the memory verses.
- Add 5 more attributes of God to your list.
- Begin your daily prayer time by halaling for at least 5 minutes using your list of attributes.
- Pray in the Spirit 15 minutes a day.

Assignment Results and Comments

LESSON 12 – Be Released

Memory Verse

But be ye doers of the word, and not hearers only, deceiving your own selves. (James 1:22 KJV)

Personal Release

You have come to the conclusion of our journey through the Word of God which focused on the subject of healing and deliverance. During our journey I believe I have accomplished my first purpose for writing this study manual: I have presented a Scriptural foundation for the Biblical truth that Jesus made atonement for both our spiritual healing and our physical healing. He made provision for both at the Cross of Calvary. This Biblical truth gives you, the believer, a solid foundation on which to release your faith to receive healing in your spirit, soul, and body.

The above memory verse clearly teaches us that it is not enough to receive knowledge of the Word; we must obey it. The Bible we know must be translated into action in order for it to be a benefit in our lives. We should never go to the Scriptures without allowing them to change our lives for the better. If we profess to have a great love God's Word or pose as a Bible student and fail to let it produce an increasing likeness to the Lord Jesus in our lives, we truly do deceive ourselves. We must become a "doer" of the Word.

You, as a believer and Bible student, have received an abundance of knowledge of the Scriptures throughout this study. If you have gone through this study and all you have done is acquire more knowledge, you have done a disservice to yourself and you fall into the category of being a "hearer only."

The word "doer" is a Greek word used to describe a poet. It carries the idea of creativity. It depicts someone putting forth his fullest creativity to do something.

The purpose of the activations and assignments in each lesson were designed to help you, the student, apply the truths you learned to your daily life and thereby become a "doer" of the Word.

Example

> ➤ Halaling and praying in the Spirit on a daily basis was to encourage you to develop a lifestyle of entering into and spending time in the presence of God.

- The exercises on hearing the voice of God and asking for words of knowledge were to help you to realize, many of you for the first time, that God wants to speak to you and you can hear Him. They were also designed to help you to become more aware of what the voice of God sounds like on the inside of you and give you a safe place to practice hearing the voice of God.
- You have received a Biblical foundation on which you can build and release your faith. At the end of each session you were given an opportunity to release your faith and see God move.
- Maybe for the first time you learned that since you have the Holy Spirit you have the potential for all the manifestations of the Spirit listed in 1 Corinthians 12 to be manifest through you. The activations and assignments were designed to encourage you to step out in faith and allow God to use you in any way He wants.
- After completing this study you are now aware of many issues that could hinder you and others from receiving healing and what to do when those issues are exposed.
- Opportunities to pray for the healing of others were available after you received instructions on how to do so.

James tells us that we must put forth our fullest efforts and most creative abilities in doing what we have heard preached. If you have been diligent to do the activations and the assignments you have become a "doer" of the Word and I am sure that you have experienced the benefits of the knowledge you received.

Many have received complete healing both emotionally and physically. Others have received a breakthrough and their healing process has begun. If this is the case I encourage you to continue to apply the Word and principles you have learned. Continue to be a "doer" of the Word.

> *So shall my word be that goeth forth out of my mouth: it shall not return unto me void, but it shall accomplish that which I please, and it shall prosper in the thing whereto I sent it. (Isaiah 55:11 KJV)*

Continue to declare your healing. Do not give up! Remember this is not a one time shot and you are done. It must become the lifestyle of the believer. The full manifestation of your healing will come.

> *God is faithful, by whom ye were called unto the fellowship of his Son Jesus Christ our Lord. (1 Corinthians 1:9 KJV)*

Once your healing is manifest you have also learned how to keep your healing and walk in the divine health that was purchased for you by Jesus at the Cross of Calvary.

> *For the wages of sin is death; but the gift of God is eternal life through Jesus Christ our Lord. (Romans 6:23 KJV)*

> *For the law of the Spirit of life in Christ Jesus hath made me free from the law of sin and death. (Romans 8:2 KJV)*

Be a "doer of the Word" and be "released" from not only the bondage of sin but also the bondage of the recompense of sin; sickness and disease which if left unchecked leads to death.

Released for Ministry

It has been prophesied that the next great move of God would come through ordinary believers who are walking in the power of the Holy Spirit. The Body of Christ, as a whole, leaves ministry in the church and to the world to pastors, evangelist, prophets, and apostles.

And he gave some, apostles; and some, prophets; and some, evangelists; and some, pastors and teachers; (Ephesians 4:11 KJV)

For the perfecting of the saints, for the work of the ministry, for the edifying of the body of Christ. (Ephesians 4:12 KJV)

Scripture plainly teaches us that Jesus gave the church apostles, prophets, evangelist, and pastors for the purpose of equipping the believer to do the work of the ministry so the Body of Christ would be edified and increase.

It has been my experience that most believers do not step out to minister to others because they do not believe God can or wants to use them or do not believe they were called to minister to others or they do not feel equipped to do the work of the ministry.

That brings us to the secondary purpose of this teaching manual: to make the believer aware of the fact that God wants to use them to equip them to do the work He has called them to do and then release them to do the work in their sphere of influence — at the grocery store, on their job, at the sports event, in their church, wherever the opportunity presents itself for God to manifest Himself in the life of a believer or to even the unbeliever.

Verily, verily, I say unto you, He that believeth on me, the works that I do shall he do also; and greater works than these shall he do; because I go unto my Father. (John 14:12 KJV)

Needless to say most believers live far below our calling and level of power and victory that has been made available to them through the blood of our Lord Jesus Christ.

What were the works of Jesus? His earthly ministry revealed the perfect will of God for mankind. Jesus went about teaching the truths found in the Scriptures. He preached the Kingdom of God. Jesus also cleansed the lepers, healed the sick, and raised the dead, thus fulfilling the "full" gospel. The "full" gospel must include the preaching of the Kingdom of God and the demonstration of the power of God.

And as ye go, preach, saying, The kingdom of heaven is at hand. (Matthew 10:7 KJV)

Heal the sick, cleanse the lepers, raise the dead, cast out devils: freely ye have received, freely give. (Matthew 10:8 KJV)

When Jesus sent the twelve out to minister He instructed them to do the same works that they had observed Him doing.

Matthew 28:18-20

And Jesus came and spake unto them, saying, All power is given unto me in heaven and in earth. (Matthew 28:18 KJV)

Go ye therefore, and teach all nations, baptizing them in the name of the Father, and of the Son, and of the Holy Ghost, (Matthew 28:19 KJV)

Teaching them to observe all things whatsoever I have commanded you: and, lo, I am with you always, even unto the end of the world. Amen. (Matthew 28:20 KJV)

We recognize the above Scriptures as the commission to the church given by Jesus himself. Notice we, as believers, are to do "all" the works Jesus commanded His disciples to do.

You now know how to lead somebody to a saving knowledge of Jesus and how to lead them into receiving the baptism of the Holy Spirit. You are also equipped to pray for others you need healing or deliverance.

For our gospel came not unto you in word only, but also in power, and in the Holy Ghost, and in much assurance; as ye know what manner of men we were among you for your sake. (1 Thessalonians 1:5 KJV)

And my speech and my preaching was not with enticing words of man's wisdom, but in demonstration of the Spirit and of power: (1 Corinthians 2:4 KJV)

The Father has provided you with everything you need to be successful in ministering to those in need. You are prepared to share the gospel not only in word, but also in demonstration of the power of the gospel.

Be "released!" Step out in faith and allow the Holy Spirit to manifest Himself through you. Be a "doer" of the Word!

Activation and Assignment

As an individual student continue to develop and cultivate a daily lifestyle of:

- Meditating on and memorizing Bible memory verses.
- Halaling at least 5 minutes a day.
- Praying in the spirit a minimum of 15 minutes a day.
- Spending time in the Word of God.
- Spending quality time in His presence listening and recording what He says to you.
- Continue to ask God for divine appointments and opportunities to lead people to Jesus, pray for others to be filled with the Holy Spirit, and to pray for others to receive healing.
- Stay sensitive to the Holy Spirit's leading and guidance.
- When opportunities and divine appointment occur be obedient and allow God to use you to be a blessing to others.
- Keep a journal. Record the signs and wonders He does through you. Refer back to your journal any time discouragement tries to creep back into your life.

Suggested Assignment for Study Groups

Night of Healing

- After completing this study, schedule a Night of Healing.
- Have each member invite 1 or 2 people who need healing to attend the Night of Healing.
- Allow the members to pray for those who come using the process outlined in Lesson 9 and the Ministry Guidelines provided at the end of Lesson 9 in this manual. If the group consists of 6 or more divide the members into teams of a minimum of 3 per team. Separate the teams a little so one team won't be distracted by the others.
- Give each guest a copy of "How to Keep Your Healing" (also found at the end of Lesson 9).
- After every guest has been prayed for gather the members together to share what they experience and to ask any questions that they may have as a result of the ministry experience.

Allowing believers to experience being used by God in a controlled environment such as a group study is beneficial in building confidence that God will use them in the market place on a daily basis. Be a "doer" of the Word. Be "released" for ministry in your sphere of influence.

Suggested Assignments for Pastors Using This Study in Leadership Training

Healing Clinic
- Schedule and promote a "Day of Healing" clinic for your congregation.
- The clinic should be about 3 hours in length.
- Invite those who are in need of healing to attend. A registration of those attending would be helpful in determining the number of guests to expect but it is certainly not necessary.
- Secure large enough space (sanctuary, fellowship hall, chapel, etc) to separate the teams so

Lesson 12 – Be Released

---

they will not be distracted by each other. Obviously the number of teams you have and the number of guests you expect will dictate the size of space needed. Multiple rooms can also be used for ministry if needed.
- Students should arrive at the clinic one hour prior to the scheduled time of the clinic. This is preparation time for the students. The time should be spent in worship, prayer, and praying in the Spirit.
- Divide students into teams of three.
- Instruct the teams to use the process outlined in Chapter 9 of this manual. Each team member should have their own copy of the Ministry Guidelines found at the end of Chapter 9. There should also be pens, tables, a box of tissues, a small trash can, and a copy of "How to Keep Your Deliverance" for each guest receiving ministry available in each team's ministering area. (If you require a ministry release form to be signed you will need a manila folder available to put the collected forms in.)
- Each team will need to decide who will lead the first time of ministry, who will intercede, and who will record the issues revealed during the interview process. (Note: instruct students to rotate their assigned duties each time they receive a new guest for ministry. This will ensure each team member an opportunity to record, to intercede, and to lead the ministry to at least one person.)
- Assign one person to be the "greeter" for the clinic. This person will greet the guests, sign the guest in as they arrive, inform the guest that those who will be praying for them are students from the Healed and Released class, thank the guest for allowing the student to practice on them, and direct the guests to the assigned seating area for guests while they wait for their time of ministry. The greeter should be in his or her assigned area at least 30 minutes prior to the scheduled start time for the clinic to guest who come early. (You may also want to provide a ministry release form for each guest to sign. The greeter can provide the form at sign in and instruct the guest to read and sign the form then give the form to their ministry team.)
- Students should be in their assigned areas at least 10 minutes before the scheduled start time of the clinic.
- At the established start time the pastor or teacher of the training will instruct the "greeter" to begin escorting the guests to the ministry teams, starting with the first person on the list. As a person receives ministry and leaves the team, the next guest can be escorted and introduced to that team. (Note: Give the team a minute or two to rotate responsibilities of ministry within their team before taking them a new guest.)
- The pastor or instructor of the training is to be available to oversee and assist the teams during this time of ministry. They should be ready answer any questions that may arise, or to assist in ministry in any of the teams, if necessary. Also be available to assist the greeter if necessary.
- When all the guests have received ministry gather the students together for a time of testimonies of the healings and any comments or questions that may have come up during the ministry time. Praise God for what He did.

Again, experiencing being used of God in a controlled setting like this will encourage the student to continue to step out in faith to minister to those they come in contact with on a daily basis.

You have "equipped" them, now step out in faith and "release" them to do the work of the ministry.

Other Suggested Ways to Activate and "Release" Students

- Use them to pray with people who come to the altar in your church.
- Use them to staff a Healing Room in your church.
- Use them to develop healing teams to go to people's homes to pray for shut-ins.
- Use them to develop healing teams to go to the hospital and pray for member of your congregation.
- Schedule a night of healing in your church for your congregation, teach on healing, invite those who need healing to come forward, and use them to pray for the people who come.
- Line your students up on the platform in your church and ask them to pray and get a word of knowledge as to what the Holy Spirit wants to heal that day. Ask anyone in the congregation who is dealing with the stated sickness or issue to stand and release the students to go pray for them and see what GodRelease them to teach a Sunday school class on healing.

The list can go on and on. The point is: you have equipped them now look for ways to release them and do it. Give them opportunities to grow in the gifting God has placed on the inside them.

As believers we all need to experience our God given right to be "Healed and Released."

Your testimony of what God has done for you and through you is powerful. Testimonies can cause others to step out in faith for the first time and believe God for their situation. They can also encourage others to stand firm when they are tempted to give up.

If you are still believing God for the complete manifestation of your healing, I invite you to visit my website (www.dorothylparker.com) and record your prayer request so I can pray in agreement with you for your healing.

If this study manual has helped you in any way, again, I ask you to please go to my website and record your testimony so others may be encouraged to be "Healed and Released."

CPSIA information can be obtained at www.ICGtesting.com
Printed in the USA
BVOW09s1319230916

463123BV00008B/31/P